More Mirrors in the Classroom

About the Series

The Kids Like Us series published by Rowman & Littlefield Education is designed to support educators in discovering the world of high-quality urban children's literature and to demonstrate the potential for culturally relevant texts to increase literacy. *More Mirrors in the Classroom: Using Urban Children's Literature to Increase Literacy* is the first book in the series. It includes research summaries, guidelines for text selection, and a step-by-step guide to increasing the cultural relevance of literacy instruction with urban children's literature. The second book in the series will provide practical guidance for building high-quality, culturally relevant classroom library collections and for utilizing the classroom library as a central part of daily literacy instruction. The third book will document practice in urban classrooms, showcasing how teachers have used urban children's literature in a range of inquiry-based projects and thematic units to support children's reading and writing development. The Kids Like Us website (www.kidslikeus.org) provides additional resources to accompany the series, including access to descriptions, cover art, and reading levels of high-quality multicultural and urban children's literature, as well as links to teaching guides, author and illustrator websites, and other resources.

More Mirrors in the Classroom

*Using Urban Children's
Literature to Increase Literacy*

Jane Fleming, Susan Catapano, Candace M. Thompson,
and Sandy Ruvalcaba Carrillo

ROWMAN & LITTLEFIELD
Lanham • Boulder • New York • London

Published by Rowman & Littlefield
A wholly owned subsidiary of The Rowman & Littlefield Publishing Group, Inc.
4501 Forbes Boulevard, Suite 200, Lanham, Maryland 20706
www.rowman.com

Unit A, Whitacre Mews, 26-34 Stannary Street, London SE11 4AB

British Library Cataloguing in Publication Information Available

Library of Congress Cataloging-in-Publication Data

Library of Congress Cataloging-in-Publication Data

Names: Fleming, Jane, 1967- author.
Title: More mirrors in the classroom : using urban children's literature to increase
  literacy / Jane Fleming, Susan Catapano, Candace M. Thompson, and Sandy
  Ruvalcaba Carrillo.
Description: Lanham, Maryland : Rowman & Littlefield, 2016. | Series: Kids like us ; 1
Identifiers: LCCN 2016006166| ISBN 9781475802153 (cloth) | ISBN 9781475802160
  (pbk.) | ISBN 9781475802177 (electronic)
Subjects: LCSH: Reading (Elementary)—Social aspects—United States. | City
  children—Books and reading—United States. | Children with social disabilities—
  Books and reading—United States. | Classroom libraries—United States. |
  Culturally relevant pedagogy—United States.
Classification: LCC LB1573 .F54 2016 | DDC 372.4—dc23
LC record available at https://lccn.loc.gov/2016006166

Printed in the United States of America

Contents

~

Preface

I'm a city child.
I love the dizzy heights,
the concrete,
the steel,
the bright neon lights.

In the United States, more than 14 million children attend school in our nation's cities, accounting for approximately 30 percent of the public school student population (U.S. Department of Education, 2013). We wrote this book with all of our "city children" in mind who are eager to find themselves, their families, and their communities represented and valued among the vast collections of children's books they find in school.

When learning how to read and write, children use language and experiences that are familiar to them to recognize words, understand texts, and tell stories. However, the large educational publishers that serve urban public school districts generally develop basal readers and trade book collections to reach a national mainstream audience. As a result, few text selections include urban settings, multicultural and multilingual communities, and the urban architecture and ecology with which young children in urban public schools are familiar. When urban selections are included, they often depict

(From *Looking Like Me* by Walter Dean Myers. Text copyright © 2009 Walter Dean Myers. Published by Egmont US Inc. and used with permission.)

communities, families, and children from a deficit perspective, rather than presenting authentic and affirming images of urban life.

Although teacher education and library science programs typically include coursework in *multicultural* education, fewer urban public school teachers and librarians have extensive knowledge of the range of high quality *urban* children's literature available to them and the important role it can play in the development of reading and writing skills. It is our goal to build greater awareness among preservice and inservice teachers, administrators, and teacher educators about literature that authentically reflects and celebrates urban life and how it can be used to engage students and support their literacy learning.

In addition, the research summaries, text recommendations, and instructional examples contained throughout the book should be useful for educators in any type of setting who are interested in learning more about culturally relevant instruction and discovering a range of outstanding children's books to add to their collections.

Organization of the Book

We begin with several chapters that summarize research in culturally relevant instruction and the key role that urban children's literature can play in student engagement, reading and writing development, and dual language learning. In addition to building our collective background knowledge about the impact urban children's literature can have on students' academic achievement, these chapters are designed to help culturally responsive teachers and administrators justify their practices and "make the case" for supplementing published curricula with more culturally relevant texts.

Chapters 6 through 8 provide guidance on text selection, outlining characteristics of high-quality urban literature and informational texts, as well as guidelines for considering cultural and linguistic authenticity in text selection. The final chapters focus on how to use these books as effective tools for reading and writing instruction. Chapter 9 includes practical examples of text sets and instructional units that utilize urban children's literature in real classroom practices. Chapter 10 wraps it up with a step-by-step process that educators can take to get started in using urban children's literature to increase literacy and help students connect with content.

Additional Resources

The collection of children's literature featured in this book is one that we have developed over many years and countless hours of public library and Internet searches and scouring the shelves of classroom libraries in the schools in which we work. The reference list on page 183 includes the complete list of recommended children's books featured throughout the chapters.

You'll find these and even more titles on the Kids Like Us website at www.kidslikeus.org. Kids Like Us is a nonprofit organization established to raise awareness of these titles and to promote the use of multicultural and urban children's literature in city schools. The idea for Kids Like Us grew from the challenges we experienced when searching for high-quality urban children's literature to build our own collections: there was no established "list" or central resource for locating books with city settings and urban themes, and searching individual publishers' websites with random keywords to try to hit on the occasional title was incredibly inefficient and frustrating.

In the hopes of making your job easier, we've developed this searchable website as a one-stop resource for locating high-quality multicultural and urban children's literature. You'll find cover art, descriptions, and reading levels of each of the books, as well as teaching resources and links to author and illustrator websites that may be useful.

Acknowledgments

We draw on, and are inspired by, the work of a long line of exceptional scholars, educators, and activists who have been championing this cause for years. Most notably, our work has been motivated by the scholarship and advocacy of Dr. Rudine Sims Bishop, Professor Emeritus at the Ohio State University and foremost authority in the field on research in multicultural and African American children's literature. This book would not have been written without her legacy lighting our path.

In addition, Vanessa Irvin made us think much more carefully and critically about the literacy experiences of students of color from lower income communities. Her scholarship on the validating effects of urban fiction on teen readers and its potential for creating voracious readers and critical thinkers has furthered our thinking about the role that urban children's literature can play in young children's development. In addition, her work has pushed us to review books for more subtle cultural, linguistic, and social markers of city life and urban culture that may ring true for our students. Other noted scholars whose contributions have paved our way include James Banks, Lisa Delpit, Eugene Garcia, Geneva Gay, Gloria Ladson-Billings, Luis Moll, Jaime Naidoo, Sonia Nieto, and Teresa Perry, among many others cited throughout the text.

We would like to collectively acknowledge the incredibly talented authors and illustrators of the children's books referenced throughout these chapters, including Gregory Christie who provided the spectacular cover illustration for this book. Without their efforts and commitment to increasing diversity in children's literature, there would be no book to write. In particular, we would like to recognize the remarkable body of work of Walter Dean Myers. In the process of completing this book, we learned of Mr. Myers's passing. His artistic legacy has provided an essential source of validation for so many young people and will continue to inspire our students to find their own literary voices. Thank you for sharing your stories and for encouraging our students to share theirs.

Many thanks to our colleagues Tracy Reynolds and Lisa Jordan who share our passion for urban children's literature and helped develop early versions of our text selection criteria. We are also indebted to our many teacher-reviewers for their time and thoughtfulness in reading and reviewing the scores of books that have gradually evolved into the Kids Like Us collection.

We are grateful to our team at Rowman & Littlefield Education, especially Nancy Evans, Sarah Jubar, Carlie Wall, and Rachel Wing for their expert guidance throughout this process. Many thanks go to our graduate assistants, Bethany Meighan for her research and technical support and for pushing us along to bring this book to reality, and Kevin Derajtys for his careful attention to many details. We also thank Priti Ahuja, Iara Fuenmayor, Sarah Huisman, Christen Park, and Ashley Smith for their research assistance back when this book was just a kernel of an idea.

This book is the result of our collective work with teachers in dozens of schools in Chicago, St. Louis, New York, and other cities. A special thanks to Amy, Christel, Clarissa, Colleen, Jill, Karenne, Kim, Lauren, Lindsey, Marella, Maria, Mary, Michael, and Sinora for letting us hang out in your classrooms, talk with your students, and ask you endless questions about the amazing jobs you do as teachers in urban schools. The examples and applications in this book are all true stories that you shared with us.[1] You are all an inspiration, and your lasting influence on your students can never be fully measured in the myriad of assessments that we currently use.

We have seen firsthand on countless occasions how children respond when they see themselves and their experiences represented in real books; the enthusiasm and investment in reading and writing that culturally relevant texts instill in young readers and writers is tremendous. We wrote this book for them, in hopes that even more of their teachers will come to recognize the power and potential for urban children's literature in increasing literacy and a love of learning. We hope you find it useful.

Notes

1. Psuedonyms are used in place of many students' and teachers' names throughout the book.

Acknowledgments

Jane Fleming

Heartfelt thanks to Candace, Sandy, and Susan for your friendship, collegiality, and persistence in seeing this project through. Special thanks to my colleagues at UIC and Erikson Institute, especially Rebeca Itzkowich, my long-time teaching partner from whom I learn more about culturally relevant instruction every day. Thanks also to Mary Hynes-Berry for your encouragement, insight, and practical advice on this project. Infinite thanks to my Chicago and St. Louis public school teacher colleagues who have so generously shared their experiences to help bring this content to life, and to their students whose enthusiasm for reading and writing has been the inspiration for this book and for the work at Kids Like Us. Thank you to my family for your constant encouragement and long-distance cheerleading. And to Mimi, my fiercest ally, for your unwavering support of this cause that is so important to me.

Susan Catapano

I would like to thank all of the passionate and gifted teachers who work in urban schools and opened their classrooms to me so I could have access to observe, document, question, and learn about the importance of culturally relevant literature from their students and from them. I want to acknowledge the children and families who bring an unlimited enthusiasm for learning to the urban classroom every day and their teachers who support their goals for success. I would also like to thank my writing partners, Jane, Candace, and Sandy, as I have learned so much from all of you and look forward to our continued collaboration.

Candace M. Thompson

Big thanks to the mighty young poets of Williston Middle School and my daughter Journey—divine readers, writers, and poets all. You all inspire me and make me better with each meeting. And to my fellow authors whose combined expertise and explosive passion open books and doors for children (and us grown folks, too!) in ways great and small. It is their vision and love that moved this book from daydream to reality. Thank you!

Sandy Ruvalcaba Carrillo

Everything we accomplish is the result of the woven threads of our experiences and the influential individuals in our lives. I would like to begin by thanking Jane, Susan, and Candace for all of the work they have put into writing this book and for giving me the opportunity to contribute to this wonderful project. I would also like to acknowledge my teachers, mentors, colleagues, but most importantly, my students, who make me strive to be a better teacher every day. Lastly, I would like to thank my family, who continually encourage and support me in doing the things that I love.

CHAPTER ONE

~

Increasing Cultural Relevance
with Urban Children's Literature

I am the city in many different ways.
I am the city on its busiest days.
I'm not powerful or loud, breathtaking or proud:
I come from 99-cent stores, beauty parlors, and nail salons.
I come from the smell of sea salt and the curve of carousel horse hair.
I come from honey dripping off baklava at Lefkos Pyrgos.
I come from rare steak au poivre with potatoes au gratin,
Arroz con pollo with black beans, Belgian fries, bagels, shrimp lo mein,
and seared salmon with soy sauce.
I come from mangu with salami, and beans with sweets.
I come from a falafel.
I come from dark Atlantic waves and silent echoes.
I come from break dancing in Inwood in the wind.
I come from Are you Dominican, Mexican, Boricuan, or Nuyorican?
I come from What ya gonna do is take the A train . . .
I am from crowded streets full of figures
with thoughts that aren't said out loud
I am from everywhere and anywhere I call home . . .

When New York City public-school students attending Teachers and Writers Collaborative workshops were asked to "write about what it is like to live, learn, and play" in their city, their words readily captured the soul of the city and celebrated the diversity of their communities. Compared to when most of today's teachers were in school, greater numbers of American public school students embrace a variety of cultural traditions and speak more than one language. Many students were born in other countries or were born to parents who recently immigrated to, or sought refuge in, the United States. Family composition has also become more diverse, as many students are cared for in multigenerational extended families, or in adoptive, blended, or foster families. Others split time with parents who have divorced, have parents who are single, or have two moms or two dads.

At the same time, there is a growing class divide in America. Increasing numbers of American public school students experience poverty, food insecurity, and uncertain living situations or homelessness at various points in their lives. In a time when high school completion and college and career readiness is being stressed more than ever, success in school still remains closely tied to socioeconomic status.

DID YOU KNOW?

Almost two-thirds of urban public school students attend schools in which more than 50 percent of children are eligible for free or reduced lunch (U.S. Department of Education 2013).

With large numbers of urban public-school students underachieving on standardized measures of reading and writing, there is ongoing concern among educators that these children are often disengaged from the process of learning, especially in the area of literacy and language arts (e.g., Lazar, Edwards, and McMillon 2012; Lee 2000). Many prominent researchers in teacher education and social justice, including Linda Darling-Hammond (2010), Lisa Delpit (2012), Sonia Nieto and Patty Bodi (Nieto and Bode 2011), and Charles Payne (2008), point to a challenge that many students from lower-income communities and students of color face when trying to succeed in school. In the words of Howard Gardner, "much of the material presented in school strikes students as alien, if not pointless" (Gardner 1991, 149).

Culturally Relevant Teaching

In her book, *Multiplication Is for White People*, Lisa Delpit (2012, 156) challenges us to consider the following questions to this point:

- Are we making connections between young people's lives and the content we attempt to teach?
- Do our students feel welcomed into the school environment, or do they feel they must change who they are to be accepted?

Research on what teachers and educational institutions can do to provide meaningful and rigorous education for *all* students has evolved into the concept of culturally relevant teaching (CRT). Geneva Gay (2010) defines CRT as an approach that draws upon students' cultural knowledge and prior experiences in ways that affirm students' cultural heritages, forge connections between home communities and school, and provide a foundation for meaningful and effective instruction.

In describing culturally relevant approaches to literacy instruction, Gloria Ladson-Billings (1992) emphasizes that CRT not only helps provide a better "fit" between the school culture and students' home cultures, but is the kind of teaching that is designed "to *use* student culture as the basis for helping students understand themselves and others, structure social interactions, and *conceptualize knowledge* [italics added]" (314).

In her work with teachers of African American students, Ladson-Billings observed how successful teachers used their students' culture as a frame of reference for learning in all subjects, regardless of the teachers' own race or ethnicity. Teachers spent a significant amount of time getting to know their students and building strong, trusting, positive relationships with learners and their families. They could reference the social language of their students, helping them make connections to the academic materials, and even modeling linguistic code-switching. When the content for a particular lesson was outside of students' experience, teachers often drew on cultural understandings, resources in the neighborhood, and familiar experiences in the lives of their learners as a bridge to learning new material (Ladson-Billings 2009).

DID YOU KNOW?

Almost 80 percent of public school students in large cities are children of color, compared to 46 percent of students nationwide (U.S. Department of Education 2013).

Similarly, Luis Moll (2014) advocates for a culturally relevant pedagogy informed by community funds of knowledge. Among working-class families in his Tucson, Arizona community, diverse social networks were formed among neighbors to share information and to help families support each other, distributing responsibilities for childcare, making connections to employment, and sharing technical skills to avoid costly home or automotive repairs. These networks provided opportunities for "funds of knowledge" to be passed on from adults to children through informal apprentice-type situations.

Teachers were able to learn more about these community practices and integrate knowledge gained from conversations with families into academic content at school. For example, when one teacher learned about some families' expertise in ranching, she developed an integrated unit on the topic to draw on community funds of knowledge while expanding students' learning through the theme. By tapping into students' already strong background knowledge about horses and ranching, learning could quickly extend beyond basic fact learning to more abstract and critical investigations.

Students were challenged to carry out their own research-based inquiry projects. As a result, the content of the unit spanned many disciplines, including study of the history of horses and the role of Spanish explorers in bringing horses to the Americas, the science of anatomy and gestation, the mathematics of horseracing, even law as it pertained to raising animals in the city. Parents and community members with expertise in animal management and care were invited to meet with the class to give interviews and provide demonstrations. These community experts helped students with their research projects and supported their content area learning and acquisition of the technical vocabulary of the field. An additional important benefit of these projects was the development of closer relationships between teachers and family members, which led to a greater collective investment in students' learning (Moll 2014; see also Amanti 2005).

In addition to drawing on students' funds of knowledge, culturally responsive literacy instruction involves tapping into students' cultural interactional styles and ways of sharing information. Kathryn Au studied teachers who encouraged Hawaiian students to respond to literature through talk story, an informal conversation pattern prevalent among people from the islands. When discussing a story, children did not have to wait their turn to talk and were able to work together to answer the teacher's questions. Kathryn Au (2001) calls this type of reading activity a "hybrid event" because it incorporates the strengths students are bringing from home with teaching methods used in school. Building on the values and strengths of the home culture helps students gain access to high levels of literacy.

Unfortunately, this type of culturally relevant instruction is still the exception in our nation's schools. Rather than recognizing discontinuities in the curricula, schools often take more of an "assimilationist approach" that expects children to adjust to and learn from the materials and methods traditionally used for instruction (Ladson-Billings 1992, 314). Too frequently, the result is that instruction and curricula for young children from working-class or poor communities gets narrowed to focus on lower-level literacy skills using watered-down readers lacking rich language, cultural content, or even any real story to speak of. With all we know about effective teaching, this cannot be allowed to persist.

Increasing Cultural Relevance with Urban Children's Literature

In this series, we make the case for building a culturally responsive practice by using urban children's literature as a key component of the literacy curriculum. Use of literature in which learners see themselves and their communities reflected and valued can increase the effectiveness of instruction by making important cultural connections between students' home and school. Culturally relevant literature increases students' engagement and interest in learning, and also allows them to draw on funds of knowledge—their cultural and linguistic assets and lived experience—to engage with, interpret, and respond to texts as they develop as readers and writers.

A Relatively Rare Subgenre
Unfortunately, finding themselves in the text or, as Moll (2000) writes, "at least in some texts" is an experience that is rare for many urban public school students in the United States, particularly in underresourced city schools serving children of color. Despite the fact that teacher education and library science programs typically include coursework in multicultural education, few urban public school teachers and librarians have extensive knowledge of the range of urban children's literature available and the important role it can play in their students' literacy development. There is also a lack of funding to expand classroom and library collections to include these materials.

In general, the publication of children's literature featuring people of color is severely limited and has been at a relative plateau over the past decade. Each year, the Cooperative Children's Book Center (CCBC) at the University of Madison-Wisconsin reviews newly published children's books with close attention to books by and about people of color. In 2014, 393 (11 percent) of approximately 3,500 children's books reviewed featured "significant content" about people of color, which was actually a slight *increase* over previous years (Cooperative Children's Book Center 2015). Compare this with the population in the United States that is comprised roughly of 37 percent people of color (U.S. Census Bureau 2015) or to the percentage of young *children* of color in the United States, which is near 50 percent (Laughlin 2014). Better yet, compare this with the percentage of students of color in an urban public school district like Chicago, currently at about 91 percent.

Many of the titles featuring people of color that are published are what CCBC calls "formulaic nonfiction" books offering informational profiles of countries around the world rather than contemporary, relevant, family, or friendship stories, such as *Last Stop on Market Street* (De La Peña 2015) and *Niño Wrestles the World* (Morales 2013), or informational text sets in a familiar contexts, like *Machines Go to Work in the City* (Low 2012). Typically, the majority of books that are published about people of color each year do not contain content that reflects the current diversity of our nation or the realities of the lives of students today. Among those that do, there is even a smaller subset that features urban settings.

Altogether, it is not difficult to imagine the dearth of contemporary, culturally relevant books there may be in urban public school students' classrooms. Given the sheer numbers of urban public elementary school students in United States—nearly one-third of children in the country—this raises significant concern about the availability of high-quality, culturally relevant instructional materials.

Multicultural ≠ Culturally Relevant
It is important to make a distinction between *multicultural* and *culturally relevant* children's literature. Multicultural literature, defined broadly, includes "books that reflect the racial, ethnic, and social diversity" of our society and our world (Bishop 1997). Culturally relevant literature, on the other hand, refers specifically to books in which students can find themselves, their families, and their communities reflected and valued. Culturally relevant texts allow students to make personal connections to literature and explore their cultural identities through texts.

They are books in which the primary characters remind students of themselves or people they know, or where the setting reflects their neighborhoods and communities, or places they've lived. They may be informational texts that describe the lives of people who have had similar experiences to them, or that include concepts and content that are culturally familiar. As such, not all multicultural literature will be culturally relevant to all students, even when they share some central dimensions of culture, such as race or ethnicity, with the characters or subjects of study.

Many elementary-school teachers incorporate a variety of multicultural children's literature into the curriculum through a genre study of folktales from around the world. Sometimes teachers put a lot of thought into choosing folktales that have some relative match with students' racial, ethnic, or religious backgrounds in an effort to bring more "cultural relevance" to the curriculum. However, a folktale set in Kenya with characters that live alongside mammals of the Serengeti may be no more relevant to African American students who live on the west side of Chicago than a folktale from Vietnam or Poland.

This is not to suggest that a unit on folktales is not worthwhile. Indeed, the study of traditional literature exposes students to a genre deeply rooted in our histories and a format for passing on cultural traditions and values. Folktales can serve as mentor texts for the teaching of complex literary elements such as symbolism and personification. Comparison and contrasting of folktales from around the world may also help students recognize commonalities we may all share. However, when working to increase the *cultural relevance* of collections, it is critical to consider contemporary content that reflects students' everyday lives and to which students can make meaningful, personal connections.

Rudine Sims Bishop describes books as "mirrors" and "windows," sometimes reflecting our lives and experiences, and sometimes offering views of the broader world (Bishop 1990). This book is about ensuring that urban classroom collections and school curricula include a substantial proportion of "mirrors" so students can see that they are included and valued in the life of school and so they can draw on their knowledge and experiences as a foundation for literacy learning.

"They know Junebug. They know Jolita. They know Darnell. They get it."

—writer Alice Mead, after discussing her book *Junebug in Trouble* with a group of third graders at a St. Louis public school

Defining Urban Children's Literature

In defining urban children's literature for the purposes of this book, two scholars serve as guides: Rudine Sims Bishop, whose groundbreaking scholarship has served as a cornerstone in the study of multicultural children's literature for more than three decades, and Vanessa Irvin, librarian, educator, expert, and advocate of street literature for teens, young adults, and older readers. Irvin defines "urban fiction" as stories set in urban settings that "highlight the socio-economic realities and culture of the characters that are at the center of the story" (Morris 2012, 4).

Although all cities include residents that span the socioeconomic spectrum, the focus of this book series is on helping urban public-school teachers, librarians, and other educators develop collections that are most relevant to the lives and experiences of the children in their classrooms, the majority of whom are likely to be children of color from lower income neighborhoods. As a result, the multicultural children's literature that is highlighted will be, in large part, books written by and about people who have "traditionally been marginalized" both in the canon of children's literature, and in society in general (Bishop 1997, 2).

Definition of Urban

Urban areas across the United States are as diverse as the people who populate them. From large urban centers like Chicago, Los Angeles, New York, and Philadelphia to midsized cities like Baltimore, Detroit, and San Francisco, or smaller cities such as Atlanta, Fresno, Miami, or St. Louis, the architecture, landscape, language, culture, and feel of a city can be considerably unique. Urban children's literature includes those books that re-create "scenes and activities that realistically occur in daily life" for children in the city (Morris 2012, 4).

Reflecting the geography of many cities, these stories are often set in neighborhoods featuring particular cultural groups, like Chinatown (Low 1997) or El Barrio (Chocolate 2009). Characters often reside in multiunit buildings or in homes including multiple or extended families. They may rely on public transportation, or walk to shop in nearby delis or bodegas. Their blocks are more frequently distinguished by brownstone steps than by private green space.

The topics addressed in urban fiction are realistic, sometimes revealing challenging aspects of city life while also celebrating the love of the city, its diversity, and its possibility. Characters in stories or poems may experience economic hardship (e.g., Gettin' Through Thursday, Cooper 1998), temporary homelessness (e.g., *A Shelter in Our Car*, Gunning 2004), and loss or separation (e.g., *From North to South*, Laínez 2010), but they also treasure their families as in *The Have a Good Day Café* (Park and Park 2008), *My Feet Are Laughing* (Norman 2006), and *We Had a Picnic This Sunday Past* (Woodson 1997). They enjoy exploring their communities in books like Ina Cumpiano's (2009) *Quinito's Neighborhood* and Sharon Dennis Wyeth's (2002) *Something Beautiful*, and they often get into typical, playful mischief with friends (e.g., *Danitra Brown, Class Clown*, Grimes 2005).

Like many of the students in urban classrooms, the protagonist in an urban children's book may also have concerns about adjusting to a new culture or learning a new language, similar to Juanito in *The Upside Down Boy* (Herrera 2006). Or, like Madlenka (Sís 2010), she may simply be reveling in the multicultural, multilingual oasis that is her apartment building.

Informational Texts

Our definition of urban literature is also extended to include informational texts in addition to literature. With the Common Core State Standards' (CCSS) emphasis on exposing students to a balance of literature and informational texts, it is important to teach with a variety of concept books, biographies, and other informational texts that support content area learning in mathematics, science, and social studies.

As with all genres of texts used for instruction and enjoyment in the classroom, nonfiction collections should include a healthy dose of culturally relevant texts that features people of color who are accomplished in diverse fields and industries, as well as informational texts that feature urban architecture (e.g., *Urban Animals*, Hill 2009) or urban ecology (e.g., *City Critters: Wildlife in the Urban Jungle*, Read 2012) to provide a familiar foundation for learning new mathematics and science concepts.

> "How do we give students access to the kind of literacy achievement that will open doors to opportunities in the larger society?"
>
> —Kathryn Au (2001)

The primary focus of this book is on the selection and use of developmentally appropriate urban children's literature for emergent, beginning, and intermediate readers ranging from preschool through the middle grades.

While Irvin's research examines "street lit," a more vivid and gritty subgenre of urban fiction typically geared toward teens, young adults, and older readers, this book on urban children's literature shares its central goal: to identify developmentally appropriate books that invite children to "make movies in their heads" (Morris 2012, 4) by engaging with texts in which they find themselves, their communities, and their experiences reflected.

For young children, urban children's literature can play a critical role in fostering emergent literacy skills, supporting productivity in oral language when exploring texts that draw on familiar experiences. For more capable young readers, connecting with urban children's literature can spark the motivation required to develop fluency and stamina, as well as support students in mastering strategies for comprehending texts in deep and meaningful ways. In the chapters to follow, this book will demonstrate how urban children's literature can generate interest and engagement in early reading experiences and provide an important foundation on which to build early reading skills.

Considering Many Dimensions of "Urban"
Gay notes that descriptions of culture and cultural behaviors, even in texts that some might consider culturally authentic literature, are merely "approximations of reality" (2010, 12). In addition, not all urban settings are the same. Urban landscapes, architecture, dialects, and pastimes can vary widely across regions and even within cities. Care should be taken to identify books that reflect contexts and experiences relevant to the children living in a particular urban community.

When considering the cultural relevance of urban children's literature, it is also important to consider the interplay of many aspects of a child's background, including race, ethnicity, social class, language, gender, family structure, residence, and religion. While the city setting may be central, also consider the extent to which books capture the context, rhythm, and spirit of those settings, including racial and cultural diversity, language and dialect variation, aspects of immigrant life, familiar urban ecology and architecture, and the pace, activities, and cultural routines of life in the city.

In addition, the social context of students' lives comes into play: who they spend time with, where they go to school, what they do for fun, and so on. The goal of focusing on urban children's literature is to ensure that children can find themselves reflected in the curriculum—that the books selected for instruction can help to tell their stories now and also provide a world of possibilities for imagining their futures.

Using Urban Children's Literature in Literacy Instruction

Research has strengthened educators' understandings about the foundational skills needed to become a strong reader and writer and the types of teaching methods that help support acquisition of literacy skills for emergent and beginning readers (Shanahan et al. 2010; National Institute of Child Health and Human Development 2000). Not only is the method of instruction important, the materials used in teaching literacy are also critical to students' success.

In practice, the inclusion of people of color in the curriculum can often get reduced to the study of certain genres of literature, such as folktales like *Lon Po Po: A Red-Riding Hood Story from China* (Young 1989), historical fiction such as *Sweet Clara and the Freedom Quilt* (Hopkinson 1995), or biography like *Harvesting Hope* (Krull 2003). This can result in making invisible the friendship, family, neighborhood, and school experiences of "everyday" kids (Martin 2004, 52) that might be better reflected in realistic fiction, poetry, and information texts.

Many classroom libraries in underresourced urban public schools still have few books with characters of color. In some cases, those books are relegated to a single "multicultural" bin, even in cases where 100 percent of the students are African American or Latino. This results in a form of "curricular segregation" (Gay 1990, 56) through which teachers, however unintentionally, may be promoting inequity and marginalization of students in their own classrooms. Even among engaged readers, urban educators often hear students of color yearning for more relevance in the curriculum, exasperated at the thought of having to "keep reading that book about Martin Luther King, Jr. until [I die]" (Dyson 1994, 160).

This type of curricular segregation ignores the realities of urban students' lives and the multilayered self-conceptions of urban youth that are represented by more than racial and ethnic membership (Gay 2010; Heath 1983). As a result, many children develop the impression that books are not about them or for them, and they can start to feel disinterested and excluded from school. Unless there is full inclusion of urban youth and children of color in the curriculum, there is the risk of further marginalizing students and potentially limiting their interest and willingness to engage in literacy learning.

> *"My son learned to read with dinosaur books, and clearly he's never seen one."*
>
> —A parent questioning the necessity of culturally relevant texts in learning to read

Funds of Knowledge to Support Reading Development

Arguments like this can be heard in many schools, and on its surface, this may be a fair question to ask. In reality, however, that same child probably had plenty of dinosaur books or dinosaur puzzles at home, and probably "played dinosaurs" with those little plastic toy creatures. He has probably had an adult or older sibling talk with him about dinosaurs and scaffold his learning about the different types, names, and kinds of things that dinosaurs would do, such as which ones are herbivores or which are carnivores. Maybe he has been to a museum of natural history to see the dinosaur collection, or maybe he has just seen every dinosaur video available to a five-year-old.

So, yes, when he picks up that dinosaur book in his kindergarten classroom, *he brings with him all of this experience, this cultural capital, and these funds of knowledge.* When he sees the picture of the dinosaur with that curvy long neck and the big long tail, and he sees that gargantuan word that starts with a "b," maybe he *can* read it as "brontosaurus," even though he has never seen one.

Unfortunately, the language, experience, cultural capital, and funds of knowledge about the world that many urban public school students bring with them to school is often very different from the kinds of language, experiences, and knowledge that are represented in the books that teachers are trying to use to teach children how to read. Our goal is to help educators think more critically about text selection and to find books that draw on students' cultural capital as a foundation for literacy learning.

Understanding Urban

In addition to increasing the cultural relevance of schooling with a stronger presence of urban children's literature, it is equally important that teachers develop competence in effectively utilizing these in instruction. Culturally relevant teaching requires more than simply integrating a few more multicultural children's books into the curriculum. Achieving real curriculum transformation that purposefully and intentionally includes culturally relevant experiences requires not just the availability of materials, but how they are used. Teachers should be intentional in planning instruction that involves students as firsthand resources of knowledge and engages students in thinking critically about the social issues that impact their lives, such as discrimination and economic inequality (Banks 1993; Gorski 2012).

For many teachers, this can be a challenge on several fronts. Much of the research in culturally responsive teaching underscores the centrality of teachers' cultural self-knowledge and competence in rejecting a colorblind or color-neutral stance that serves to further marginalize children from diverse ethnic, racial, linguistic, and cultural backgrounds. In order for teachers to tap into the funds of knowledge that children bring with them to school, Carol Weinstein and colleagues (2004) contend that teachers—the majority of whom are European American, white, and middle-class—must first examine their own cultural identities and recognize biases before they can make use of the knowledge of their students' cultural backgrounds. This is important because "[m]ulticultural competence is directly related to an understanding of one's own motives and beliefs, biases, values, and assumptions about human behavior" (29).

Getting beyond deficit-based perceptions of urban communities is essential. A key characteristic of teachers in Ladson-Billings's (1992) momentous study of successful teachers of African American children was that they viewed the urban community "as a good place to live and work" (317) and that they recognized the significance of the community and the culture of their learners as part of the learning process.

Maintaining a positive view of urban communities does not mean teachers can ignore or "sugar coat" the social and economic realities that children and families face when living in a significantly impoverished community. Teachers unaware of or not sensitive to the effects of stressful life circumstances, poor environmental conditions, or children's roles and responsibilities in their families may make misguided assumptions about students' investment in school, the quality of parenting they receive, or their overall learning capabilities. Authentic, culturally relevant teaching requires a willingness to have "real" conversations with students. Some teachers may be reluctant to open that door, but keeping it closed denies students inclusion of their whole selves in the learning process.

One thing is clear: we must engage children from diverse cultural, racial, ethnic, and linguistic backgrounds with curricula and teaching that is relevant to their lives, affirms the important knowledge students bring with them to the school, and supports them as they build meaningful connections between home and school.

Alejandra's Story:

From the time I was a young child, I realized that there was a divide between my home and school life. I imagine it was confusing going from being a competent girl who could tell stories, recite poetry, and sing and dance to songs taught to me by my mother and grandmother to a girl who couldn't answer a simple question in English. One day, I went to school and my confidence and rich vocabulary evaporated into a wide-eyed stare and pressed lips because nobody spoke my language. Every day, my mom stood at the door and sent me to school with a blessing and a reminder to listen to my teacher. In her eyes, teachers knew best and she wanted to make sure I knew that, too.

As the years went on, I began to dislike school. To me, school was like watching a black and white, silent movie. I would go through the motions and be the quiet, obedient student who can easily be forgotten in the classroom. I couldn't wait to rush home and enter my world of color, laughter, loudness, family, and the smell of the delicious arroz and frijoles my mom had prepared for me. It was like I was two different people and the person I was at home had absolutely nothing in common with who I was at school.

My teachers began to have meetings with my mom and told her that I wasn't learning. "She doesn't really talk much. She hasn't learned her letter sounds and doesn't know how to read. Maybe, she'll need to be retained." "You know, you're confusing your child by speaking to her in Spanish. You should really try to speak to her in English." The teachers who are never to be questioned and are never wrong were telling me I was not good enough for school.

It took me many years to catch up and eventually succeed in school. It took me even longer to overcome the feelings of "not being good enough" for school. It definitely affected the paths I took in school (choosing not to participate in a lot of school-related activities, choosing not to take more accelerated courses even though I tested into them). To this day, I often wonder, what if . . . What if I hadn't been able to eventually form that wobbly bridge between my school persona and who I really was? What if that bridge would have existed, strong and sturdy, from the beginning?

This brings the conversation back to reflecting on the questions posed by Delpit (2012): Are we making connections between young people's lives and the content we attempt to teach? Do our students feel welcomed into the school environment, or do they feel they must change who they are to be accepted? This book examines the contribution of urban children's literature to culturally responsive teaching and literacy development. Readers are encouraged to keep these questions in mind. If the answers seem elusive, keep reading. There are suggestions, ideas, and experiences shared by teachers and students throughout the chapters.

Summing It Up:
Academic and Social Benefits of Culturally Relevant Instruction

Academic Outcomes for Students

- Increases engagement and interest in learning
- Draws on students' cultural and linguistic assets in engaging with, interpreting, and responding to text as children develop as readers and writers
- Sparks the motivation required to develop reading fluency and stamina
- Supports students in mastering strategies for comprehending texts in deep and significant ways

Social Outcomes for Students

- Helps students make personal connections to literature
- Children can explore their cultural identities through texts
- Engagement and investment increase when children see they are included and valued in the life of school
- Builds meaningful connections between home and school
- Increases relevance of curricula by connecting with students' lives

CHAPTER TWO

~

The Power of the Mirror

Identity, Academic Self-Concept, and Motivation to Learn

> *"I think I might know him."*
>
> —a fourth grader, responding during literature discussion of *Junebug* by Alice Mead

When a group of fourth graders in a St. Louis public school read the book *Junebug* by Alice Mead, they made such strong, personal connections to the text that it was hard for some of them to imagine that the book was a work of fiction. The students could envision and describe what life might be like in Junebug's neighborhood around the Auburn Street housing project in New Haven. They could relate to ten-year-old Junebug's role as a big brother and caregiver to little Tasha, they understood the challenges that Junebug, his friend Robert, and other boys growing up in their neighborhood sometimes faced, and they identified with Junebug's hopes and dreams for his future.

This chapter discusses why these types of connections are so important for students' literacy learning. It reviews the research on the relationship between identity and academic achievement, and describes how affective connections with texts can lead to increased engagement, effort, and skill. Many examples of students making connections with urban children's literature are woven throughout the chapter, concluding with ideas for using author and illustrator study to help students envision themselves as readers and writers with stories of their own to tell. In subsequent chapters, we discuss specific

17

methods through which urban children's literature can be used as a tool to accelerate literacy learning.

The Relationship between Identity and School Achievement

The connection between identity and learning is well documented. When learning activities are connected with one's sense of self as an individual or as a member of a group, student participation and engagement is especially strong (Brophy 2008; Faircloth 2012). Students are motivated when learning activities connect to their daily lives or lived experiences. This makes the activities meaningful and worthwhile to students. They will take learning seriously and put forth more effort in order to accomplish what they set out to do when they see the value and connection in what is being learned.

While there are many dimensions of student identity, a students' racial identity may play an especially important role in engagement. Racial identity refers to the beliefs, opinions, and attitudes one holds about his or her racial group (Swanson et al. 2009). The development of racial identity begins in early childhood. Even preschoolers can categorize racial groups by skin color, for example, and can express preferences and beliefs about race and social class.[1] By age ten, children are well aware of racial stereotypes (Swanson et al. 2009). There is a well-established body of research that indicates that a positive racial identity is associated with positive academic attitudes and outcomes.[2]

How a child's racial identity gets negotiated in school can have a significant impact on his or her academic self-concept—the perceptions she forms about herself through her experiences in school (Marsh and Martin 2011). Not surprisingly, teachers and school leaders can play a significant role in either embracing or disregarding students' cultural identities in school. Those who value diversity and engage in culturally responsive teaching can contribute to children's development of a positive racial identity, which promotes resilience and helps to increase student achievement.[3] When children find themselves, their families, and their communities reflected in the curriculum and included in the "conversations of schooling," they are more likely to be engaged in learning, feel capable and competent as learners, and experience greater school success (Shields 2004, 122).

> *"When we see ourselves, we are reminded of our existence, our humanity, and that we are worth rooting for."*
>
> —Mara Brock Akil (2013)

Making intentional connections between students' home and academic lives provides opportunities for children to stay connected with their cultural identities while engaging at school. Unfortunately, many students face day-to-day struggles when they do not feel a sense of belonging in their school environment. This disconnect can have a strong negative impact on students' academic self-worth, even among competent learners. Consider Javier's story, below:

Javier's Story:

At some point, the mere feeling of being an "outsider" at school began to creep its way into my academic performance. When I was in elementary school, the teacher assigned each of us a country that we had to research to learn about its cultural customs and present to the class. Parents were invited, but like most school activities, this one was during school hours. Although it would have meant the world to me to see my father there, I understood that he could not justify jeopardizing our livelihood and take a day off from work to come see me at school. My mother planned on going and that was enough for me.

The day of the presentation came and I was both excited and nervous. I had done my work and was ready to tell the group everything I had learned about India through my memorized speech that I had practiced over and over. Our presentations began promptly at 11 a.m. and ended exactly before lunch time. The whole time I was in front giving my presentation, I was scanning the crowd looking for my mother's reassuring, proud face. Of course, I didn't see her because my mom still was not used to the rigidness of time that is involved in all school activities. She was running late, and I forgot most of my speech.

Afterward, the teacher had a long talk with me about how upset and disappointed she was with my lack of preparation. I was sad and frustrated too, but I didn't try to explain. This was a series of misunderstandings on all sides and the beginning of many failures that I encountered at school. The irony of this is that the very assignment that was intended to help us better understand other cultures made me realize that I did not understand nor was I understood in the very world I was living in.

Despite his commitment and preparation for the assignment, Javier's confidence in learning was negatively impacted by this misunderstanding with his teacher. Rather than try to explain what had happened, Javier felt a need to compartmentalize his cultural identity in a way that resulted in much longer-term effects on his academic achievement. In addition, his teacher's perception of him was altered by this exchange, likely calling into question his capabilities and lowering her expectation for his preparation in the future. Willis Hawley and Sonia Nieto (2010) call this an "inconvenient truth"—that race and ethnicity affect how students respond to instruction and this, in turn, impacts teachers' assumptions about students' capabilities and how much they can learn (1).

Teachers and schools play a critical role in helping children maintain a positive cultural identity while solidifying their sense of selves as learners (Brown and Chu 2012; Cummins 2001; García Coll and Marks 2009). Seeing oneself represented in the characters, authors, and illustrators in a classroom and school library can go a long way in making sure we are conveying a message to children that school is *for* and *about* them.

Literacy and Identity

The selection of texts that intersect with various dimensions of students' identities can have an impact on reading and writing achievement through its influence on motivation and engagement in literacy learning activities. Readers tend to be more interested in books that they can connect with personally, and they often seek out books with characters with whom they can identify (Francios 2013; Graff 2010; McNair 2013; Sims 1983; Smith 1995). In turn, there is substantial evidence that children who value reading and see it as an interesting activity tend to engage in reading more frequently and subsequently develop better reading skills.[4]

"It matters when a book has characters named Tameka and Shanice, not named Sarah and Lynn."

—Jill, first-grade teacher, referring to My Best Friend by Mary Ann Rodman

---

This relationship between reading interest and reading skill is especially important for urban public-school teachers to consider, because it holds true for *all* students, including children from lower income families or students whose parents may have less formal education (Guthrie, Shafer, and Huang 2001). There also seems to be a reciprocal relationship between motivation, engagement, and reading skill; as children become more capable readers, they are motivated to read more and more (Morgan and Fuchs 2007), which in turn, continues to support reading development.

Increasing Motivation and Engagement with Urban Children's Literature

Our willingness to engage in any activity depends both on how much we value the activity as well as the degree which we expect to be able to complete it successfully (Wigfield and Eccles 2000). Using urban children's literature that reflects students' experiences can increase engagement in literacy learning because it taps into students' funds of knowledge and invites them to share their expertise and insights. Being able to offer expertise is satisfying and empowering to learners, and contributes to their investment in what is being taught in school (Brophy 2008).

Teresa's Story:

When I use texts which students can relate to, it really does engage my students in discussions. It is easier to participate in discussions when you are familiar with the topic or when you understand what a character might have gone through. Students can easily make connections to stories which remind them of home, their traditions, their language. I always find that when a read aloud is about someone who resembles them in some way, even the most introverted student has something to share.

For example, in her work in a predominantly African American urban school, Jeane Copenhaver (2001) reported a dramatic increase in second- and third-graders' participation and engagement in a literature discussion of Walter Dean Myers's (1989) *Malcolm X: A Fire Burning Brightly*. Teachers were "floored" by children's connections with the text as they related themes from the story to their own lives and shared opinions about the characters' situations (355). Children were more invested in understanding the text and demonstrated independent use of comprehension strategies such as making connections, asking questions, and rereading throughout the literature discussion.

Gayla Lohfink and Juana Loya (2010) reported similarly high levels of engagement when reading culturally relevant texts with their bilingual, Mexican American third-graders. Sharing dual language picture book memoirs such as *The Upside Down Boy/El niño de cabeza* by Juan Filipe Herrera (2006) and *My Very Own Room/Mi propio cuartito* by Amada Irma Pérez (2000) led to a wealth of text-to-self connections in literature discussion among their students. Having access to books by authors and illustrators who shared their cultural backgrounds also had an empowering effect on students' identities as writers. After reading a number of culturally relevant texts, students "became the authors" as they transferred their connections into writing their own dual language personal narratives (Lohfink and Loya 2010, 361).

In essence, these teachers are helping children connect their "funds of identity" with literacy learning (Esteban-Guitart and Moll 2014)—actively making use of family and community experiences as they begin to define themselves as readers and writers. As a result, children can begin to see their experiences as assets to learning, that their cultural funds of identity can be compatible with their literacy identities, not something to be "left at the door" when they enter the classroom.

> *"Most helpful to me was simply reading the ground-breaking book* The House on Mango Street *by Sandra Cisneros. It was a revelation to see that the stories of my own life/culture could make a compelling book. It is easy to overlook the simple fact that seeing examples of your heritage in books empowers you, but there it is."*
>
> —Meg Medina, author of *Mango, Abuela, and Me*

As Moisès Esteban-Guitart and Luis Moll (2014) point out, educators can offer "possibilities" or constrictions" with the choices they make (33), which will no doubt have different effects on the ways children respond to instruction. It is up to us to determine whether to rely on a traditional or "popular" literary canon or to be intentional about text selection that allows our students to bring their whole selves to the learning process.

Tapping into Multiple Identities

The selection of texts that intersect with a number of dimensions of students' identities may have an especially strong impact on reading and writing achievement though its influence on motivation and engagement in literacy learning activities. Consider "Carter's Story" below, which describes a group of second-graders' responses to a read aloud of the book *My Steps* by Sally Derby (1996).

The story in *My Steps* included many elements with which children in Carter's classroom in Chicago could identify: the book features an African American primary character; she is about the same age as the children in

---

Carter's Story:

So as we were reading My Steps, *we got to this one page. I'm not from Chicago, so this wasn't very familiar to me, but when I read it to my kids they made an immediate connection.*

It says:

> I have another friend, that's Nicholas, and when he comes, we all play stone school. Here's how we play: I'm teacher first, because they're my steps. I put my hands behind my back and hide a little stone. Then I put my hands out in front. Essie and Nicholas sit on [step] One (that's kindergarten), and they take turns guessing which hand [the stone is in]. When they guess right, they get to move up to the first grade. And whoever gets to fourth grade first [the fourth step] gets to be teacher next. (Derby 1996, 20)

When my students saw that, they started shouting, "That's Rock Teacher! That's Rock Teacher!" and started making connections to this game they play all the time. They were really excited to see that something in the story was totally related to what they do on a regular basis. So now the book goes from just being some book that my teacher read, to "Man, I can make connections with this book," so I want to read this book and reread this book. So if I do this two or three times a week with a text, they now have these books that they are reading and rereading. Comprehension is going up. Vocabulary is increasing. Fluency is increasing. Their love of reading is increasing."

---

the classroom; she lives in a city where residents experience changes of seasons, similar to what might be experienced in Chicago; and, to the students' delight, the children in the story played a game very similar to one Carter's students played all the time.

There are many more studies that demonstrate how the use of culturally relevant texts can transform the level of literacy engagement in classrooms (e.g., Boston and Baxley 2007; Carrillo 2012; Feger 2006; Fleming and Clark 2014; Kirkland 2011). In one urban public school serving dual language learners, adding culturally relevant texts to the mix contributed to nearly doubling the frequency of students' reading (e.g., Brassell 1999). Creating stronger links between "what children learn and what they live" may be especially important for supporting the academic engagement of children living in poverty, especially when the realities of these students' lives are seldom acknowledged in the day-to-day of school curricula (Hunsberger 2007, 422).

In addition, there is substantial evidence that culturally relevant texts can support motivation and persistence of struggling or disengaged readers (Al-Hazza 2010; Faircloth 2012). Increasing engagement by connecting learning with identity and inviting children to share expertise and insights from their experience may be particularly important for these students.

Michael's Story:

When you have a reluctant and struggling reader, you have to do everything possible to find books that they can relate to and understand. Every child has a spark in them; it is our job to ignite that spark. I have found that many students who were not [initially] interested in reading were the first ones to go to the classroom library and pick out a book.

Increasing Family Engagement

The connection between identity and reading engagement is also strong for adults. Because of this, urban children's literature may be a useful tool for increasing family engagement around reading. For example, as part of an after-school parent literacy program, Clarena Larrota and Jesse Gainer (2008) used books like *The House on Mango Street* by Sandra Cisneros (1984) to spark the interest of their adult learners and support them in making personal connections to texts.

The discussion that followed provided a rich context for participants to practice application of reading comprehension strategies that they could then use with their children at home. Similar programs have demonstrated that family members subsequently sought out similar books to read with their children that captured familiar family and community experiences (e.g., Madrigal et al. 1999; Ortiz and Ordoñez-Jasis 2005).

Books to Explore Emotions

Reading culturally relevant literature not only has an effect on student engagement, but it may also impact how students learn to confront and address emotional concerns that can hinder academic achievement in the classroom. Research suggests that literature is an excellent tool for promoting children's social and emotional learning because it provides a forum for children to discuss the causes and consequences of emotions, and it provides opportunities for teachers to teach social and emotional learning strategies (Ahn 2005; McCoy and McKay 2006; Morrell and Morrell 2012).

As they read about characters going through challenges, children can discuss and debate a range of problem-solving strategies and weigh the outcomes and potential consequences of characters' decisions (Prater et al. 2006). Children also tend to experience less apprehension when discussing situations involving storybook characters versus their own situations. When shared in a trusting, caring environment, urban children's literature may encourage some students to more openly discuss issues they might not have

---

Jill's Story:

I think about [my students making] connections along the lines of socioeconomic situations, like when we read Gettin' Through Thursday *[about a family that's living paycheck to paycheck] or when we had read* Junebug *and they were talking about living in public housing. When you have those kinds of experiences in books, then that makes the kids feel like it's ok. There is some part of [these types of books] that I think other people might look at and think, "Oh, that's not good," but the flip side of it is that it makes my kids feel like, "Oh, somebody else is going through that, too."*

shared otherwise (e.g., Berns 2004; Nicholson and Pearson 2003). It may be an especially useful tool in empowering immigrant children as they adjust to the many changes that come with moving to a new country (Baghban 2007).

Addressing the Need for More Mirrors

Despite its great potential for increasing student engagement, frequency of reading, and reading skills, urban public school students often are not seeing enough "mirrors" in the books they are being asked to read in school. Indeed, the gap between students' lived experience and schooling may be a primary contributor to a lack of student engagement in reading and school (Fairbanks and Ariail 2006; Tatum 2008).

This critical role that text selection plays in literacy learning is often a "glaring omission" (Tatum 2006, 45) in discussion of urban public school students' achievement. Most publishers of literacy curricula that service public schools tailor selections to reach a national mainstream audience. As a result, few story selections include images of city living, multicultural and multilingual communities, and familiar urban landscapes. Texts may be selected to represent more "generically" diverse families or neighborhoods without authentically representing any student or family in the school community (see chapter 8 for discussion). Moreover, reading curricula in the early grades rarely include stories that discuss the experiences of children in poverty (Hunsberger 2007).

Instead, too often texts are selected solely for their utility in teaching accuracy and comprehension strategies. This focus on improving technical skills tends to outweigh consideration of more "enabling texts" that can help students make connections, sustain intense engagement in literature discussion, and support their exploration of their identities as young people and as readers and writers (Tatum 2006, 47).

Similarly, the omission of books by authors and illustrators of color from school-based book club catalogs contributes to restriction in access to culturally relevant texts (McNair 2008). Especially concerning is the limited availability of culturally relevant transitional chapter book series that are so popular among second- through fourth-grade readers and can contribute significantly to reading fluency and stamina (Fleming and Carrillo 2011a; Hughes-Hassell, Barkley, and Koehler 2009; Rich 2012).

It is a rare occurrence to find series like *The Carver Chronicles* (English 2013), *Make Way for Dyamonde Daniel* (Grimes 2010), or *Zapato Power: Freddy Ramos Takes Off!* (Jules 2010) among the library shelves in any classroom. Not only are there few series featuring primary characters of color, the series that are available are limited in how many books are published and where they are distributed.

Research has shown that positive attitudes toward reading tend to decrease over the course of the elementary grades (McKenna, Kear, and Ellsworth 1995). When students do not see themselves represented in the texts that are utilized and valued in school, they may be left with the impression that this reading "club" is not for them. This can contribute to even greater disengagement, resulting in a lack of investment in reading as a valued activity and limiting the regular practice necessary to build reading skills and keep them strong.

Teacher Beliefs and Actions

When a teacher picks a book to share with students, it sends a very important message to children. Even if we do not explain to children why we chose a particular text, the sheer fact that we selected that book tells them something about its importance in our eyes; it tells them a lot about who we are, what school is about, and what we value. As a result, it is critically important to examine our literacy curricula and trade book collections to determine the extent to which children can see that their families, communities, and experiences are valued in what we teach.

Fortunately, when we find our curricula may be lacking these "mirrors," we *can* do something about it. Even in schools with prescribed curricula, teachers, librarians, and school administrators have options when it comes to text selection. This chapter has highlighted many examples of how urban children's literature can support the development of a positive racial identity and the strong academic self-concept that can contribute to interest and engagement in literacy activities. Chapters 3 and 4 provide additional detail about the critical role urban children's literature can play in children's reading and writing development, as well as in the language and literacy learning of dual language learners. These initial chapters are designed to support educators in "making the case" for inclusion of more urban children's literature in the curriculum. Subsequent chapters in this book provide specific guidance for the selection of high-quality texts, as well as strategies for integrating those texts with the core curriculum.

Summing It Up: The Impact on Racial Identity, Academic Self-Concept, and Motivation

- Connections between school and cultural identities of children promote engagement, participation, and academic resilience
- Culturally relevant texts support positive racial and cultural identities and strong academic self-concepts
- Culturally relevant texts provide important pathways for connecting the experiences and perspectives of children, their families, and their communities to the classroom
- Urban children's literature can increase family engagement in literacy activities
- Urban children's literature can promote children's social and emotional learning through reading and discussion
- Recognize and nurture connections between student cultural identity and literacy development

Notes

1. Results of several studies indicate that these findings hold true for very young children of various racial backgrounds. See Doyle and Aboud (1995), Ramsey (1991), Spencer (1982), and Spencer (1984). More recent studies continue to confirm these findings (e.g., Pahlke, Bigler, and Suizzo 2012).

2. Much of the research on the relationship between racial identity and academic achievement involves adolescents, rather than younger children. The results of this research consistently reveal positive associations between these constructs: having a positive racial identity is generally associated with more positive academic attitudes and outcomes. Since the development of one's racial identity starts at a very young age, the connection between racial identity, school engagement, and academic achievement should be an important consideration for educators at all levels. See Chavous et al. (2003); Eccles, Wong, and Peck (2006); and Wong, Eccles, and Sameroff (2003) for a more comprehensive discussion.

3. Many studies indicate the important role that teachers and the school environment can play in contributing to students' racial identity as it relates to school and academic achievement (see Eccles [2006] for an excellent review). Teachers' attitudes toward students of color and schools' valuing of diversity can contribute significantly to students' beliefs in their academic abilities and their willingness to engage fully in school. Feeling positively about one's ethnic group is especially impor-

tant for maintaining positive engagement in school, particularly when students are faced with discrimination in the school environment (Brown and Chu 2012; Smalls et al. 2007). The opposite is also true. When students perceive that teachers hold low expectations for their achievement based on race, this can have substantial cumulative negative effects on motivation and achievement (see Eccles and Roesner [2011] for review). Given the impact teachers' attitudes and actions can have on student achievement, teacher-preparation programs that incorporate teachers' examination of their beliefs about race and engage them in learning about cultural responsive teaching methods is of critical importance (Bryan and Atwater 2002).

4. Seminal research documenting the strong, stable relationship between interest, reading frequency, and skill development has been conducted by the team of researchers including Linda Baker, John T. Guthrie, and Allan Wigfield since the 1990s. Children who find reading interesting engage in reading more frequently and develop stronger reading skills (see Baker and Wigfield 1999; Guthrie and Wigfield 2000; Wang and Guthrie 2004; Wigfield 2004; Wigfield and Eccles 2000; Wigfield and Guthrie 1997). Additional recent studies support these findings (e.g., Unrau and Schlackman 2006; Becker, McElvany, and Kortenbruck 2010).

CHAPTER THREE

~

Enhancing Reading and Writing Instruction with Urban Children's Literature

Imagine that you are five years old, and that you are just starting school at Melody Elementary in West Garfield Park, a predominantly African American neighborhood on Chicago's west side. Adjacent to one of the largest public parks in the city, West Garfield Park is a largely lower-income, residential community with a vintage feel, comprised of some single-family homes amidst two- and three-flat apartment building rentals. Residents can make the thirty-minute commute downtown via the green line "El" train on Lake Street or on one of the major bus routes on Madison or Harrison, through city streets lightly peppered with local retailers, Mom-and-Pop restaurants, childcare centers, and places of worship.

Now imagine that your kindergarten teacher, Ms. Price, is searching for the perfect book to introduce you to the excitement and the possibilities and the power of reading. Ms. Price has a lot of books to choose from, but she picks *Hot City* by Barbara Joosse and R. Gregory Christie. It's a story about siblings Mimi and Joe who seek cool refuge in the local library on a hot summer day, where they spend the afternoon in the world of adventures they discover in the books on those library shelves. Now imagine, as a five-year-old at Melody Elementary, watching intently as Ms. Price opens the book, and there—right there on the page—is your block, your bus, your street, your world. . . .

Most kindergarteners at Melody Elementary know this story. In fact, it looks as if Mr. Christie could have been standing right in front of the school when he illustrated this scene. That looks just like the #7 Harrison bus that

Figure 3.1. From *Hot City* by Barbara Joosse. Illustration © 2004 by R. Gregory Christie. Used with permission.

comes west down Van Buren Street. Many children may know Miss Trudy who drives that bus most weekday mornings. Just like the characters Mimi and Joe, children can describe what that bus looks like, what it sounds like, and what it smells like. Many children have stepped off of that cool CTA bus and onto the hot pavement at the bus stop. Even if a kindergartener at Melody Elementary cannot yet read the words on the pages of this book, *she can tell this story*. And this is a critical factor in learning to read and write.

In the previous chapters, the importance of urban children's literature has been discussed for increasing the cultural relevance of schooling, supporting students' positive identities as learners, and fueling students' interest in reading and writing. Most of the existing research on the use of multicultural children's books speaks to this power of culturally relevant texts for "teaching *literature*" [emphasis added] (McGinley et al. 1997, 44). But integrating multicultural children's literature with a distinctly urban focus into the curriculum can also play a crucial role in the reading and writing development of students in urban schools. This chapter draws on current research and provides practical examples to illustrate the power of urban children's literature for teaching *literacy*.

How Urban Children's Literature Impacts Literacy Development

According to Klingner et al. (2005, 8), "culturally responsive educational systems are grounded in the belief that all culturally and linguistically diverse students can excel in academic endeavors when their culture, language, heritage, and experiences are valued and *used to facilitate their learning and development*" [emphasis added]. Despite the fact that educators have become increasingly attuned to the importance of including multicultural children's literature in the classroom, surprisingly little empirical research has been done to demonstrate the specific role that culturally relevant texts may play in facilitating reading and writing development.

Still, there are substantial bodies of research on reading acquisition and reading comprehension that illustrate the mechanisms through which urban children's literature can accelerate literacy learning for students in city schools: (1) research on emergent literacy; (2) research on how readers respond to text; (3) the use of language as cultural capital in literacy learning; and (4) the role of cultural schemata in supporting reading fluency and comprehension. Each of these is explored in the sections that follow.

Supporting Emergent Literacy

The selection of books used in the kindergarten classroom at Melody Elementary School has a far-reaching impact on that kindergartner's development as a reader and writer. Before they are able to read and write, children first use pretend play to begin to construct and act out stories of their own, often based on everyday activities prevalent in their particular communities and cultural contexts (e.g., Paradise and Rogoff 2009).

As early as age three, many children are able to engage in complex dramatic play, often taking on the roles of adults and attempting to use the more sophisticated language that adults use (Anderson 1986; McNamee 2015). A look into any preschool classroom or childcare center may reveal "doctors" managing triage on patients in the pretend hospital waiting room, "restauranteurs" taking orders in the classroom deli, or "postal workers" serving customers and sorting mail. Engagement in this type of dramatic play can be directly linked to literacy development.[1]

Ms. Price will use the opportunity of pretend play to write down the stories students act out, helping them make books about their stories that they can then "practice" reading (Howes and Wishard 2004). As children participate in this shared story writing, they will be encouraged to represent some words with scribbles or letters, gradually learning more about letter-sound relationships over time (Bredekamp 2004).

When children engage in interactive storybook reading—often about those same topics that are the focus of their play—they begin to develop a literacy orientation through the teacher's scaffolding (Pransky 2009) and to begin to understand concepts about print (Clay 2000). These books will find their way to the library shelves so everyone can enjoy them, and they will be a central part of the first parent–teacher conference Ms. Price holds for the students and families in her kindergarten classroom.

One of the critical moments in reading development is the realization that the words in the book describe the pictures. What better set of words to describe a picture than the words of the child reading the story? As children begin to internalize some formal reading behaviors through adults' repeated readings of favorite books, they start to participate in the storytelling, *first using their oral language to read the story in the pictures, and then gradually getting closer and closer to oral reading of the actual words in the text* [emphasis added] (Teale and Sulzby 1987).

Once children begin to relate their speech to print in "pretend" reading, it matters if the language children are using—some of the words in their home language or the words that students would typically use to describe the story or a particular scene—actually does show up on the page. Thus, while young students enjoy listening to all kinds of stories, the use of culturally relevant literature, including the words and stories they create, is important for supporting emergent literacy.

Imagine that you are that five-year-old just starting school at Melody Elementary. Imagine the language you might use to describe what's happening in the illustration from *Hot City* shown in Figure 3.1. Imagine some of the words, the inflection, and the cadence you might use to tell this story. Now imagine your kindergarten teacher, Ms. Price, as she begins to read the text aloud:

> "It's one of those days in the city when the sidewalk is as hot as a fry pan, and Mimi and her little brother, Joe, are sweatin' out rivers . . . Out on the street, the buses are huffin' out dragon-hot smoke." (Joosse 2004) From *Hot City*. Text copyright © 2004 by Barbara Joosse. Used with permission.

Does the text match some of the words you used to describe the scene? The same is true for our kindergarteners. Grounding reading instruction in books that carry this potential for a match between a students' oral language with the written text is an important factor for supporting the development of concepts of print and beginning word recognition skills. Adding the support of familiar illustrations and situations to engage children in their own rich retellings of stories is key.

Responding to Reading with Cultural Capital

Theories about how readers make meaning from texts can also help explain how urban children's literature can support literacy learning.

DID YOU KNOW?

Reader-response theory focuses on readers' engagement with text, such as the ways readers identify with characters, visualize settings and events, and relate personal experiences to texts (Beach 1993).

Reader-response theory views reading as an active process in which readers derive meaning from print using a variety of cultural resources and background knowledge. In her highly influential book on transactional theory, Louise Rosenblatt (1978) described how meaning is created in the interaction of the reader with the text. Because readers are inseparable from their social and cultural selves, students' thinking is always influenced by their cultural understandings, their background knowledge, and their prior experiences with others when they engage in making meaning from texts.

Under the right circumstances, this cultural capital can be used as a cognitive resource to help students engage in higher levels of information processing during reading and writing activities. For example, Jeane Copenhaver (2001) examined African American second-graders' responses to the reading of *Malcolm X: A Fire Burning Brightly* by Walter Dean Myers (1989) and found that students were readily able to use their cultural understandings to make self-to-text connections and respond to other students' insights about the text. Similarly, Gayla Lohfink and Juana Loya (2010) documented how bilingual Mexican American third-graders' engagement with culturally relevant picture books like *The Upside Down Boy* by Juan Felipe Herrera (2006) and *My Very Own Room* by Amada Irma Pérez (2000) facilitated high levels of critical analysis and evaluation.

TRY THIS TOMORROW:

1. Select a book for read aloud that has strong potential cultural relevance for your students.
2. Notice what difference it makes in your students' level of participation in discussion and their ability to make text-to-self and text-to-world connections.

In these ways, urban children's literature not only encourages high levels of interaction around texts, but it can also provide the means for beginning readers to practice applying background knowledge in making meaning, likely increasing the efficiency of literacy learning. As students gain facility in making connections, comparing and contrasting their experiences with situations presented in texts, and making inferences about characters' motivations and feelings, these comprehension skills will more readily transfer to making meaning with all types of texts.

Harnessing the Power of More Than One Language

Language is a cultural resource that students bring to the classroom that serves a central role in thinking and problem solving (Gee 2004; Moll 2014). Urban children's literature, especially that which incorporates a dual language format or integrates authentic language and dialect with familiar contexts and themes, such as *Quinito's Neighborhood* (Cumpiano 2009) or *Young Cornrows Callin' Out the Moon* (Forman 2007), can serve as an invitation for students to use their home language, and thus, their cultural knowledge, as a tool for developing reading and writing skills in the classroom.

Terry Meier (2008) outlines numerous ways in which linguistic abilities and dispositions associated with African American English can provide a rich foundation for successful literacy instruction when they are valued and utilized by teachers. Traditions honoring linguistic agility and verbal debate, storytelling, the use of rhythmic and poetic language, and the ability to "read between the lines" in discerning meaning in Black Communications provide opportunities for even very young children to develop sophisticated oral language capabilities that are important precursors for the development of strong literacy skills, (see Meier 2008 for excellent discussion).

The extent to which teachers understand and are able to capitalize on these capabilities can make a big difference, not only in children's confidence about their capabilities, but in helping children see how these strengths can be assets in school. Culturally relevant text selection, coupled with a teachers' openness to a range of ways of participating and communicating,[2] can create opportunities for children to leverage these strengths in literacy learning.

For example, Elizabeth Smith (1995) described how reading and discussing books with African American characters, such as *Aunt Flossie's Hats (and Crab Cakes Later)* by Elizabeth Fitzgerald Howard (1991b), led to her fifth-grade students' spontaneous use of call and response in asking questions and sharing comments about the text, similar to participation patterns used in their African American church services. Meier (2008) also relates how, when African American children in one second-grade class were encouraged to spontaneously share their wonderings and comments during discussions of books like *The Hard-Times Jar* (Smothers 2003), rather than adhere to more strict turn-taking procedures, their questions often "push[ed] everyone's thinking in new directions" (114).

In similar ways, culturally relevant literature may be a particularly powerful tool for supporting the development of reading comprehension and writing skills of bilingual students at the emerging and developing stages of English language literacy. Julia López-Robertson (2011) describes how her students' sharing of life stories prompted by the reading of *Friends from the Other Side/Amigos del Otro Lado* (Anzaldúa 1993) led to her English language learners' effective use of questions as a tool for clarifying meaning and expressing opinions.

Studies have revealed comparable effects on students' writing. For example, after reading works by African American writers and poets, students were more readily able to recognize features of African American English and replicate the format, cadence, and linguistic patterns in their own writing (Brooks 2006). Similarly, Sandy Carrillo (2012) found that grounding language and literacy instruction in culturally relevant memoirs by Latino authors had a significant impact on her bilingual fourth graders' understanding of figurative language, evidenced by more frequent and accurate use of similes and metaphors when writing their own personal narratives.

While a number of studies have demonstrated student progress using informal literacy measures in the classroom, there is also some evidence that these effects may translate to standardized measures. An examination of high-school students' writing scores on the National Assessment of Educational Progress (NAEP) revealed that African American students who were able to incorporate the "voice" of their communities in their writing, using African American discourse features such as rhythmic language or the rhetorical style of traditional black churches, received higher NAEP scores than those who did not (Smitherman 1993).

Urban children's literature that incorporates authentic language and dialogue can be used as a tool for instruction that invites students to use their home language as an asset in literacy learning. Encouraging students to draw on the "intellectual power" of their biliteracy (Moll and Dworin 1996) often allows for different kinds of thinking and creativity that may not be possible using one language alone.

Activating Schema for Reading Comprehension

A critical factor in how students respond to text is the extent to which they possess and can apply cultural knowledge to the process of comprehending what a passage or book is about. The term "schema" (or its plural, schemata) refers to a network of knowledge and mental representations that help students organize and interpret information. Readers use their existing schema to interpret information in texts, in essence, to try to find a mental "home" to place information or to modify existing knowledge to accommodate new ideas (Anderson and Pearson 1984).

While cultural schemata include general background knowledge of the topic, situation, or problem presented in a text, they also involve a more complex network of knowledge, including the language used to describe those topics, the settings and social contexts in which students may have

Jill's Story:

"I see differences in students' feedback [when reading urban children's literature]. They talk much more about how the characters feel, or what the characters want to do, or how they once did what the character did. The text-to-self connections are much stronger."

experience with a problem, knowledge of how individuals typically react in those situations, and emotions associated with those experiences. Indeed, good readers construct in their understanding the voice, the tone, the rhythms and inflections, and even the persona of the author as part of what they decode from the text (Rosenblatt 1978, 77).

There is substantial evidence that indicates when people read texts to which they can bring more cultural schemata to bear, they are able to make better predictions about the text, read more accurately and fluently, and are able to produce more accurate retellings or summaries.[3, 4] This same effect has been found on the reading comprehension of second-language learners.[5] Much of this research comes from work with adult readers, but those studies that do involve children have found similar results.

The effects of relevant cultural schemata on reading accuracy, fluency, and comprehension can be explained, in part, by their impact on working memory. Readers use working memory to "hold" and manipulate information gleaned from the text while working to make meaning. Working memory allows readers to apply what they know about letter–sound relationships and morphology while simultaneously retrieving word meanings, accessing their knowledge of story grammar or informational text features, and activating a relevant schema through which to interpret and integrate new information gleaned from a particular combination of symbols and images on the page.

Unfortunately, working memory does not come in unlimited supply. Humans can only hold so many pieces of information in working memory at one time; the more "moving parts" one has to work with, the greater the cognitive load of the learning task. As a result, for novice readers who may not yet have developed automaticity in any one of these areas, the cognitive load is high and the demands on working memory are great.

Fortunately, there are ways in which the cognitive load of learning tasks can be reduced. One important way is by using schemas to organize multiple elements of information, essentially consolidating many pieces of information into a collective single "part," allowing readers to process information much more efficiently (see Rueda [2011] or Hammond [2015] for a much more detailed and nuanced description of how these cognitive processes operate).

Research demonstrates how reducing the cognitive load of a reading task by situating it in a culturally relevant context allows for more working memory to be allocated to meaning-making. For example, in one investigation of reading by fourth-, fifth-, and sixth-grade students of different religious affiliations, Marjorie Youmans Lipson (1983) found that comprehension of passages about religious customs was significantly improved when students had culturally familiar schema into which to incorporate new information. When there was a significant mismatch, such as Catholic school students reading about a bar mitzvah, students read passages more slowly, recalled less information, and had more frequent misconceptions about the content.

In a more recent study of African American eighth-graders' responses to multicultural literature, Ruanda Garth McCullough (2013) found that knowledge of the language patterns and cultural content of a story had a significant impact on reading comprehension. African American students who recognized cultural scripts that were similar to their own (e.g., descriptions of Baptist church services or family reunions) performed more strongly on measures of reading comprehension than on similarly challenging passages that were more oriented toward Chinese American or European American culture.

The effect of schema on reading comprehension may be particularly strong for struggling readers. Beverly Adams, Laura Bell, and Charles Perfetti (1995, 307) found a "trading relationship" between reading skill and background knowledge in their investigation of middle-grades boys' comprehension and fluency in reading passages about football. Strong knowledge about football helped some boys compensate for weaker reading skills, while strong reading skills could help compensate for less background knowledge.

This same finding was replicated in the Garth McCullough (2013) study, in which students with lower reading levels but high levels of cultural knowledge related to a passage outperformed strong readers who had low levels of cultural knowledge. Again, the level of cultural relevance of the passage had a greater impact on reading comprehension than students' independent reading levels.

Unfortunately for many urban public school students, these opportunities to "trade" background knowledge to compensate for challenges with accuracy and fluency often come few and far between when culturally relevant literature is limited among selections used for reading instruction. The disadvantage to readers who do not have sufficient relevant background knowledge to apply to making-meaning may lead to significant misconceptions or frustration when reading.[6] In some cases, studies have found that students had difficulty integrating ideas from culturally unfamiliar texts, *even when they were able to read relatively accurately* (e.g., Garth McCollough 2013; Malik 1990).

This is a finding that is very familiar to many urban public school teachers whose students may "read" print well but are not always able to make meaning from text. When students read accurately but struggle with reading comprehension, teachers often work to develop students' use of various comprehension strategies, such as activating schema, making predictions, asking questions, or using visualization to support understanding of text. While reading comprehension strategies generally do help with meaning-making, some studies have found that they cannot compensate for a lack of relevant cultural schema if the gap between a students' cultural knowledge and the content of text is too large (e.g., Erten and Razi 2009).

Of course, our goal is that students are able to apply comprehension strategies to make meaning from all kinds of texts. A challenge for urban public-school teachers often comes in the form of published curricula, in which many of the texts recommended for the teaching of reading skills contain content that is unfamiliar to their students.

When beginning or struggling readers are regularly asked to practice applying reading strategies to texts whose content is far outside their lived experience, the gap may be too wide for strategy instruction to take hold. It may be especially important to choose some texts to which students can bring their cultural schemata and background knowledge to bear, until they become sufficiently proficient to apply these strategies to less familiar content and are able to "trade" their reading skill for less background knowledge.

Learning in "The Zone"

Research in child development and constructivist learning theory can help explain these findings. According to Lev Vygotsky (1978), the most effective learning occurs in the "zone of proximal development" (ZPD). The ZPD is defined as "the distance between the actual developmental level as determined by independent problem solving and the level of potential development as determined through problem solving under adult guidance or in collaboration with more capable peers" (Vygotsky 1978, 86).

The potential for learning is dependent on many factors, including what a child currently knows, the nature of the task to be learned, the circumstances under which the learning is taking place, the materials or tools being used, and the quality of instructional scaffolding provided by teachers or other more skilled learners (Bruner 1975). Good teaching should support a student in developing capabilities beyond what he or she could do without assistance, but should not extend "beyond the links to what a student already knows" (Lee and Smagorinsky 2000, 2).

Urban children's literature can serve as more than just a tool for student engagement; it can actually help create the atmosphere and provide the foundation for using students' cultural knowledge as a link to literacy skills. Educators should carefully consider the cultural relevance of the text selections

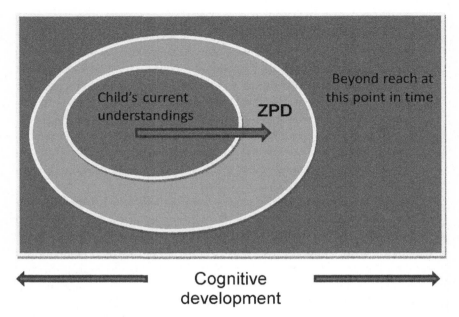

Figure 3.2. The zone of proximal development. Adapted with permission from Atherton (2013).

used for reading and writing instruction, as well as the sequence in which those texts are used, in order to ensure that the curricula is complementing instructional goals. Some examples are provided below. Chapter 9 provides additional guidance on text selection with respect to unit planning.

Incorporating Culturally Relevant Literature into the Curriculum

The first step in assuring a more culturally relevant curriculum is for educators to purposefully and intentionally plan to blend a rich collection of urban children's literature into the mix of text selections from the core literacy curricula that are commonly found in urban public schools. When provided some flexibility, teachers can make the curriculum more relevant while maintaining consistency with the learning objectives and expected language and literacy outcomes set forth in the core curriculum.

Some published literacy curricula take a thematic approach to literacy learning while others focus more explicitly on strategy instruction. Here is an example from the *Opening the World of Learning* (OWL), a comprehensive thematic curriculum for prekindergarten in which "themes, skills, and concepts are developed through quality children's fiction and nonfiction trade books" (Pearson 2012). Unit 3 is entitled "Wind and Water." The unit theme centers on the importance of wind and water in supporting life, as well as how they can sometimes be dangerous for living things. One of the core storybooks selected for this unit is *Rabbits and Raindrops* by Jim Arnosky (2001). It is a story about a family of rabbits that goes out to play in a field, gets caught in a rainstorm, and has to seek shelter in the hedge.

There are several language arts learning objectives for children identified in this unit:

1. to be able to use their own experiences to understand story events;
2. to be able to relate events from familiar stories in sequence; and
3. to use new words (e.g., lawn, raindrops, soaked, shelter, shower) and relate dialogue from stories (Pearson 2012, 19).

In addition, there are several science objectives in this integrated unit related to describing the effects of basic forces of nature and understanding seasonal weather changes.

In general, *Rabbits and Raindrops* is an appropriate and effective story choice for a Wind and Water unit for PreK. The cover art is visually interesting and provides useful clues about the content of the story, it follows a logical sequence of events, it incorporates developmentally appropriate language in a rhyme scheme, and it provides colorful, engaging illustrations that complement and enhance the story (Fleming et al. 2007). In addition, practically every four-year-old loves a bunny and enjoys stories about animals.

However, when thinking about meeting the wind and water learning objectives from a culturally relevant teaching perspective, *Rabbits and Raindrops* may not be the most relevant text to support children living in the city in drawing on their cultural capital to understand this new content. Instead, teachers might seek an alternative selection to open this unit—one that would allow emergent literacy learners to better draw on their own experiences to understand the story events and that would situate this new science content instruction more solidly within children's zones of proximal development.

Rain Play by Cynthia Cotten (2008) is a story about a family that goes out to play in a city park, gets caught in a rainstorm, and has to seek shelter. This story is almost identical to *Rabbits and Raindrops*. *Rain Play* includes very similar content, covers the same concepts, and includes similar vocabulary to the book included in the OWL curriculum. For students in an urban context, many of whom may have never seen a rabbit playing in a field but who have likely had experience getting caught in the rain at the park, *Rain Play* may be a little more familiar, providing students with an opportunity to see themselves in the text, better capitalizing on their cultural schemata, and helping situate new learning a little closer inside the ZPD.

Use of *Rain Play* does not rule out also using *Rabbits and Raindrops* in this unit. It is important to expose students to a wide variety of texts to support their content learning, vocabulary development, and enjoyment of literature. If they are not familiar with rabbits nesting in the hedges, here is an opportunity to introduce the topic of habitats, tying in science concepts and expanding students' learning. The purpose of blending rich urban children's literature with a curriculum's recommended text set is not to replace all the books in the core curricula, but to enhance students' opportunity for learning and understanding.

Ideally, teachers will utilize both books in the Wind and Water unit example above. A teacher could use *Rain Play* to launch the Wind and Water unit, drawing on students' experiences for the first entry into this content. Reading *Rabbits and Raindrops* then provides an opportunity to engage children in comparing and contrasting settings and characters, deepening their understanding of how forces of nature can have similar effects on living things in different contexts.

Teachers can support student learning about animals and habitats, develop vocabulary that is not familiar, and engage children in considering scenarios beyond the urban setting. Connecting a student's current schema with new information broadens their conceptual understanding and widens the range of content knowledge they will utilize as they progress through school.

Another example comes from Harcourt's *StoryTown*, a literacy curriculum used widely in urban districts (Harcourt Publishers 2011). One of the units in the third grade *StoryTown* curriculum focuses on using visualization as a comprehension strategy—teaching children to make pictures in their minds in order to understand and remember what they read.

The core text choice for this unit is *Bat Loves the Night* by Nicola Davies (2001), where the nocturnal wanderings of a pipistrelle bat are described. This beautifully illustrated informational text provides students with opportunities to explore the structure of narrative nonfiction. It is an effective selection for learning about animals and their habitats, where bats live and what they do in the night, how they raise their young, and how they search for prey. But is it the best core text choice for starting a unit on visualization with third-graders in urban public schools? Below is some text from *Bat Loves the Night.* Think about what background knowledge and cultural schemata might be required to make a movie in your mind about what's happening here:

> Bat is waking, upside down as usual, hanging by her toenails. Her beady eyes open. Her pixie ears twitch. She shakes her thistledown fur. . . . Gliding and fluttering back and forth, she shouts her torch of sound among the trees, listening for her supper. (Davies 2001)*

This text is excellent for teaching science content, and it includes wonderful descriptive language and robust vocabulary to discuss the bat's use of echolocation to identify its prey. However, for introducing and practicing this particular comprehension strategy—visualization—teachers in urban schools might consider opening the unit with a text with more familiar content so students are more readily able to "make a movie in their minds" of what is going on in the book.

In contrast to *Bat Loves the Night,* consider this excerpt from *Black Cat* by Christopher Myers (1999), which captures a cat's wanderings around the city at night. *Black Cat* is written at approximately the same reading level as *Bat Loves the Night,* and it includes rich vocabulary and appropriately complex text for this grade level. When reading this selection, think about the cultural capital many urban public schools students might bring to the task of visualization here:

> Black cat, black cat, cousin to the concrete, creeping down our city streets
> Where do you live? Where will we meet?
> Sauntering like rain water down storm drains
> Between Cadillac tires and the curb
> Sipping water from fire hydrants
> Dancing to the banging beats of passing jeeps. (Myers 1999)†

This selection describes the urban landscape at night and the cat's journey among places that are likely familiar to many students in city schools. It has the potential to create conditions for students to experience how using visualization can support meaning-making and recall of text.

This is not to suggest that urban educators *only* use urban children's literature for literacy instruction. Students must be able to apply comprehension

---

*Bat *Loves the Night.* Text copyright © 2001 by Nicola Davies. Reproduced by permission of the publisher, Candlewick Press, Somerville, MA on behalf of Walker Books, London.

†From *Black Cat* by Christopher Myers. Scholastic Inc./Scholastic Press Copyright © 1999 by Christopher Myers. Reprinted by permission.

strategies with all kinds of texts. However, when *first* introducing comprehension strategies such as visualization—especially for beginning readers,
struggling readers, or students less experienced with reading in English—it
makes sense to start with text that is better grounded in student's lived experience, one that helps activate their cultural schemata, and invites them
to leverage some of their cultural capital in creating those images. Once students have the opportunity to learn and practice these strategies in a familiar
context with a book that is closer to the ZPD, teachers then work to transfer
those skills to all kinds of other texts, including those like *Bat Loves the Night*.

Of course, not just any books with an urban setting or theme will suffice.
Indeed some studies have shown that the quality of story, such as having an
interesting and realistic plot, can transcend cultural relevance in students'
responses to reading (e.g., Altieri 1993). Children are smart; they want
to read high-quality literature. Moreover, studies have found that cultural
relevance can only be supportive when the linguistic complexity of a text is
within the child's reach (e.g., Droop and Verhoevan 1998). Thus, in addition to considering cultural relevance, teachers need to be mindful of select-

---

Summing It Up: Enhancing Reading and Writing Instruction with
Urban Children's Literature

- Urban children's literature can be an important tool for facilitating reading and writing development
- Familiar illustrations and situations in storybooks support emergent literacy by allowing young children to connect their experiences and oral language with the written text
- Fosters engagement and high levels of discussion about texts
- Helps better situate learning in the Zone of Proximal Development (ZPD)
- Comprehension improves when readers have culturally familiar
  schema into which they can incorporate new information
- Children can use their background knowledge as a foundation
  for learning to apply sophisticated comprehension strategies to
  meaning-making
- Literacy skills gained through reading culturally relevant texts
  can transfer to understanding new content and developing writing skills

ing texts within students' instructional reading and listening levels. If the linguistic complexity of the text exceeds what the child is capable of reading at this time, the benefits of cultural relevance on reading comprehension tend to fade away.

Students should engage in wide reading and be exposed to as many literacy opportunities as possible. It is important, however, that included in these opportunities are examples that reflect their lives, neighborhoods, families, and experiences. This strategy will increase children's engagement, allow them to respond to text in ways that draw on their lived experience, and provide an opportunity for them to use their cultural schemata as a foundation for developing new understandings.

In upcoming chapters, there are guidelines for the selection of high-quality children's books, including *general* characteristics of quality as well as *urban-specific* characteristics to consider when selecting culturally relevant texts for our students. When teachers choose high-quality, developmentally appropriate selections, cultural relevance can accelerate literacy learning by allowing students to draw on their cultural and linguistic assets and their lived experience in engaging with, interpreting, and responding to texts as they develop as readers and writers.

Notes

1. Researchers Catherine E. Snow, Patton O. Tabors, and David K. Dickinson are well known for their studies linking this type of dramatic play to later literacy development (see Dickinson and Tabors [2001] for an extensive review). In addition, Carollee Howes and Catherine Matheson (1992b) demonstrated how complex play emerges along a developmental continuum, and that the proportion of complex play in which children engage can be influenced by both the quality of the child care environments and the nature of interactions between teachers and children.

2. As discussed in chapter 1, culturally responsive literacy instruction extends well beyond the selection of texts. It requires understanding children's cognitive and communicative systems, incorporating teaching methods that capitalize on culturally oriented cognitive and linguistic routines, and the design of activities and routines that honor group values associated with students' home cultures, among other considerations. In addition to Meier (2008), see Zaretta Hammond (2015) for an excellent discussion.

3. Chen-Hong Li and Shu-Fen Lai (2012) compared Taiwanese college-students' reading of culturally familiar texts about a Chinese Dragon Boat Festival to their understanding of an equally challenging passage about St. Patrick's Day, a holiday with which these readers had little, if any, familiarity. Being able to apply their cultural schemata to the Dragon Boat Festival passage had significant impact on

students' reading fluency, comprehension, memory for details, and accuracy of interpretation of the text. Lack of cultural schemata for the St. Patrick's Day passage had the opposite effect; not only did students have difficulty making meaning from the passage, their interpretations resulted in misconceptions and inaccuracies. Earlier studies have found similar results (e.g., Steffenson 1987; Steffenson, Joag-Dev, and Anderson 1979).

4. One recent study explored the technique of "nativization" of short stories to examine the impact on Turkish college students' reading comprehension (Erten and Razi 2009). Using a short story originally set in New York City, researchers shifted the setting to Canakkale, a coastal city in Turkey, and made simple adjustments to the names of characters, streets, and cultural content (e.g., meals involving Turkish baguettes and tea vs. rolls and coffee), while maintaining the core structure, events, and theme of the original text. Adapting the text to reflect more of the lived experience of Turkish students resulted in significant differences in comprehension of the two passages, demonstrating the powerful impact of cultural schemata.

5. In a study of Iranian college students' reading, Patricia Johnson (1981) compared the comprehension of native English speakers and English-language learners using American and Iranian folklore. As reported above, the cultural content of the text had a significant effect on students' reading comprehension. Notably, in this study, the cultural origin of the story had a greater impact on the comprehension of English-language learners than the syntactic and semantic complexity of the text. These findings seem to suggest that activation of cultural schemata helps to reduce the cognitive load on working memory (e.g., Nassaji 2007) so readers can direct more attention to second language reading comprehension.

6. Ralph Reynolds et al. (1982) showed that white eighth-grade students from a rural, agricultural area were disadvantaged in their understanding of a text featuring black characters "playing the dozens." A lack of cultural schemata related to this form of linguistic play led to greater numbers of misconceptions among the white rural students than black students from a working-class community.

CHAPTER FOUR

~

Supporting the Literacy Development of Dual Language Learners

> *"My mom is from Mexico, too!"*
>
> —Veronica, age five, after her teacher modeled writing about her own mother on Día de las Madres

Like many students in U.S. schools today, Veronica is a member of a growing population of dual language learners (DLLs). According to the National Center for Education Statistics (NCES), the proportion of school-age children in the United States who spoke a language other than English at home more than doubled between 1980–2011, increasing from 10 percent to 22 percent (Aud et al. 2012; Ryan 2013). Although dual language learners can be found in classrooms across the country, a substantial proportion of DLLs attend urban schools. For example, of the nearly five million estimated DLLs in the nation's K–12 public schools, almost 25 percent attend schools among sixty-seven large city school districts (Uro and Barrio 2013).

Students learning English make up an average of 14 percent of urban public school enrollment, ranging from 9.4 percent in small cities to 16.7 percent in large cities (Kena et al. 2015). While a majority of DLL students in the United States speak Spanish as their first language, nearly four hundred languages are represented in our nation's schools (Ryan 2013). For example, among DLLs in New York City Public Schools, the top ten languages represented include Spanish, Chinese, Bengali, Arabic, Haitian Creole, Russian, Urdu, French, Uzbek, and Punjabi (New York City Department of Education 2015). In addition, an increasing number of DLLs are relative newcomers to schools, having just recently immigrated to the United States (National Education Association 2014).

Although they are linked by the common characteristic of learning English as well as one or more additional languages, DLLs differ in age, socioeconomic status, ethnicity, place of birth, reason for migrating, native language(s) spoken, degree to which they are spoken, English proficiency, and educational background.[1] This is certainly the case in Veronica's class (above).

Veronica was born in the United States shortly after her parents arrived from Mexico. Her first language is Spanish, but she spoke some English at the start of kindergarten as a result of attending one year of preschool the year before. Her classmate, Jasmeen, who speaks Arabic, just arrived from Yemen and has had no prior schooling. In Bartek's home, Polish is spoken by his mom and Spanish by his dad, and he speaks both. Bartek did not attend preschool, but he has picked up some English from playing with neighborhood friends and watching television.

WHY USE "DUAL LANGUAGE"?

There are a variety of ways educators refer to students whose first language is different from English (e.g., ESL students, ELL students, etc.). Here, we use the term "Dual Language Learners" to emphasize the fact that these students are continuing to develop language and literacy skills both in their native language as well as English. Many organizations such as the American Federation of Teachers (AFT), the National Association for the Education of Young Children (NAEYC), and the National Head Start Association also use this term.

Differences in nonnative English speakers set them apart from other students. DLLs face the difficult task of developing their literacy as they are learning a new language. Educators, many of whom are not trained to meet the specific needs of DLLs, are challenged to find effective teaching strategies that will facilitate language and literacy development and to develop effective strategies to engage with families (Ebe 2012; Haynes and Zacarian 2010). This chapter discusses the use of multicultural and urban children's literature as an effective tool for scaffolding the language and literacy development of DLLs and facilitating transitions for students who are new to the country. In addition, this chapter provides an overview of stages of second-language development and offers specific examples of how to help students at different levels of English proficiency make connections to texts.

Increasing Engagement by Making Connections

In reviewing "Sandy's story," on the next page, we can see that Veronica is a writer. Throughout the school year, Veronica has been encouraged to write about her life experiences and things that are meaningful to her. This has allowed her to develop her writing and has added to the richness of it. She shares a similar cultural background with her teacher. Her teacher is aware of how important it is to make sure Veronica has many opportunities to see herself reflected in the curriculum.

On the particular day described, Veronica has made a connection with the writing that her teacher has shared, and that has inspired her to write on a similar topic. She does so beautifully and without hesitation. She does not know the word *lotion* so she writes the Spanish word, *cremita*. She knows that writers will sometimes use more than one language when writing and that this is a strength. She has learned this from the many "interlingual" books in her classroom library that are written primarily in English, but have many Spanish words interwoven in the story (Hadaway and Young 2010, 120), such as *Bebé Goes Shopping* (Elya 2006), *Dear Primo: A Letter to My Cousin* (Tonatiuh 2010), or *My Abuelita* (Johnston 2009). Veronica is an interlingual writer, just like the authors of the books she enjoys.

One thing that helped Veronica become engaged with writing is certainly the connection that she made with her teacher. Yet even when a student and teacher do not share the same language or cultural background, culturally relevant texts can help increase student engagement and provide a catalyst for discussions that can help students and teachers learn more about each other. For example, Dara Hill (2012) describes how an African American teacher's sharing of Patricia Polacco's *The Keeping Quilt* (2001) with a first-generation Russian American student led to his deep connections with the text and an extensive discussion with her about cultural practices that were similar or different from those of his family.

Similarly, despite their cultural differences, Mary-Virginia Feger (2006) noticed that her students read more, made more personal connections to

Sandy's Story:

As I often do, I was mentally going over my to-do list on my way to work. At the top of the list was to call my mom later that day and wish her a Feliz Día de las Madres. Although my mom has been living in the United States for almost forty years, one of many things she holds onto dearly from her native country is celebrating Mother's Day on the tenth of May. I could hear my mom's colorful stories of celebrations in Mexico, complete with folkloric dances and a mariachi band playing the mañanitas. I could not forget to call or I might not be forgiven.

Later that day, it was easy to pick a topic for my writing with my students as I often remind them that our ideas for writing are carved from our hearts and our life experiences. I shared with my students the importance of the day, explained that I was celebrating on this day because my mom is from Mexico, and wrote about the amazing influence my mom has been in my life. I gently suggested that they may want to write about an important person in their lives and began to distribute their journals, as I inquired about their topic of writing.

As I am doing this, I feel a tug on my shirt. I turn around to see Veronica motioning me to come closer to her. I bend down and she softly whispers in my ear that her mom is from Mexico, just like mine. I turn to look at her—her big, brown eyes and smile from ear to ear, sealing a magnificent bond. With that, she is off to write about her mom, a memoir of a bath-time routine.

Veronica wrote: "When I take a shower, my mom puts cremita (lotion) on me and my sister. We play a game and she kisses my feet." (Written in May of her kindergarten year.)

text, engaged in critical thinking, and made text-to-text connections in their dialogue journals with her when she incorporated culturally relevant books like Gary Soto's *Buried Onions* (1997) or Sandra Cisneros's (1984) *House on Mango Street* into the curriculum. Culturally relevant literature can help to build these bridges, not only between a student and the curriculum, but between students and teachers. The sharing of culturally relevant texts with family members has also been shown to increase parent engagement with school and encourage more reading and literacy-related discussions with children at home (e.g., Larrotta and Gainer 2008).

Supporting Dual Language Learners' Comprehension with Culturally Relevant Literature

Imagine a situation where someone is taking a cooking class for the first time. Maybe he or she is a beginner and does not have much experience with cooking. Rather than learning to make a simple dish with common ingredients, the cooking class involves a recipe for creating an exotic dish. Both the ingredients and the kitchen are unfamiliar to the novice chef. To top it off, the teacher is giving instructions in a foreign language. The fact that there are so many "unknowns" will certainly add to the challenge and might even get in the way of a successful execution of this dish. For a greater chance of success, it would help if the dish and the ingredients had been seen and used in the past and the language spoken by the chef was the learner's first language.

As discussed in chapter 3, having background knowledge when approaching a new task is important, and it is especially helpful for reading comprehension. Similar to the cooking example above, when DLLs are presented with books that are not relevant to their lives, they may face the "double task" of trying to comprehend unfamiliar cultural events and concepts (e.g., new characters, unfamiliar settings, novel situations, unusual facts) while simultaneously trying to interpret unfamiliar English words and specialized vocabulary (Agosto 2007, 28). It is important that teachers balance these

---

"The pictures in the book have happy colors, just like the houses in Colombia."

—Mariana, age nine, talking about the illustrations in *My Diary from Here to There* by Amada Irma Pérez (2009)

cognitive demands of learning activities with the language demands so that students do not get "overloaded" (Hadaway 2009, 41).

As discussed in chapter 3, urban children's literature can help with this by providing contexts and content with which students have some experience and can make connections, which reduces some of the cognitive load of the learning task. Readers can construct meaning from texts that resonate with them. They relate to characters who are like them, who have lived similar experiences, and who have walked similar paths. They can visualize and imagine the colors, sights, sounds, and smells of familiar events and settings. Including culturally relevant literature in the curriculum provides DLLs the opportunity to relate to what they already know while building on their background knowledge to allow them to focus on strengthening reading strategies and vocabulary in the new language.

Consider a project in which Sandy Carrillo (2012) read a series of memoirs including *My Diary from Here to There/Mi diario de aqui hasta alla* by Amada Irma Pérez (2009) and Juan Felipe Herrera's (2006) *The Upside Down Boy/El niño de cabeza* with a group of fourth-grade DLLs. Like Amada and Juanito in the stories, many of Carrillo's students had experienced recent moves to the United States from places like Colombia and Mexico. Students were able to make self-to-text connections, relating feelings similar to those the characters were feeling when trying to adjust to a new life in the city or when being temporarily separated from family members who had left ahead of them to get things situated in the United States.

> "My favorite part of the story was when she travel [sic] to California because I felt the same thing when I came here."
>
> —Daniel, fourth grade, responding to Amada Irma Pérez's *My Diary from Here to There*

Using texts that presented opportunities for students to draw on their personal experience also reduced the cognitive load of the reading and helped to support comprehension. Children were able to better understand the authors' use of figurative language and subsequently were able to include similar language in their own written narratives. For example, after reading about Juanito's worry that his tongue might "turn into a rock" because he doesn't speak English (Herrera 2006, 7), one student conveyed a similar sentiment in her own memoir about her first days at school in the United States: "I felt that a mouse ate my mouth . . . because I didn't know what to talk."

Children's productivity in writing also increased dramatically through access to culturally relevant books. Some students who had dreaded writing prior to this unit were eager to get started on their own stories and were able to compose several pages of writing when describing their own journeys to the United States (Carrillo 2012).

"Can we write our stories today?"

—David, age nine, after studying personal narratives written by Latino authors

---

Culturally relevant literature is an important tool for supporting the literacy development of DLLs. Students will be drawn into books that they connect with and can understand, which, in turn, can foster reading motivation, persistence, and stamina (e.g., Freeman and Freeman 2004). The more students read, the more academic vocabulary they acquire, which helps expand their oral language proficiency in addition to strengthening their reading comprehension and their writing.

Not only is the selection of texts critical, but the ways in which teachers engage children with diverse language proficiencies matters as well. The next section provides examples of how teachers might consider DLLs' language levels when engaging them in literature discussion around a culturally relevant text.

A Bridge to Language Development

Teachers take many things into consideration when choosing a book: age-appropriateness, interest, cultural relevancy, and connections to the curriculum, among other things. (For criteria on text selection, please refer to

---

"Hey, I went there before!"

—Axel, age eight, in response to a picture of the Mercado (market) in *The Birthday Swap* by Loretta Lopez

chapters 6 and 7.) In order to understand the needs of DLLs and to differentiate instruction to best serve their language needs, it is also important to keep in mind the developmental sequence of language acquisition when choosing and using books.[2]

To illustrate, we use *The Birthday Swap* by Loretta Lopez (1997).[3] When considering the selection of culturally relevant texts for DLLs, educators are encouraged to think broadly about cultural relevance, focusing on experiences and themes that may resonate with DLLs and students who may be newer to the country, such stories including extended family networks, bicultural experiences, family members residing in more than one home country, and themes related to learning new language or understanding a new culture.

In *The Birthday Swap*, Ms. Lopez tells an autobiographical story of the best surprise she ever received when she was a young girl. In this story, the main character, five-year-old Lori, and her family live in a border town between the United States and Mexico and frequently cross the border to shop and visit family. Every year on her older sister Cookie's birthday, the family gets together for a big family reunion and summer celebration. Since Lori's birthday is in the winter, she never gets to have such a big party, but this year, Cookie has secretly decided to swap birthdays with her little sister. Unbeknownst to Lori, the party she is helping to plan for Cookie is actually for her. While Lori is searching the local Mercado Central for the perfect gift for Cookie's birthday, the rest of the family is planning the surprise party for Lori.[*]

Many children may find familiarity in the annual family reunion that includes "everyone"—friends, relatives, and neighbors from Mexico and the United States. They might also recognize the fruit and vegetable stands and curio shops of the crowded Mexican mercado as similar to markets they have visited. Even the vibrant colors of Lopez's illustrations and the various objects featured in their borders, such as the tools used to make piñatas, or the maracas, muñecos, or the caja sopresa de viborita (snake-in-the-box toy), may resonate with many children. It is these elements of cultural authenticity that may ground comprehension of the content of the text in familiar experiences, allowing some students to focus more of their cognitive effort on the language-learning demands of the task.

Levels of Language Proficiency

Listed below is a sequence of descriptors based on levels of language proficiency outlined by the TESOL International Association (2015). These

---

[*]*The Birthday Swap*. Copyright © 1997 by Loretta Lopez. Permission arranged with Lee & Low Books Inc., New York, NY 10016.

levels correspond closely with the English language proficiency levels of the *WIDA* Consortium English Language Development Standards, for educators who may be more familiar with WIDA. After each description, suggestions are provided for how to involve students at different levels of English proficiency in making connections when reading the book, *The Birthday Swap*, by Loretta Lopez.[4]

The examples are meant to serve as a guide that can be used with many books, as well as with questions that focus on other reading comprehension strategies, such as predicting, determining main idea, or making inferences. The intent is to not only develop reading strategies, but to foster *language development* as well. Choosing a culturally relevant book to use in a lesson, either as the focus or as an addition to a curriculum-prescribed text, will allow DLLs to focus more on the language and reading skills that are being presented.

Level 1—Starting

Students are beginning to build their receptive language and have little understanding of English. They require the use of visuals and context to make sense of what is being said. Many students will go through a "silent period" that may last varying lengths of time. Since they do not have the language to respond verbally, they should be encouraged to draw a picture, point or gesture, copy simple written words depending on their age, answer yes-or-no questions, or imitate others to show comprehension. They may begin to use simple words or phrases that they hear repeatedly, such as greetings. The use of illustrations when reading to students at this point is crucial as they require them to construct meaning.

Level 1 Questioning Strategies. Ask a yes-or-no question: "Here Lori is breaking the piñata at her birthday party (point to picture). Do you like to break piñatas?"

"Here is Lori with her sister (point to picture). Do you have a sister?" Students may expand on their answer in their native language.

Level 2—Emerging

Students are beginning to understand and use simple phrases and sentences. As in the previous level, they will most likely use phrases that they have memorized from repeated exposure. They can understand and use simple academic vocabulary that is taught with visual support. Students can label and write simple sentences with support, but grammatical errors may impede understanding. Students still strongly benefit from the use of illustrations to make meaning from text.

Level 2 Questioning Strategies. Point to the picture of Lori and her birthday cake. Ask students if the picture reminds them of anything. Expect students to answer in a short phrase or simple sentence with grammatical errors. A student might say, "I eat cake my birthday." As in level 1, students may want to say more about this in their native language.

Level 3—Developing

Students are understanding more complex speech through repeated encounters. However, their English vocabulary is still limited, which may make it difficult for them to express themselves. Students can write simple, multiparagraph compositions with support. Their writing still presents itself with grammatical errors, but these no longer impede understanding. Reading abilities vary, but most students are still not reading at grade level when they are "developing" their English. Students will be most successful when they read books for which they have background knowledge that will assist in their comprehension.

Level 3 Questioning Strategies. Point to the picture of Lori and her mom at the market in Mexico. Ask students, "Have you ever been to a market like this one?" Expect a complete sentence or sentences as a response with possible grammatical errors. A student might say, "I go to the market with my grandma. We buyed watermelon and oranges."

For students who have had the experience of visiting an outdoor market, a prompting question may not even be necessary. As noted in a quote earlier in the chapter, students will usually enthusiastically share that they have been there before and provide details of that experience. Sometimes, they cannot get the words out fast enough. This happens even with students who may not typically speak up in class—and this is exactly what we want—for students to generate ideas and discussions and have the opportunities and space to practice their language skills.

Level 4—Expanding

Students at this level are nearing the English proficiency of a native English speaker. They can read fluently and recall the facts of the text, but they still may have difficulty with comprehension if concepts are presented without much context, or if sentence structure or vocabulary is complex. In particular, students may require support understanding more complex academic concepts.

Level 4 Questioning Strategies. At one point in *The Birthday Swap*, Lori and her Mom stop by her aunt's house. Tía Sabina asks Lori to think about what kind of present she might get for her sister while "your mother and I discuss cake business" in the kitchen. Although the illustrations do not provide much visual support to suggest this, it is presumed the reader might infer that Lori's mother and aunt take this opportunity to secretly discuss plans for Lori's party. Ask direct questions to support Level 4 readers in understanding the nuances of the story, such as "Why did Tia Sabina want to talk with Mom in the kitchen?" "What do you think they talked about?"

Level 5—Bridging

Students are able to express themselves in a variety of settings on a range of topics. They have good command of technical and academic vocabulary and often require minimal language support. Students at the Bridging level of language development can be challenged to respond to higher-level comprehension questions that require them to use more sophisticated comprehension strategies, such as comparing and contrasting different texts, making inferences to explain character motivations, or describing cause-and-effect relationships.

Level 5 Questioning Strategies. Ask students, "Does this story remind you of something else you've read?" In levels 4 and 5, students have more age-appropriate vocabulary and grammatical structures and are able to provide more detailed responses. Students may respond, "It reminds me of *The Flower Garden* [by Eve Bunting] because the mom got a birthday surprise like Lori. Lori got a party and a puppy and the mom got a garden."

Summary of Questioning Strategies for Dual Language Learners

Table 4.1. TESOL Levels of Language Proficiency.

TESOL Level of Language Proficiency	Characteristics of Language Level	Questioning Strategies
Level 1—Starting	• Little understanding of second language • May repeat words or phrases they hear often • Go through "silent period" while observing others using new language	• Yes/No questions • Emphasize key words • Allow for nonverbal responses (e.g., Show me, Point to, Draw, Gesture, Copy)
Level 2—Emerging	• Use of simple words and phrases • Can understand basic vocabulary • Can label and write sentences with support	• Couple questions with strong visual support • Expect answers in short phrases with some grammatical errors

Table 4.1. *(Continued)*

TESOL Level of Language Proficiency	Characteristics of Language Level	Questioning Strategies
Level 3—Developing	• Understand more complex speech • Expressive English vocabulary still limited • Background knowledge will assist reading comprehension	• Make predictions using prior knowledge and experiences • Make self-to-text connections • Expect response in complete sentences but with possible grammatical errors
Level 4—Expanding	• Nearing conversational proficiency • Can read fluently and recall basic facts • Require support with more complex academic concepts	• Provide support for concepts presented out of context • Ask direct questions to support inferencing
Level 5—Bridging	• Can express themselves in a variety of settings and on a range of topics • Good command of technical and academic vocabulary	• Challenge to respond to high-level comprehension questions • Practice use of sophisticated comprehension strategies to compare/contrast, identify cause and effect, etc.

Adjusting to School in a New Country and a New City

In addition to the challenges of learning a new language, many dual language learners, especially those born in another country, face social and environmental changes and challenges that can oftentimes be stressful. DLLs often feel "set apart" linguistically, socially, and emotionally from other students in their classrooms (Agosto 2007, 27). In addition, many have left behind family, friends, possessions, and everything they knew to come to a different place with a new language and new ways of doing things. They go from a place of competence to not being able to do what other children can do because they do not yet speak the language.

Large "gateway" cities, such as Los Angeles, San Francisco, New York, and Chicago, have long been traditional entry points for many immigrant families (Price and Benton-Short 2008). While this continues to be the case, an increasing number of families are also heading for mid-sized and smaller metropolitan areas like Detroit, Minneapolis, and El Paso, Texas (Painter and Yu 2008). Urban environments can present another layer of challenge, particularly for students who are immigrating from more suburban or rural settings in their home countries.

Adjusting to the Urban Environment

The unique set of challenges presented in learning a new language, in a new school, in a new culture, but also, in a place as busy and chaotic as an urban setting may seem insurmountable to young children and their families. The activity level, the sights, sounds, pace, and congestion of the city may feel overwhelming. Urban children's literature may serve as a useful tool to help organize all of this new information and provide some of the new language needed to describe and process it.

For young children, books like *123 NYC: A Counting Book of New York City* (Dugan 2007), *City Colors* (Milich 2006), or *Wow! City!* (Neubecker 2004) capture many of the new sights and sounds children may be experiencing while labeling photographs and illustrations with helpful, basic vocabulary. Other selections such William Low's (1997) *Chinatown* or George Ancona's and colleagues (2004) *Mi Barrio/My Neighborhood* in which children explore the people, resources, and activities in their urban neighborhoods may also provide a context to which children can relate many of their new experiences in the city.

Maintaining a Strong Bicultural Identity

Oftentimes, children who are new immigrants feel they lose their identity as they leave their name and language at the door of the school. As Marcia Baghban (2007) points out, "all children live between the worlds of home and school, but for immigrant children, there is a clear disparity between their home and school worlds" (72). Immigrant children must establish their identity in their new country as well as at their new school. Children who grew up in the dominant culture must establish their school identity only.

As discussed in chapter 2, seeing oneself represented and valued in the curriculum can help strengthen all students' connections to school and support development of positive academic self-concepts. Who we are is shaped by our culture and our experiences (Rogoff 2003). Despite language differences, our students enter our schools with a rich background and a wealth of lived experiences. Culturally relevant urban children's literature can help children understand who they are and help them become confident that their experiences matter when they see themselves represented in the curriculum. As described above, books like *My Diary from Here to There* and *The Upside Down Boy* can help teachers get to know students better by fostering communication and helping students feel comfortable talking about their own lives (e.g., Rodriguez 2009).

> *"I know that in the United States I will have a better life, but I will never forget my home."*
>
> —Mahdi, age eleven, translated from Arabic on his first day in a U.S. school

Urban children's literature can also support maintenance of a positive bicultural identity. For example, in his autobiographical book of poems, *A Movie in My Pillow/Una pelicula en mi almohada*, Jorge Argueta (2007) captures how "Jorgito" gradually develops into an expert resident of San Francisco's Mission District while he still holds close the memories and values of his native El Salvador. Similar themes are present in Argueta's (2008) *Xóchitl and the Flowers/Xóchitl, la Niña de las flores*. Books like *Madlenka* by Peter Sís (2000), while not specific to any one cultural group, demonstrate how a group of neighbors with roots all over the world form a close-knit community in a New York City neighborhood while continuing to value and share traditions and stories from their homelands.

Learning a New Language

Successes and challenges in learning a new language can play a central role in shaping DLLs' sense of self and feelings of competence (Igoa 1995). Many books like *The Upside Down Boy* and *My Diary from Here to There* can serve as a forum for students to open up about the frustration that can come with learning English. *Cooper's Lesson* (Shin 2004) puts the shoe on the other foot, showing how Cooper, a biracial, second-generation Korean American student, struggles to learn Korean in order to communicate and fit in with the owner and patrons of his neighborhood grocery store.

For some children, their roles in their families change as they begin to learn more and more English and are called on to help parents and extended family members with translation. These experiences may lead to feelings of disconnect between children and their families. In Tony Johnston's (2001) *Uncle Rain Cloud*, young Carlos initially resents being asked regularly to translate for his often-grumpy Uncle Tomás (aka "Uncle Rain Cloud" in Carlos's mind). Over time, Carlos comes to understand that his uncle's disposition is the result of feelings of fear and displacement in the largely English-speaking-world of Los Angeles.

While *Uncle Rain Cloud* does draw attention to the ways children who translate sometimes take on adult responsibilities, it also can be used to emphasize the students' asset of being bilingual. Johnston makes clear in *Uncle Rain Cloud* how skilled Uncle Tomás is with language in general—he's a virtual master of storytelling and tongue-twisting—just not in English yet. It also makes clear that while learning English is definitely important, it is also important for Carlos to continue to learn Spanish and to learn about his heritage.

Educators should also note a difference between *Uncle Rain Cloud* and some other books that highlight children's experience as translators (e.g., *A Day's Work* [Bunting 1997]). Sometimes books that touch on this theme can infantilize the adult characters, making it seem as if the children are in charge (Mendoza and Reese 2001). Even though Carlos does translate for Uncle Tomás during his parent–teacher conference and at the grocery store, it is clear throughout the book that Uncle Tomás is the one taking care of Carlos, not the other way around.

Coping with Separation

Culturally relevant urban children's literature not only helps students form a positive self-concept but can also help alleviate the stress encountered by DLLs, especially those new to the country (Baghban 2007; Celic 2009; Ebe 2010). Many children experience short- or even long-term separation from close family members when they move to the United States. Books like *A Movie in My Pillow* (Argueta 2007), *Tía Isa Wants a Car* (Medina 2011), and *Sitti's Secrets* (Nye 1997) may help students work through these experiences as they discuss characters who are going through similar situations of separation or loss. In a rare find in picture books for young readers, René Colato Laínez (2010) takes on the subject of separation via deportation in *From North to South/Del Norte al Sur* when José's Mamá is deported from their home in San Diego to Tijuana.

As discussed in chapter 2, books like these might be especially useful recommendations for families experiencing separation or for a child who has experienced the deportation of a parent or other family member. Children may find comfort in discussing situations involving storybook characters rather than their own personal situations. Even in the context of a fictional story, discussing characters' emotions can be a useful outlet for exploring students' own feelings about a similar situation.

Support Through Context and Connection

When incorporated into the curriculum, urban children's literature is an effective tool that teachers can use to support DLLs' language and literacy development. As with other students, urban children's literature can increase student engagement in reading and writing and can help students make connections that can increase comprehension of texts. For DLLs in particular, culturally relevant urban children's literature can support language development by grounding potentially challenging language tasks in a familiar context, allowing students to build on familiar experiences, and freeing up cognitive energy to apply to the task of learning new vocabulary and language structures.

Summing It Up: Supporting the Literacy Development of Dual Language Learners

- Culturally relevant texts can provide a vehicle for discussions that can help students and teachers learn more about each other
- Urban children's literature can support students' development of a positive bicultural identity and a stronger sense of belonging in school
- Urban children's literature may help alleviate the stress encountered by dual language learners, especially those new to the country
- Culturally relevant texts help balance the cognitive and language demands of learning activities so students do not get overloaded
- Consider a range of appropriate questioning strategies to support language and literacy development for students at various levels of language proficiency.

In addition, DLLs can often feel disconnected from other students in their classrooms because of language and cultural differences. Seeing their home language, aspects of their culture, and familiar settings and experiences represented in texts can contribute to a sense of belonging among DLLs and can foster a stronger connection to school. Urban children's literature may also help students who are new to the country and to a new environment cope with the many changes they are experiencing. Educators are encouraged to keep in mind both cultural relevance and levels of language development in selecting texts to best serve the needs of our dual language learners.

Notes

1. See Hadaway and Young (2010, 10) for an extensive discussion of "The Many Faces of English Language Learners."

2. For more extensive reading related to the overview provided here, we again recommend Nancy Hadaway's and Terrell Young's (2010) *Matching Books to Readers: Helping English Learners in Grades K–6.*

3. Current limitations in the availability of urban children's literature that incorporates the experiences of children from diverse language backgrounds may make it difficult to find texts that are "perfect" mirrors for DLLs in urban schools. Books like *The Birthday Swap*, which includes a close, extended family network, bicultural experiences, and family members residing in more than one home country, may resonate with many DLLs because of its connection with other aspects of students' identities. Educators are encouraged to consider a broad range of multicultural and urban children's literature that may be most culturally relevant to the students in your classrooms. Limitations in the urban subgenre are discussed in more depth in chapter 5. *THE BIRTHDAY SWAP* copyright © 1997 by Loretta Lopez. Permission arranged with LEE & LOW BOOKS Inc., New York, NY 10016.

4. See Celic (2009) for additional examples and question frames for helping students connect with text.

CHAPTER FIVE

~

Urban Children's
Literature as a Critical Subgenre

The purpose of this chapter is to define urban children's literature as an important subgenre of multicultural children's literature and to help educators situate this subgenre in the broader world of children's books. The chapter begins by establishing definitions of various formats and genres of children's books and providing examples of urban children's literature that fall within those categories.

In addition, the chapter explores diversity and gaps in this subgenre with respect to various formats and genres, and makes suggestions for how educators might begin to fill these gaps. This chapter should serve as a useful overview for building classroom collections and utilizing urban children's literature of a variety of genres for instruction across the content areas so children can see themselves and their communities reflected and valued in all aspects of the curriculum.

Formats, and Genres, and Subgenres—Oh, My!

In schools and public libraries, children's literature is generally organized by subject matter (Dewey Decimal System) and type (fiction vs. nonfiction). Teachers, however, often organize literature in classrooms in a variety of different ways that include content area topics or curricular themes, favorite authors, illustrators or characters, genre of literature, and reading levels (e.g., Accelerated Reader, Fountas and Pinnell A–Z Text Levels). The organization system one chooses typically depends on the developmental level of the children and how the teacher utilizes the classroom library in instruction. For purposes of this chapter, we will use format and genre as our framework for discussing urban children's literature and its place in the broader curriculum.

Definitions

Many of these terms may already be familiar to many readers, but it is important to establish some shared understandings here.

Literature for Children, as opposed to literature for adults, needs to provide information, enjoyment, and entertainment about topics and emotions that are developmentally appropriate for children (Kiefer 2007). Children manage and respond to emotional situations in different ways as they mature and experience the world around them. Many picture books, while outstanding, are not necessarily intended for young children (e.g., Peter Sís's *The Wall* or Walter Dean Myers's *Harlem*). It is important to select books appropriate for the age, maturity levels, and language and literacy skills of the children who will be reading or listening to them.

Book Format describes the design or layout in which the story or information is presented. We draw from respected sources in the field, including Irene Fountas and Gay Su Pinnell (2012) and Barbara Kiefer (2007) to identify commonly agreed upon formats for preschool, primary, and intermediate grades.

Forms of Language in books can include *prose* and *poetry*. Prose generally includes sentences organized into paragraphs and is the form of language commonly used in newspapers, magazines, and literature to explain or describe things. Poetry, on the other hand, consists of more condensed language and frequent use of imagery and various types of rhythm to express the author's thoughts. Both prose and poetry can be found in fiction and nonfiction texts.

Genre is a term to designate a category of a literature or informational text having specific content and characteristics. All book formats (e.g., picture books, chapter books) will include a range of genres. There are a number of fiction and nonfiction genres that are generally agreed upon by classroom teachers and literature experts to describe the categories of books that are written specifically for enjoyment by children. We draw from Lee Galda and Bernice Cullinan (2006), Fountas and Pinnell (2012), and Duke et al. (2011) in describing these common genres here.

Multicultural Literature is often defined as "literature that represents any distinct cultural group through accurate portrayal and rich detail" (Yokota

Table 5.1. Book Formats

Format	Description
Board Books	Often identification or naming books; might include simple narrative. Allows the child to point to and identify familiar objects. Some board books include flaps or moving parts that assist in helping children predict or identify the item.
Predictable Books	Includes repetitive language, familiar sequences, and rhyme. Emergent readers can identify refrains by memory and through illustrations to understand the text whether or not they can read each word.
Wordless Picture Books	Books in which a story is told completely through illustrations. Though lacking any words, these books can often involve sophisticated stories that require close reading and inferencing, making them appropriate for use with a range of readers.
Picture Books	Combine illustrations and text to tell a story or convey information. Many times the illustrations are as important in contributing to meaning as the text.
Big Books	Favorite stories and poems in oversized format for ease of use in instruction with large groups of young children. Allows children to "read along" to familiar stories and poems.
Easy Readers	Short, illustrated storybooks developed to help beginning readers gain confidence in reading independently. Carefully controlled vocabulary and length of story. Often part of a basal or guided reading series for emergent and transitional readers.
Transitional Chapter Books	Combine text with illustrations in short chapter book format, often in a series. These books are for children who have moved beyond Easy Readers but are continuing to build reading fluency and stamina for reading longer texts. Typically geared toward children in second through fourth grades and include characters and themes that are reflective of that age group.
Chapter Books	Books that are long enough to break into chapters with more complex plot and character development or depth of coverage of content. Typically absent of illustrations for intermediate and older readers who can access meaning solely from text. The story may span a longer period of time than books geared toward younger children.
Short Stories	Brief narratives, often including few characters and focused on a short period of time or a single incident. Individual short stories are typically intended to be read in one sitting. Often sold in collections.
Graphic Texts	Information or stories conveyed primarily through panels of artwork. Stems from the long history of comics and manga, and includes novels and nonfiction texts. Require readers to make meaning from illustrations with just a small amount of text.
Digital Texts	Books in electronic form. Unlike books in print, digital texts may include embedded hyperlinks to provide readers with supplemental information via links to websites, videos, or other digital content.

Table 5.2.   Genres of Children's Literature

Genre	Description
Fiction Genres	
Contemporary Realistic Fiction	Fictional stories taking place in contemporary settings, featuring realistic characters and events that could happen in real world. This genre can provide excellent "mirrors" in which children might recognize themselves or be reminded of people they know and experiences they have had.
Historical Fiction	Set in the past, could have happened. Story reconstructs events of past age, things that could have or did occur.
Traditional Literature	Stories passed down through history. Includes folktales, fairy tales, legends, nursery rhymes, and songs from the past. Often derived from oral tradition with no known original author.
Modern Fantasy	Stories set in imaginative worlds about characters or creatures that could not exist, and events that could not happen. Includes animal fantasy (e.g., walking and talking animals), magical fantasy ("real" world with magical elements), and high fantasy (involves an alternative or parallel universe).
Science Fiction	Stories grounded in real physical laws and scientific principles. Often futuristic, employing technological advances or space travel and presenting possibilities for what life in the future might be like.
Nonfiction Genres	
Concept Books	Provide information on basic concepts by using brief narratives, labels, rhyme, and repetition. Includes alphabet, counting, shapes, colors, days of the week, sounds, opposites, and so on.
Informational texts	Nonfiction texts that provide facts about the real world. Describe events that have actually occurred or explain a subject or concept to instruct the reader. Often include features such as tables of contents, headings, glossaries, photographs, and diagrams.
Narrative Nonfiction	Nonfiction texts that provide information using a narrative structure. Reads like a story, but includes factual information about a topic.
Biography	A nonfiction account of a person's life, or a part of someone's life history, written by another. Typically based on significant research of historical events. May draw on primary source documents such as letters, diaries, and journals.
Autobiography	A biography of one's own life. Written by or told by the subject of the book.
Memoir	Autobiographical account of specific events or a particular time period in one's life. Draws on the author's memory of events in his or her life, rather than on historical research. Generally written in more of a narrative style.

1993, 157). As discussed in chapter 1, we also embrace Rudine Sims Bishop's specific definition of multicultural literature as "literature written by and about people who are members of groups considered to be outside the socio-political mainstream" (Bishop 1992, 39).

Multicultural literature can be identified within each of the genre categories. One can find multicultural literature in realistic fiction (*The Butter Man*, by E. L. Alalou and A. Alalou), historical fiction (*Chickadee* by Louise Erdrich), poetry (*Tan to Tamarind: Poems About the Color Brown* by Malathi Michelle Iyengar), traditional literature (*La Llorona /The Weeping Woman* by Joe Hayes), fantasy (*Raising Dragons*, by Jerdine Nolen), and science fiction (*Galaxy Games: The Challengers* by Greg R. Fishbone), as well as in nonfiction concept books (*Opuestos: Mexican Folk Art Opposites in English and Spanish* by Cynthia Weill), informational texts (*What is Religion?* by Bobbie Kalman), biographies (*Jackie Robinson: Champion for Equality*, by Michael Teitelbaum), and memoirs (*The Circuit: Stories from the Life of a Migrant Child* by Francisco Jiménez).

Urban as a Subgenre of Multicultural Children's Literature

Where does urban children's literature fit into the discussion of genres? Urban literature is a subgenre of multicultural children's literature that has specific settings and situations designed to "highlight the socio-economic realities and culture of characters" and re-create "scenes and activities that realistically occur in daily life" for children in the city (Morris 2012, 4).

The large majority of urban public school students are from groups outside the sociopolitical mainstream and, as a result, are often less visibly represented in published curricula. Most are children of color. Many are first- or second-generation immigrants negotiating bicultural identities and maintaining strong ties to their heritage cultures. Some are recent refugees to the United States or are migrant children, many of whom are adjusting to life in a new country or learning English as a new language. Many reside in lower-income communities, which are infrequently represented in the world of children's literature. All are deserving of "mirrors" in which they can see themselves, their families, and their communities reflected and valued, yet many live in urban locales that are often maligned, feared, or resented, rather than celebrated.

As such, we see urban children's literature as a distinct and important body of work within multicultural children's literature. Connecting with urban children's literature can provide a familiar foundation for learning new content, can spark the motivation required to develop reading fluency and stamina, and can support students in mastering strategies for comprehending texts in deep and meaningful ways.

The Emergence of a Subgenre

The term "genre" comes from the French word meaning "kind" or "sort." As described above, it is generally used to designate a category of texts having specific content and characteristics. Subgenres (or subtypes) of literature often emerge when thematic groupings within genres can serve as useful organizers. These groupings may be related to subject matter (e.g., "mysteries"), form (e.g., "diaries"), time period (e.g., "Medieval fantasy") or setting (e.g., "Westerns") (see Chandler [1997], for discussion).

Although we often discuss genres and subgenres as fixed, distinct categories, in practice, there are "no rigid rules of inclusion and exclusion" (Gledhill 2000, 60). In addition, as new works are published, new subgenres can emerge, particularly when that subgenre serves a useful purpose or tells us "something theoretically important" about that classification (Miller 1984, 155).

In the previous chapters, we have described the theoretical and practical importance of urban children's literature, illustrating the mechanisms through which it can support development of a positive academic self-concept and the ways it can be used to promote and accelerate literacy learning. Consequently, we believe it is warranted and critically important to identify the subgenre of urban children's literature in this way. Heightening urban educators' awareness of "urban" as a subgenre of multicultural children's literature will inform selection of the particular types of texts that can be most effective in connecting students' lives with the content we teach and supporting children in using their knowledge and experiences as a foundation for literacy learning.

A Brief History of Urban Children's Literature

There is a long, rich history of multicultural children's literature in the United States that can be traced back through the nineteenth century in church publications, oral tradition, music, and folklore. Several turn-of-the-century publications by American Indian writers were written specifically for children, including *The Middle Five: Indian Boys at School* by Francis LaFlesche(1900) and *Indian Boyhood* by Charles Eastman (1902). Print publications for children emerging through the Harlem Renaissance such as W.E.B.

Du Bois's (1920) *The Brownies' Book* magazine and the early twentieth-century works of Pura Belpré and Langston Hughes would pave the way for a new era of multicultural picture books for young readers emerging in the 1960s through the Civil Rights movement (see Bishop [2007], Gilton [2007], Martin [2004], and Naidoo [2011] for excellent histories).

Early Images of Urban Life

The earliest American works of urban children's literature appeared around this same time, beginning perhaps with Arna Bontemps's *Sad-Faced Boy*, published in 1937, which follows the adventures of three African American boys who travel to New York City's Harlem from Alabama. Other early works include Leo Politi's (1946) *Pedro, The Angel of Olvera Street* and *Juanita* (1947), whose young protagonists were depicted enjoying cultural traditions and holiday celebrations amidst the markets, musicians, and shops of historic downtown Los Angeles. Ellen Tarry was also an early, key contributor to the subgenre, with several works set in Harlem, including *Hezekiah Horton* (1942), the story of a boy fascinated by the parade of cars streaming up and down Lenox Avenue and *My Dog Rinty* (1946, with Marie Hall Ets) about a family and their mischievous pet.

Gwendolyn Brooks's *Bronzeville Boys and Girls* (1955) was also a notable addition to the subgenre during this time, for a number of reasons. First and foremost, Brooks's collection of fictional poems beautifully captured the joys and experiences of children growing up in Bronzeville, Brooks's predominantly African American, South Side Chicago neighborhood. Despite her intention, however, HarperCollins's original release with illustrations by Ronni Solbert featured line drawings of white children. It was not until fifty years later that *Bronzeville Boys and Girls* was reissued with more authentic illustrations painted by Faith Ringgold.

The Works of Ezra Jack Keats

Perhaps most well known by teachers and educators is the collection of urban picture books by Ezra Jack Keats. A prolific writer and fine artist of Polish and Jewish descent, Keats often drew inspiration for his stories from his own childhood experiences growing up in Brooklyn during the Great Depression. Similarly, he looked to the community for his characters, and he was committed to featuring children of color in urban settings as protagonists in his picture books from the very start of his publishing career. His first coauthored children's book, *My Dog is Lost!*, published in 1960, features a boy named

Juanito, who has recently arrived in New York City from Puerto Rico and is in search of his lost dog, Pepito. Next came *The Snowy Day* in 1962, a landmark in children's literature as the first book featuring a black protagonist to win the Caldecott medal.

Designed for emergent and beginning readers, Keats's collection of family and community stories "reflect the simple pleasures and more complex problems that a child often encounters in his daily routine" (Ezra Jack Keats Foundation 2014). Keats's protagonist, Peter, is seen by many parents and educators as the "American Everychild" (Bishop 2007, 116). Although Keats has received some criticism for his generic portrayal of Peter that is absent of any significant cultural content in the story, the series of urban picture books in which Peter and his friends are featured, including *Whistle for Willie* (1964), *Peter's Chair* (1967), *A Letter to Amy* (1968), and *Pet Show!* (1972) continue to be staples in contemporary classrooms (see chapter 8 for a discussion of the importance of culturally specific texts).

In addition to these more "everyday" family and friendship stories, others of Keats's books published around that same time present more complex predicaments that can serve as a catalyst for critical conversations about real-life circumstances (Ladson-Billings 1992). *Goggles* (1969), *Apt. 3* (1971), and *Louie's Search* (1980), for example, invite young readers to grapple with true-to-life issues in developmentally appropriate ways, as characters try to evade neighborhood bullies, confront their notions of disability, or explore feelings about living without a father. Simultaneously, African American authors like Lorenz Graham were writing more culturally specific texts for older children. His book series, including *North Town* (1965), follows a young man working to keep his dream of becoming a doctor alive in the face of discrimination and bigotry.

Stevie—A Major Breakthrough in Urban Children's Book Publishing

Then came John Steptoe's *Stevie* (1969), representing a major milestone in urban children's literature. *Stevie* was first published in *Life* magazine when John Steptoe was just eighteen years old. It captured the essence of an urban, working-class community through the eyes of young Robert, an African American boy not thrilled with the prospect of putting up with a younger tag-along, when Robert's mother offers to help care for a friend's son while his parents are working.

In contrast to the "Everychild" nature of *The Snowy Day*, *Stevie* was written with a very specific audience in mind: "Steptoe wanted his readers to see themselves in his work" (Bishop 2007, 118). Steptoe's well-developed characters are distinctly urban and African American, not "color-me-brown" caricatures only recognizable as black based on skin tone (Bishop 2007, 118). Robert reluctantly plays games on the stoop with Stevie and takes him to the nearby park with his friends. Robert's family uses dialect characteristic of African American English, and they share childcare arrangements with friends, similar to many working families.

The fact that *Stevie* was featured—in its entirety and in full color—in the leading American news magazine of the time was a tremendous accomplishment and a significant breakthrough in the recognition of urban children's literature as an important subgenre. Steptoe went on to write more books capturing urban life in Brooklyn through his young characters' eyes, including *Uptown* (1970) and *Train Ride* (1971). Indeed, a substantial proportion of picture books written by African American writers in the 1970s were set in the city and were designed to fill the chasm of culturally relevant text for children in urban schools (Bishop 2007).

Walter Dean Myers, A Champion for Urban Youth

Around the same time that *Stevie* was written, another writer who grew up just across the river in New York City's Harlem neighborhood received an award from the Council on Interracial Books for Children (CIBC) for what would become his first published picture book, *Where Does the Day Go?* (Myers 1969). This was the start of a prolific and highly acclaimed writing career for Walter Dean Myers, who went on to publish more than one hundred books over the next forty-five years (see walterdeanmyers.net for a complete bibliography).

Although he was a voracious reader as a teenager, Myers recognized an absence of characters he could truly identify with as a young black man growing up in Harlem. Myers credited James Baldwin's short story "Sonny's Blues" (1965) for helping solidify his identity as a writer by giving him "permission to write about my own landscape" (Myers 2014). Indeed, Myers went on to dedicate his career to creating more "mirrors" for urban children and teens, and his contributions to the subgenre of urban children's literature are unparalleled.

Myers's canon has incredible depth, comprised of picture books, chapter books, short stories, and graphic texts written in prose and poetry across a wide range of genres. His nonfiction works include informational texts

(*Antarctica: Journeys to the South Pole*, 2004; *Jazz*, 2006), narrative nonfiction (*Toussaint L'overtoure: The Fight for Haiti's Freedom*, 1996), biography (*At Her Majesty's Request: An African Princess in Victorian England*, 1999; *Ida B. Wells: Let the Truth Be Told*, 2008), and memoir (*Bad Boy: A Memoir*, 2001), while his fictional works include historical fiction (*Fallen Angels*, 1988; *Sunrise Over Fallujah*, 2008; *Riot*, 2010), animal fiction (*The Blues of Flats Brown*, 2000), modern retellings of classic works (e.g., *Amiri and Odette*, 2009; *Carmen*, 2011), and more recently, science fiction (*On a Clear Day*, 2014).

Still, he is perhaps best known for his wealth of realistic fiction titles, often set in Harlem, featuring young, African American male protagonists. Whether writing *Fast Sam, Cool Clyde, and Stuff* (1975), *Scorpions* (1988), or *Darnell Rock Reporting* (1994) for younger readers or *Monster* (1999), *Lockdown* (2010), or *Darius and Twig* (2013) for high schoolers, Myers filled his books with compelling characters, familiar language, credible scenarios, and absorbing plots that have rung true with urban youth for decades. Like his own experience reading James Baldwin, Walter Dean Myers's work has had a similarly profound effect on countless young people who have recognized themselves in his stories, often for the first time.

More Pioneers of the Subgenre

Other distinguished writers of urban children's literature during this time include Eloise Greenfield and Lucille Clifton. Greenfield's contributions to the urban subgenre have been significant, starting with her first book, *Bubbles* (1977, later reprinted as *Good News*) about a little boy who is eager to share his new-found ability to read with anyone in his family who will listen.

In another touching family story, *She Come Bringing Me That Little Baby Girl* (1974), Greenfield delicately captures young Kevin's initial jealousy over the attention being paid to his new baby sister, and the guidance of a perceptive mom and kind uncle who help him realize his uncle was his own mother's "big brother" at one time. A prolific writer, Greenfield has continued to publish dozens of picture books, novels, and poetry collections over

---

"I could see how African American children could miss seeing themselves in books. I wanted them to see their reflections and see how beautiful they are and how wonderful their lives are sometimes."

—Eloise Greenfield (Teachingbooks.net 2011)

the past four decades, many of which feature African American families in urban settings.

Clifton was a poet and a writer who believed her role was to "authenticate the world of Black children . . . providing them with information that allows them to understand their connections to others like themselves, [and] to take pride in belonging to a particular social/cultural group" (Bishop 2007, 120). Clifton's *The Boy Who Didn't Believe in Spring* (1973) follows a typical adventure of two young boys, but in the specific cultural context of the city. Pals King Shabazz and Tony Polito are pessimistic about finding any "blue birds" or "crops coming up" in their chain-linked, pavement-laden, pedestrian-heavy, traffic-filled block, resulting in quite a surprise when their quest proves them wrong.

Clifton's eight-book Everett Anderson series (e.g., *Some of the Days of Everett Anderson* [1970] to *Everett Anderson's Goodbye* [1983]) includes poems about a young boy who lives in an urban housing project. In describing a wide range of Everett's experiences over time, Clifton presents "matter of fact" socioeconomic realities in the context of loving family relationships and friendship stories, making visible a population that had not been well represented in children's books at the time (Bishop 2007).

Similarly, Cruz Martel's *Yagua Days* (1976) provided a rare, authentic look at a Latino family living in New York City. Adan, whose family owns a bodega on the Lower East Side of Manhattan, gets discouraged on rainy days when he can't get out to play in East River Park. But on his first visit to Puerto Rico, Adan meets his extended family and develops a new appreciation for rain-filled "yagua" days. Martel's story, coupled with Jerry Pinkney's beautiful black-and-white pencil illustrations, presents one of the first positive and accurate depictions of a Puerto Rican family in a time when stereotypes of Latinos were pervasive in children's books (see Naidoo [2011] for discussion).

Contemporary Writers of Urban Children's Literature

Social, legal, and educational forces in the 1960s and 1970s contributed to a gradual recognition of the demand for multicultural children's literature and an expansion of opportunities for writers of color over the next several decades. The ongoing efforts of the Civil Rights movement, new funding streams provided through the Elementary and Secondary Education Act and the Bilingual Education Act, and the continued activism of organizations like the CIBC resulted in an uptick in multicultural and urban children's literature in the latter part of the twentieth century (see Bishop [2007] and Naidoo [2011] for more extensive discussion).

Many of today's well-known writers got their starts during the 1970s and 1980s and continue to contribute to the subgenre of urban children's literature today (e.g., Angela Johnson, Sharon Bell Mathis, Faith Ringgold, Gary Soto). In turn, their efforts helped pave the way for a new generation of exceptional writers of urban children's literature, a number of whom have

Table 5.3. Prominent Contributors of Contemporary Urban Children's Literature for the Elementary Grades

Author	Selected Texts
Monica Brown	Butterflies on Carmen Street; Marisol McDonald Doesn't Match/Marisol McDonald no combina
Sandra Cisneros	The House on Mango Street; Hairs/Pelitos
Nina Crews	The Neighborhood Sing Along; One Hot Summer Day
Sharon G. Flake	Pinned; The Skin I'm In; Unstoppable Octobia May
Nikki Grimes	Make Way for Dyamonde Daniel; My Man Blue; Words with Wings
Monica Gunning	America, My New Home; A Shelter in Our Car
Juan Felipe Herrera	Grandma and Me at the Flea/Los Meros Meros Remateros; The Upside Down Boy/El niño de cabeza
Angela Johnson	The Leaving Morning; One of Three; The Sweet Smell of Roses
Tony Johnston	Any Small Goodness; My Abuelita; Uncle Rain Cloud
Barbara Joosse	Hot City; Stars in the Darkness
William Low	Chinatown; Machines Go to Work in the City
Sharon Bell Mathis	Sidewalk Story; Ray Charles
Meg Medina	Mango, Abuela, and Me; Tía Isa Wants a Car
Christopher Myers	Black Cat; Fly!; Wings
Walter Dean Myers	The Cruisers; Darnell Rock Reporting; Harlem; Jazz; Looking Like Me
G. Neri	Chess Rumble; Ghetto Cowboy
Faith Ringgold	Tar Beach; Cassie's Word Quilt
Hope Anita Smith	The Way a Door Closes; Keeping the Night Watch
Gary Soto	Taking Sides; Neighborhood Odes
Javaka Steptoe	The Jones Family Express; Rain Play
Carol Boston Weatherford	Sidewalk Chalk; Sugar Hill
Rita Williams-Garcia	One Crazy Summer; P.S. Be Eleven; Gone Crazy in Alabama
Janet S. Wong	Apple Pie 4th of July; Minn and Jake's Almost Terrible Summer
Jacqueline Woodson	Brown Girl Dreaming; This Is the Rope; Visiting Day

emerged in the past decade (e.g., Kwame Alexander, Claudia Guadalupe Martinez). Readers may recognize many of the prominent contributors listed in table 5.3, along with select titles for elementary readers from their often extensive collections. Educators are encouraged to explore these and other titles by these writers.

This list is meant to be illustrative of some contributors to urban children's literature for the elementary grades. Readers are likely familiar with many more writers, including those who have regularly contributed excellent works to the subgenre of urban children's literature aimed at older students and young adults, such as Coe Booth, Sharon Draper, Matt de la Peña, Daniel José Older, and Ashley Hope Pérez. Numerous additional authors and texts are recognized throughout the following chapters and in the list of Recommended Children's Literature that is included at the end of this book.

The Central Role of Illustrators

It is important not to underestimate the contribution of a great artist. The degree to which urban picture books and transitional chapter books serve as authentic mirrors for students in urban communities is substantially impacted by the quality and authenticity of their illustrations. Like writers, illustrators' choices help propel the stories they are trying to tell. They engage the reader, establish the mood as a story unfolds, and complement and enhance its meaning.

Illustrators of urban picture books have played an essential role in the emergence of the subgenre since the early works of Moneta Barnett (e.g., *Timothy's Flower*, 1967) and George Ford (*Walk On!*, 1972). Several contemporary illustrators stand out for their ability to capture the look, feel, and vibrancy of the city. Readers familiar with the subgenre may immediately recognize some key artists' work: the striking, emotion-filled faces in the vibrant acrylic paintings of R. Gregory Christie (*DeShawn Days, Stars in the Darkness, Yesterday I Had the Blues*); the lanky and lively characters of Frank Morrison (*I Got the Rhythm, Jazzy Miz Mozetta, My Feet Are Laughing*); the gouache paintings and photo collages of David Diaz (*El Barrio, Smoky Night*); or the colorful cityscapes and construction scenes in William Low's digital paintings (*Chinatown, Machines Go to Work in the City*).

Similarly, authors Nina Crews, Christopher Myers, and Javaka Steptoe (noted above) have each become well known for their individual and immediately recognizable illustrative styles: Crews with photographs of children who revel in the city, Myers for his bold and brilliant paintings, and Steptoe for his mixed-media collage. These and other artists such as E. B. Lewis

(*Bippity Bop Barbershop, Keeping the Night Watch*) and Eric Velasquez (*Rain Stomper, Grandma's Gift*) have each made significant contributions to urban children's literature and to the field of children's literature more broadly, publishing many of the best illustrated picture books in recent years. Artists who have more recently made their mark on the subgenre include Christian Robinson (*Last Stop on Market Street, Rain!*) and Sara Palacios (*Marisol Mc-Donald and the Clash Bash/Marisol McDonald y la fiesta sin igual*).

Similar to author studies involving the examination of a collection of titles by a single writer, educators are encouraged to engage children in illustrator study, providing opportunities to closely examine an artist's body of work. Illustrator study can expose children to various art forms and illustrative techniques, and give them ideas for conveying meaning in their own writing through a variety of verbal and nonverbal means. Learning about contemporary illustrators from diverse backgrounds may also inspire children to discover the artists within themselves and envision new avenues for pursuing their talents.

Urban Children's Literature across the Genres

Urban children's literature can be found in all genres, as illustrated by the sample titles included in Tables 5.4 and 5.5. There are many more titles available than these, but this selection is presented to illustrate the range of available literature across genres, and to encourage educators to ensure that contemporary, culturally relevant selections are included across the curriculum (see www.kidslikeus.org for additional recommendations by genre).

TRY THIS TOMORROW

Browse the shelves or bins of your classroom collection, and ask yourself the following questions:

- Does your collection include many urban children's literature titles?
- Can your students see themselves well represented in literature across all topics and genres?
- Are there some genres (folktales, historical fiction, biography) that include much more diversity than others?

Table 5.4.   Urban Children's Literature in Fiction Genres

Fiction Genre	Sample Titles
Contemporary Realistic Fiction	*Cooper's Lesson* (Shin and Cogan 2004)
	Last Stop on Market Street (de la Peña and Robinson 2015)
	My Abuelita (Johnston and Morales 2009)
Historical Fiction	*Across the Alley* (Michelson and White 2006)
	¡Sí, Se Puede!/Yes, We Can! Janitor Strike in L.A. (Cohn and Delgado 2005)
	Sweet Music in Harlem (Taylor and Morrison 2004)
Traditional Literature	*Jack and the Beanstalk* (Crews 2011)
	The Neighborhood Mother Goose (Crews 2003)
	The Neighborhood Sing Along (Crews 2011)
Modern Fantasy	*H.O.R.S.E.: A Game of Basketball and Imagination* (C. Myers 2012)
	The Sound of Colors: A Journey of the Imagination (Liao 2006)
	The Magic Paintbrush (Yep and Wang 2003)
Science Fiction	*Marina and the Little Green Boy: In the City/Marina y el niño verde: en la ciudad* (Vicente and Ordóñez 2012)
	Oh No! Or How My Science Project Destroyed the World (Barnett and Santat 2010)
	When You Reach Me (Stead 2011)
Poetry	*DeShawn Days* (Medina and Christie 2003)
	My Chinatown: A Year in Poems (Mak 2001)
	My Feet Are Laughing (Norman and Morrison 2006)

In some classroom collections, multicultural children's literature gets represented primarily in the study of certain genres, such as historical fiction, biography, or traditional literature (e.g., reading several different versions of familiar folktales). Urban children's literature often gets underrepresented in genres like realistic fiction, poetry, memoir, and informational texts. It is important to ensure that children can see themselves reflected in all aspects of the curriculum and that they are invited to bring their knowledge and experiences to bear in all kinds of learning.

Limitations of the Urban Subgenre

Despite the exceptional contributions of so many authors and illustrators, the availability of urban children's literature—and the diversity of selections within the subgenre—continues to be somewhat limited. As discussed in chapter 1, there is a critical need for greater diversity in children's book publishing that cuts across all subgenres, and urban children's literature is no exception. Some restrictions in representations of diversity are discussed here.

Table 5.5. Urban Children's Literature in Nonfiction Genres

Nonfiction Genre	Sample Titles
Concept Books	*The City ABC Book* (Milich 2003) *Yesterday I Had the Blues* (Frame and Christie 2008) *Urban Animals* (Hill 2009)
Informational Texts	*Dreaming Up: A Celebration of Building* (Hale 2012) *Machines Go to Work in the City* (Low 2013) *Meadowlands: A Wetlands Survival Story* (Yezerski 2011)
Narrative Nonfiction	*Pale Male: Citizen Hawk of New York City* (Schulman and So 2008) *Redwoods* (Chin 2009) *March On: The Day My Brother Martin Changed the World* (Farris and Ladd 2008)
Biography	*Sonia Sotomayor: A Judge Grows in the Bronx/La juez que crecio en el Bronx* (Winter 2009) *Farmer Will Allen and the Growing Table* (Martin 2013) *When the Beat Was Born: DJ Kool Herc and the Creation of Hip Hop* (Hill 2013)
Autobiography	*Knock Knock: My Dad's Dream for Me* (Beaty 2013) *To Dance: A Ballerina's Graphic Novel* (Seigel 2006) *We Beat the Street: How a Friendship Pact Led to Success* (Davis et al. 2006)
Memoir	*Grandma's Gift* (Velasquez 2010) *A Movie in My Pillow/Una pelicula en mi almohada* (Argueta 2007) *The Upside Down Boy/El niño de cabeza* (Herrera 2006)
Poetry	*City I Love* (Hopkins 2009) *A Poem as Big as New York City* (Teachers and Writers Collaborative 2012) *Sugar Hill: Harlem's Historic Neighborhood* (Weatherford and Christie 2014)

Cultural Stereotypes in Children's Literature

There is a long history of overt stereotyping in children's literature, oftentimes occurring when writers outside of a cultural group attempt to depict

> "We are past the days where we 'explain' who we are via the foods we eat, the holidays we celebrate, etc., and into an era where we simply tell our stories, just like everyone else does."
>
> —Adriana Domínguez, on the need for more diversity in publishing (Lee and Low 2013)

a people without sufficient research or life experience in the community. For example, there is widespread agreement that many stories that focus on Native Americans, both historic accounts and modern depictions, continue to perpetuate stereotypes. Much critique has been written about overtly stereotypic depictions in books like Lynne Reid Banks's (2010) *The Indian in the Cupboard* or the more subtle misrepresentations in books like Bill Martin Jr.'s and John Archambault's (1997) *Knots on a Counting Rope*, in which very little of the cultural content of the book is accurate (see Reese and Caldwell-Wood [1997] for discussion).

Similarly, urban children's literature is not without cultural stereotypes. While the past decade has brought many high-quality text selections highlighted throughout these chapters and noted in the bibliography, there are some limitations in this subgenre that are important to note. Many of these limitations are due not to the content of particular books per se, but to trends in publishing within this subgenre as a whole.

Restrictions in Representations of Race and Ethnicity

As discussed in chapter 1, picture books with urban settings are still relatively scarce, and as a result, racial, ethnic, and linguistic diversity among their primary characters is limited. With nearly one-third of our nation's students attending urban public schools, this raises significant concern about the availability of high-quality, culturally relevant texts to support literacy instruction. Although there is a strong visible presence of African American primary characters in urban children's literature, ethnic diversity in representations of Black Americans, including African, Caribbean, and Middle Eastern cultures, is rather limited. In addition, compared with the population of many American cities, there are surprisingly few Asian American or Latino characters in picture books featuring city settings.

Asian Americans in the City

When Asian American characters appear in urban picture books, they are very often featured in stories or informational texts highlighting the Chinatown neighborhood of certain cities or in celebrations of Chinese New Year. Less common are books like *Apple Pie 4th of July* (Wong 2006), *Juna's Jar* (Bank, 2015), or *Suki's Kimono* (Uegaki 2005) featuring family and friendship stories with Chinese American, Korean American, and Japanese American primary characters. With the exception of some noteworthy titles for middle- and upper-grades readers (e.g., *Ask Me No Questions*, Budhos 2007), South Asian characters are also significantly underrepresented. Very few urban picture books feature Indian, Bangladeshi, or Pakistani characters, for example, like *Big Red Lollipop* by Rukhsana Khan (2010).

Latino Characters in Urban Children's Literature

Several studies have revealed significant gaps in the representation of Latinos in children's literature (e.g., Cooperative Children's Book Center 2013; Fleming and Carrillo 2011), and the subgenre of urban children's literature is no exception. Family, friendship, and neighborhood stories set in the city featuring Latino characters like *Quinito, Day and Night* (Cumpiano 2008) or *Lola's Fandango* (Witte 2011) are relatively hard to come by, compared with books that center on food, cultural celebrations, or immigration or border themes that more often involve rural settings.

> *"I do love colorful stories about our holidays and foods—por Dios, who doesn't love an empanada?—but we Latinos move through the US a lot like everybody else, looking for success, for happy families, for friends at schools, for a way to understand the sometimes sad things that happen to us as children."*
>
> —Meg Medina, author of *Tía Isa Wants a Car*

Among urban children's literature and informational texts that do feature Latinos, studies have shown significant underrepresentation in diversity among Latino characters, particularly with respect to Caribbean, Central American, and South American subcultures (Fleming and Fuenmayor 2013; Naidoo 2008). In addition, many texts present "generic" Latino characters, absent of many identifiable cultural characteristics. It is worth teachers' time to examine the extent to which their collections are inclusive of Latinos generally, but also representative of characters of Mexican, Puerto Rican, Haitian, Dominican, Argentinian, Venezuelan, Salvadoran, or Panamanian descent, for example.

Whose Mirrors Are Missing?

Characters from other less predominant cultural and ethnic groups, such as Middle Eastern Americans, are also virtually absent from urban children's literature, except in informational texts that are geared toward teaching others about families' immigration experiences, religious practices, or cultural traditions (e.g., *Coming to America: A Muslim Family's Story*, Wolf 2003). Most often, when books do include a Middle Eastern character, they rarely take place in city settings and are often set in the Middle East, possibly making the content seem distant or exotic, especially for children who may be second- or third-generation Americans.

Similarly, urban educators may be hard-pressed to locate authentic "mirrors" for their Native American students, since the majority of books published feature rural, Western U.S. settings. While it is important to include a range of high-quality, accurate representations of Native American history and heritage in any collection, teachers might also do well to include Cynthia Leitich Smith's *Indian Shoes* (2002), a collection of contemporary short stories about a Seminole-Cherokee boy who lives in Chicago, or *Children of Native America Today* by Yvonne Wakim Dennis and Arlene B. Hirschfelder (2003), an informational text about contemporary Native America, including urban Indians.

Representations of Multiracial Families
Another perspective to consider is the reality of multiracial and multiethnic families and experiences. According to the most recent census, the proportion of people in the United States identifying as multiracial is growing faster than any other group (United States Census Bureau 2012). As a result, it is surprising how few biracial, multiracial, or blended families are currently present in urban children's literature for younger readers. Books with multiethnic families, like *Marisol McDonald and the Clash Bash/Marisol McDonald y la fiesta sin igual* (Brown 2013), are welcome additions to the subgenre, as are books like *Grandma's Gift* (Velasquez 2010) and *Kitchen Dance* (Manning 2008), which celebrate their primary characters' Afro-Latino heritage.

Linguistic Diversity
Similarly, it is challenging to find much language diversity in urban children's literature that truly captures the "multicultural tapestry" of our cities (Morris 2012). While there are some dual language and interlingual Spanish and English books available, dual language texts in other languages, such as Korean in *Cooper's Lesson* (Shin 2004) or Tagalog in *Lakas and the Makibaka Hotel* (Robles 2006) are rare. Books like *Madlenka* (Sís 2000) and *Subway Sparrow* (Torres 1997), which feature a multilingual cast of characters sharing greetings or phrases in French, Italian, Punjabi, Spanish, and Polish, are also an exception, as are books that include any reference to languages such as Albanian, Arabic, Chinese, Jamaican patois, Caribbean Spanish, Haitian

Creole, or Russian, for example, which are prevalent in many of our nation's cities.

Socioeconomic Diversity and Race

Interestingly, there is a fair amount of socioeconomic diversity in urban children's literature, particularly among books with primary characters of color. Numerous selections include families that could be perceived as low income or poor (e.g., *A Shelter in Our Car*, Gunning 2004; *Xóchitl and the Flowers/Xóchitl, la Niña de las flores*, Argueta 2008), lower-middle or working-class (e.g., *Night Shift Daddy*, Spinelli 2000; *The Bakery Lady/La señora de la panadería*, Mora 2001), or professional middle class (*Abuela*, Dorros 1997; *Destiny's Gift*, Tarpley 2004).

Although there is some socioeconomic diversity in urban picture books that feature Caucasian characters (e.g., *A Chance to Shine*, Seskin and Samblin 2006; *Didi and Daddy on the Promenade*, Singer 2001; *Madlenka Soccer Star*, Sís 2010), white characters in urban children's literature are more frequently depicted in professional middle-class families (Fleming and Carrillo, 2016). In some cases, children might be left with the impression that most white people in the city live in high rises with uniformed doormen or spend the bulk of their lives frequenting museums and other cultural attractions. Educators should take care to examine the breadth of representation in their collections with respect to the intersection of race and socioeconomic diversity to ensure that all students can find themselves authentically reflected and to ensure that unrealistically narrow representations do not leave students with stereotypical notions of others.

A Need for More Mirrors

Despite its high potential for engaging students and supporting reading and writing development, urban children's literature is generally in short supply in city schools. While school programs and literacy curricula are getting better and better at exposing children to a range of *multicultural* literature, fewer teachers and school librarians have a broad awareness of the availability of excellent children's books that include familiar city settings and contemporary urban themes. In addition, most publishers of school literacy curricula tailor selections to reach a geographically diverse national audience, and as a result, only a few text selections may include images of city living, multicultural communities, and familiar urban landscapes.

It is time to get more "mirrors" in the classroom. As outlined in the previous chapters, a significant representation of urban children's literature can support development of students' identities as readers and writers, increase the power of literacy instruction, and provide important learning supports for students who are learning English. Educators should review their collections to ensure the inclusion of cultural relevant texts across all formats and genres so that students can see themselves represented in all aspects of the curriculum. Where there are gaps, teachers should be provided the resources and autonomy to select culturally relevant books to include in their classroom libraries, as well as text sets to supplement content area instruction. To support this, the following chapters provide specific guidelines for the selection of high-quality urban children's literature and informational texts, as well as strategies for integrating urban literature into the curriculum.

Summing It Up: Urban Children's Literature as a Critical Subgenre

- Identify urban children's literature as a subgenre of multicultural children's literature
- Explore the history of multicultural children's literature
- Note the emergence of urban children's literature across a variety of genres
- Recognize authors and illustrators of urban children's literature
- Recognize the important place multicultural literature holds for connecting with all students
- Tailor the selection of multicultural and urban children's literature for use in the classroom
- Be aware that the cultural identities of students in the classroom are not static or singular

CHAPTER SIX

~

Guidelines for
Text Selection: Literature

As discussed in the previous chapters, urban children's literature can serve as a bridge between children's lived experiences and the instructional content of school, providing a vehicle for increasing the cultural relevance of instruction that can help accelerate the acquisition of literacy skills. Having access to books in which children can see their communities and experiences represented and valued also may be key to increasing students' motivation and persistence for reading, and subsequently developing reading skill.

Despite the high potential for engaging students and supporting reading development, not just any urban children's books will do. Children want to read *good* books! Some studies have shown that the quality of the story, such as having an interesting and realistic plot, can sometimes outweigh cultural relevance in students' responses to reading (e.g., Altieri 1993). The classroom libraries found in urban schools must have a strong representation of literature that serves as a mirror for students, but this literature must also be of sufficient quality to engage students and support their learning.

Studies have found that cultural relevance contributes most to reading accuracy and comprehension when the text choice is developmentally appropriate. Factors related to the linguistic complexity, such as the sentence and passage length, the proportion of difficult words in the text, word order, phrasing, and sentence structure chosen by the writer, need to be within the child's reach. If the linguistic complexity of the text exceeds what the child is capable of reading at this time, the benefits of cultural relevance on reading comprehension tend to fade away (Droop and Verhoevan 1998). So, in addition to considering cultural relevance, teachers need to be mindful of selecting texts within students' instructional reading or listening levels.

When students are supported in selecting high-quality, just-right texts, cultural relevance clearly plays a significant role and can add an additional layer of foundation on which to build word-recognition skills, develop reading fluency, and teach comprehension skills for deepening students' understanding of texts. This chapter provides a brief overview of general characteristics of high-quality children's literature with a focus on realistic fiction. This is followed by a more in-depth discussion of *urban-specific* characteristics to help guide the selection of high-quality urban children's literature in particular. The next chapter provides guidelines for selecting high-quality, culturally relevant informational texts to support students' development of skills for reading and writing expository text and to provide a strong foundation for content area learning.

General Characteristics of High-Quality Picture Books

There are a number of factors that help define "quality" children's literature. The illustrations, the development of characters, the choice of language, and the appeal to the intended audience are a few of these. In developing the guidelines presented in this chapter, a thorough literature review was conducted to determine the criteria commonly used to gauge the quality of picture books by scholars in the field of children's literature.

To evaluate the quality of literature in which today's students might see themselves represented, the top criteria for evaluating contemporary realistic fiction from a host of well-respected researchers were reviewed, compared, and combined.[1] This resulted in identification of six dimensions for evaluating the general quality of realistic fiction picture books: cover, character, plot, theme, language, and illustrations.

- *Cover*—An interesting cover draws the reader in and provides some clues about what the story may be about.
- *Characters*—Memorable characters are about the same age as the readers and have experiences the reader can relate to.
- *Plot*—An interesting plot will keep readers engaged, encourage them to make predictions, and leave them eager to find out how problems are resolved.

- *Theme*—A worthwhile and developmentally appropriate theme can generate thoughtful and rigorous discussion about the author's message, especially if it does not "hit the reader over the head" in an overly didactic way.
- *Language*—Natural, vivid language helps evoke clear, concrete images of characters and actions and builds children's vocabulary and understanding of narrative discourse.
- *Illustrations*—Great illustrations help establish the mood as the story unfolds and they complement and enhance the story, supporting readers in making meaning.

A set of guiding questions was developed for use in reviewing texts along each of these dimensions (see table 6.1). These characteristics are in line with general instincts about what makes for a good picture book.

Urban-Specific Characteristics

In addition to considering general characteristics of high-quality picture books, a set of *urban-specific* criteria was developed for considering the quality and cultural relevance of urban children's literature. Similarly, scholars in multicultural children's literature were consulted.[2] These criteria were adapted to capture the uniqueness of the subgenre of urban children's literature. When looking for culturally relevant children's literature, the reader must think broadly about the many aspects of a person's background, including race, ethnicity, social class, and language, but also gender, family structure, residence, and religion. In addition, the social context of students' lives comes into play—where they live, what their neighborhoods are like, who they spend time with, where they go to school, what they do for fun, and so on.

Obviously, there are great cultural, linguistic, ecological, and architectural variations in urban settings across the country, from cities like New York and Los Angeles to places like Miami, Seattle, or San Antonio, versus cities like St. Louis, or Charlotte, or Cincinnati. Determining whether particular urban children's books are culturally relevant is dependent upon reviewing them with a lens for the particular cultural context in which each person lives or works.

Still, given the large proportion of public school students residing in urban locales, this collective subgenre is worthy of important consideration for its instructional implications for urban youth. As described in chapter

Table 6.1. General Characteristics of High-Quality Children's Literature—Realistic Fiction Picture Books

1. Cover	• Is the cover of the book visually interesting?
	• Do the illustrations and title on the cover give useful information about the content that draw the reader to the story?
2. Character	• Does the story contain a memorable character who is about the same age as the students?
	• Is the behavior of the characters consistent with their ages and backgrounds?
	• Are the characters well developed and convincing?
3. Plot	• Will students enjoy the story (is it interesting, fun, engaging on its own)?
	• Will students understand the problems and be able to easily follow the sequence of events?
	• Is the text segmented to add to the drama of turning the page?
4. Theme	• Is the theme worthwhile and developmentally appropriate for young children?
	• Is the author's message one that can children can relate to?
5. Language	• Does the story contain natural, vivid language that reflects the mood of the story?
	• Do the words evoke clear, concrete images of characters and actions?
	• Is the language (vocabulary, syntax) appropriate in complexity to the age of the intended audience?
6. Illustrations	• Do the illustrations establish the mood, theme, and setting as the story unfolds?
	• Do the illustrations complement and enhance the story?
	• Are the illustrations interesting and engaging?

Specific Characteristics of High-Quality Urban Children's Literature—Realistic Fiction Picture Books

1. Authenticity of Characters and Culture	• Are culture and language accurately portrayed from the point of view of someone inside the group?
	• Does the book capture experiences, values, and attitudes that resonate with members of the cultural group depicted?
	• Are gender, racial, and cultural stereotypes avoided among the characters?
	• Does the book present positive images of urban culture?
2. Familiar Context	• Does the book depict a familiar urban context?
	• Do the characters have experiences that are familiar to your students?
	• Will urban public school children be able to see themselves in the story and among the characters and settings?
3. Familiar Language	• Does the story use natural language and authentic dialogue that children will recognize?
	• If set in nonurban setting (suburban, rural), would vocabulary and dialogue change significantly?

4. Authentic Urban Scenery	• Do the illustrations and descriptions accurately and realistically depict urban settings? • Will children recognize the setting as similar to their neighborhood/community?
5. Diversity of Characterization	• Does the book show diversity within and/or across human cultures (age, race, ethnicity, socioeconomic status, family structure, lifestyle)?
6. Diversity of Setting	• Is urban diversity represented through a variety of characteristics of city settings (apartment buildings, city sidewalks, city parks, local businesses, vacant lots)?

3, high-quality urban children's literature helps to capture the specific relevance of the contemporary urban context, providing students with access to multicultural texts that value their experiences and that can be used to ground reading and writing instruction in what they know. The sections below walk through urban-specific criteria, providing examples of texts that help exemplify what to look for in high-quality urban picture books. A set of guiding questions for reviewers to consider is included in table 6.1.

Accuracy of Characters and Culture

The first of the six urban-specific criteria relates to the accuracy of characters and culture depicted in the text and illustrations. As with all multicultural children's literature, it is critically important that culture is accurately portrayed from the point of view of someone inside the group, and that gender, racial, and cultural stereotypes be avoided. With urban children's literature, the reviewer must be mindful that some of children's books present deficit views of urban culture and communities of color. Teachers should be on the lookout for books that present positive and authentic images of urban life.

Key questions about characters and culture:

- Are culture and language accurately portrayed from the point of view of someone inside the group?
- Does the book capture experiences, values, and attitudes that resonated with members of the cultural group depicted?
- Are gender, racial, and cultural stereotypes avoided among the characters?
- Does the book present positive images of urban culture?

An example of a picture book that stands out for its accuracy of characters and culture is *Bippity Bop Barbershop* by Natasha Tarpley (2002). *Bippity Bop Barbershop* presents a day in the life of Miles during an important rite of passage: taking his first trip to the barbershop with his father.

From revealing Daddy's "secret knock" to wake Miles in the morning, to their regular stop at Jack's Sweet Shop for cinnamon rolls and glazed doughnuts on their early morning walk through the neighborhood, to the encouragement that other customers provide Miles between checkers moves and cheering the NBA highlights, Tarpley captures the "unique sharing . . . between a father and son and among the men in the barbershop" as Miles attempts to overcome his fear of the barber's clippers (Tarpley 2002, author's note). Miles's relationship with his father is one that many children can relate to, and the characterization of "the regulars" in the barbershop captures the qualities of men many of us know in our own neighborhoods.

Meg Medina presents a similarly accurate portrayal of characters and culture in her Ezra Jack Keats Award–winning book, *Tía Isa Wants a Car* (2011). Vibrantly illustrated by Claudio Muñoz, the story is told from an unnamed young niece's perspective as she and her extended family work to save for a car while also prioritizing the saving of "helping money" so that family members living at a distance can come live with them one day. *Tía Isa Wants a Car* realistically captures the sacrifices the family makes, keeping close in mind the loved ones who live far away while celebrating the joy in working toward common goals that several family members share.

In each of these examples, characters are presented as multidimensional and the stories are told from an insider perspective. In selecting high-quality urban children's literature, characters and culture must be portrayed with accuracy and authenticity, capturing "the cultural values, facts, and attitudes that members of a culture as a whole consider worthy of acceptance and belief" (Mo and Shen 2003). Toward this end, it is strongly recommend that teachers work with colleagues with extensive urban teaching and living experience who are also members of the cultural community depicted to review texts for cultural relevance and authenticity. Parents and other caregivers may also be great resources in reviewing books for possible inclusion in the classroom library and curriculum. Chapter 8 includes a more in-depth discussion of cultural authenticity and provides suggestions for engaging students and family members as expert informers.

Familiar Urban Context
To gauge the level of familiarity of the urban context depicted in children's books, ask the question: *Will students be able to see themselves in the story and*

Key questions about context:

- Does the book depict a familiar urban context?
- Do the characters have experiences that are familiar to your students?
- Will children be able to see themselves in the story and among the characters and settings?

Figure 6.1. Copyright © 1995 by Nina Crews. Used by permission of HarperCollins Publishers.

among the characters and settings? Teachers are encouraged to identify texts that present situations that their students have experienced or that depict the character in contexts in which children might often find themselves. Consider, for example, Nina Crews's *One Hot Summer Day* (1995) in which a young girl's activities on a hot summer day include a visit to a city park. There she finds metal seats that are too hot for swinging so instead opts for a stop into the local bodega for an ice pop. Crews's use of photographs from her neighborhood in Brooklyn to illustrate the text allows many young readers to easily insert themselves in the place of the main character, having had similar experiences in their own urban neighborhoods.

Similarly, consider Mo Willems's very popular *Knuffle Bunny* (2004) in which on a typical trip to the laundromat with her father, Trixie inadvertently leaves her Knuffle Bunny behind, resulting in a hilarious and chaotic search for the beloved stuffed animal. Here, too, photographs of city streets, a city park, and the laundromat provide a familiar urban context in which many children can find themselves, relating to Trixie's dilemma as they make self-to-text connections from their own experiences in these settings and situations.

The *Madlenka* series by Peter Sís may provide another familiar context for many children as Madlenka goes "around the world" exploring her multiethnic city block to report the news of her loose tooth to anyone who will listen. Self-to-text connections may be especially salient for children whose families have recently immigrated to the United States, as Madlenka's neighbors share memories they have carried with them from their home countries to their new home.

Familiar, Developmentally Appropriate Language
Beginning readers use their oral language to identify words in print, so it is important that books for young readers include language that sounds natural and familiar. When looking for familiar language, a good rule of thumb is to consider whether or not the word choice or phrasing might change sig-

---

Key questions about language:

- Does the story use natural language and authentic dialogue that children will recognize?
- If set in nonurban setting (suburban, rural), would the vocabulary and dialogue change significantly?

nificantly if the story were set in a different context. For example, consider the language Tony Medina (2001) uses to capture a typical day in the life of ten-year-old DeShawn Williams through his poem "I love my block" in *DeShawn Days*:

> I love my block/and playing with my friends/
> In front of our building/the girls play double dutch/jumping fast and high/
> While us boys play skellies/with shaving cream tops and/different color clay inside. (Medina 2011, p. 23)
> "Deshawn Days Text copyright © 2001 by Tony Medina. Permission arranged with Lee & Low Books Inc., New York, NY 10016."

Medina's use of vocabulary specific to an urban setting (e.g., "block" and "building" as opposed to "neighborhood" or "house") and his naming of games that might typically be played on any city sidewalk will help many students relate to DeShawn. In addition, it provides a context for students to use their oral language and familiar experiences to support word recognition and comprehension of the poems.

When judging the developmental appropriateness of language in literature, the age of the primary character is often a good indicator of the age level of the intended audience. It is important to be sure the language of the text captures the voice and perspective of a child of that age, while also providing an appropriate level of intellectual challenge. Consider, for example the language that captures six-year-old Lily's naïveté upon meeting up with her "best friend" at the community pool in *My Best Friend* by Mary Ann Rodman and illustrated by E. B. Lewis:

> Hi, Tamika," I say. Tamika wrinkles her nose and sticks out her tongue.
> Then she jumps into the pool with Shanice. Tamika is my best friend.
> She just doesn't know it yet. (Rodman 2007, p. 7)
> "From My Best Friend by Mary Ann Rodman, copyright © 2005 by Mary Ann Rodman used by permission of Viling Children's Books. A Division of Penguin Young Readers Group , A Member of Penguin Group (USA) LLE."

Here, Rodman uses straightforward, simple sentences to describe the girls' interaction, while leaving just enough room for young readers to have to grapple a bit with the differences in perspective Lily and Tamika have with respect to their friendship.

Compare this with the much more sophisticated language used by Christopher Myers to capture the observations of Jawanza, the lead character in the friendship story *Fly!*, as he watches pigeons soaring from rooftop to rooftop from his upper-story apartment building window.

They are flying now, a cloud between the buildings, drawing circles
and patterns in the air. A hundred black, brown, and gray bodies,
winging pictures in the white city sky. I wonder where they come from,
a twisting river of birds flying patterns above my house. (Myers 2001, 5)

In this picture book geared toward intermediate readers, Myers's word choice
and use of metaphor presents a challenge to readers to adopt Jawanza's point
of view, visualizing this flock of birds flying free while he is somewhat isolated
indoors, having been asked to "stay in our apartment" safe from the traffic
and, perhaps, other hazards below. In this way, Myers's use of developmentally appropriate but sophisticated language makes *Fly!* an excellent mentor
text for the teaching of descriptive writing in the intermediate grades. In
both cases, the writers use context-specific vocabulary and dialogue to give
readers a familiar feel for the setting of the neighborhood pool where Lily and
her friends meet up to swim and play or the city block on which Jawanza's
resides.

Urban educators working with bilingual students and English language
learners often use dual language books (written in two languages) or interlingual texts that take words and phrases from one language, such as Spanish
or Korean, and intersperse them within a text written in English, so the story
might be accessible to monolingual and bilingual students. Examples of dual
language texts include *Quinito's Neighborhood* (Cumpiano 2009) and *Cooper's Lesson* (Shin 2004), compared with interlingual texts such as *Bebé Goes
Shopping* (Elya 2006) or *The Have a Good Day Café* (Park and Park 2008).
Scholars in bilingual education recommend selecting texts that provide
monolingual readers with enough information to understand the meaning of
terms or phrases in the secondary language while avoiding the "double talk"
of so much repetition or overtranslation that the story becomes redundant
and disengaging for bilingual students (Barrera and Quiroa 2003, 259).

In *Dear Primo: A Letter to My Cousin* (Tonatiuh 2010), for example,
cousins Charlie, who lives in the United States, and Carlito, who lives in
Mexico, exchange letters to get to know each other, having not yet met in
person. Rather than translating Spanish words and phrases, author Duncan
Tonatiuh supports comprehension for monolingual English readers with
engaging, labeled illustrations of the content of the cousins' letters to one
another.

In one exchange, the boys describe their daily rides to school, Carlito on
his *bicicleta* and Carlos on the *subway*. As Carlito rides "past the perros and
past a nopal" young readers can gather from the illustrations that Carlito is
referring to dogs and a cactus without the need for translation. If additional
confirmation is needed, a glossary of Spanish terms is provided.

By not providing direct translations in the context of the boys' letters, Tonatiuh is able to preserve a greater degree of cultural authenticity for bilingual readers, mirroring the code-switching the cousins might naturally do in their letter writing and avoiding the redundancy of overtranslation that would likely reduce the literary quality and linguistic rigor of the text for bilingual Spanish–English readers. As with cultural authenticity, it is important that teachers consult with colleagues and community members when reviewing dual language or bilingual texts if they are not a primary or fluent speaker or reader of the second language.

Authentic Urban Scenery

The next urban-specific criterion addresses the degree to which the book accurately and realistically depicts the urban setting. While the *familiar urban context* criterion is designed to help the teacher consider the extent to which books depict characters in situations and scenarios that reflect familiar *experiences* for urban public-school children, the *authentic urban scenery* criterion involves the look and feel of the illustrations and descriptions. When reviewing books for authentic urban scenery, teachers should ask themselves whether students might see similarities between the setting in the text and the neighborhood or community in which they live.

Key questions about scenery:

- Do the illustrations and descriptions accurately and realistically depict urban settings?
- Will children recognize the setting as similar to their neighborhood/community?

One book that stands out for its authentic urban scenery is Christopher Myers's *Black Cat* (1999) in which an inquisitive narrator follows an adventurous feline as he roams the city streets. Using an illustration technique of painting over photography, Myers captures scenes that are highly familiar to many students in city schools. Indeed, the images of Black Cat "crossing basketball courts with no-netted hoops" or slinking across the fencing while children swing in the background are striking resemblances to the many urban play lots that sit adjacent to public school buildings.

crossing basketball courts and no-netted hoops

Figure 6.2. From *Black Cat* by Christopher Myers. Scholastic Inc./Scholastic Press. Copyright © 1999 by Christopher Myers. Reprinted by permission.

Other examples of authentic urban scenery include the characteristic streetscapes and brownstone stoops inviting us to dwell out front of the five story walk-ups in Brenda Roberts's and Frank Morrison's *Jazzy Miz Mozetta* (2004), or the tai chi classes, open-air fish markets, and vibrant awnings of "lots and lots of restaurants" captured in William Low's *Chinatown* (1997).

It is important to remember that context matters when considering the *authentic urban scenery* criterion. For example, *Hot City* by Barbara Joosse (2004) or *Come On Rain!* by Karen Hesse (1999) depict communities where the landscape, architecture, and even bus traffic reflects the general look of many of the neighborhoods on the west side of Chicago or in north St. Louis, for example. As a result, children attending school in those communities might experience instant recognition of a place that could be "my" neighborhood or "my" block.

Other texts may capture a different type of urban scenery. For example, *Estela's Swap* by Alexis O'Neill (2007) appears to be set in a southern California city, as evidenced by the mission-style architecture and palm trees dotting the landscape. Indeed, O'Neill based the story on some of her visits to swap meets in Simi Valley, outside of Los Angeles, where she lives.

While the *concept* of the swap meet certainly may be familiar to many students, the urban landscape looks very different from that of many other urban communities. Teachers should employ these guidelines with a consideration of the local context as the "standard," keeping an eye out for landscape, architectural features, and plot features that might be most familiar to the students in their classrooms. In this way, the guidelines can be used to identify a set of culturally relevant picture books in which students can find themselves, and that can best help generate the vocabulary, application of background knowledge, and self-to-text connections so important to reading comprehension.

Diversity of Characters
The final two urban-specific criteria are related to the diversity of urban contexts. In reviewing books for an urban children's literature collection, it

---

Key questions about diversity of characters:

- Does the book show diversity within and/or across human cultures (age, race, ethnicity, socioeconomic status, lifestyle)?

is important to focus on stories that capture and celebrate the diversity of urban areas, including racial, ethnic, and linguistic diversity, but also books that reflect generational diversity and differences in family structure, socio-economic status, and ways of life.

Subway Sparrow by Leyla Torres (1997) is one example of a book that captures the racial and linguistic diversity of the city. When a young girl discovers a sparrow that has flown into her subway car on the D train in Brooklyn, she enlists the help of her fellow passengers to bring the bird to safety. What results is a multigenerational group of strangers working together despite their language differences to usher the little bird out of the car and through the station to freedom at the street level above.

The story is peppered with English, Spanish, and Polish phrases as this multicultural, multilingual group of passengers rely on gestures to communicate as they offer their hats, umbrellas, and scarfs as tools to help corral the unsuspecting bird and set it free. Both in and out of the station, Torres's illustrations capture the diversity and vibrancy of the city as her story reveals a "common concern" that unites these strangers, an experience those who live in the city often encounter despite the sometimes stereotypic portrayal of city-dwellers as isolated, cold, and uncaring.

John Steptoe's *Creativity* (2003) strikes a similar balance in exploring cultural and linguistic similarities and differences two boys discover when Hector, a new student from Puerto Rico, joins Charles's class in school. As these new classmates and neighbors get to know each other, the story explores the complexities of cultural heritage that allow the boys to share a similar skin tone while growing up in very different places, speaking different languages, and having distinctly different fashion sense. In the end, they come to appreciate the "creativity" of their languages and lifestyles while finding plenty of common ground on which to build a new friendship.

In addition to looking for books that represent and value diversity across cultures, it is also important that classroom library collections accurately reflect diversity *within* cultures, rather than painting a one-size-fits-all view of particular cultural groups. Urban picture books like Javaka Steptoe's *Jones Family Express* (2003), Jacqueline Woodson's *We Had a Picnic This Sunday Past* (1997), or Monica Brown's *Marisol McDonald Doesn't Match/Marisol McDonald no combina* (2011) provide wonderful representations of diversity within families. Teachers should include these and other books in the classroom library collection that help capture variations in family structure, including grandparents or extended family members as primary caregivers, multiracial and blended families, differences in lifestyles, professional paths, and socioeconomic circumstances, and even the range of personalities within families.

With the large number of students in many urban schools who are first- and second-generation immigrants, it is also important to include books that represent immigrant children's experiences and a range of perspectives within families. Janet Wong's *Apple Pie 4th of July* depicts one such experience as a first-generation Chinese American girl questions her parents' wisdom in keeping their family market open when "no one wants Chinese food on the Fourth of July" (Wong 2006, 4). Just when she thinks her parents, who were not born in the United States, cannot possibly understand this traditional American holiday, they and their diverse crowd of customers help her come to appreciate that being American means that we can celebrate in many kinds of ways, including enjoying parades, fireworks, apple pie—and yes—even sweet-and-sour pork and chow mein.

Diversity of Settings

In addition to reviewing books for their diversity of characterization, it is important for the urban settings themselves to be represented in diverse ways. Books can realistically capture a diversity of images of urban life and landscape, including apartment buildings, row-houses, local businesses, and city parks while also representing the somewhat grittier side of urban life, including boarded-up buildings, graffitied train cars, and vacant lots. Teachers should be cautioned to review books carefully for this balance, avoiding children's books that only depict the city as big, scary, dangerous place to live or choosing a majority of text that present big houses and sprawling yards as the norm.

Key questions about diversity of setting:

- Is urban diversity represented through a variety of characteristics of city settings (apartment buildings, city sidewalks, city parks, local businesses, vacant lots)?

One example of a book that strikes this type of balance is *Something Beautiful* by Sharon Dennis Wyeth (2002) in which a little girl, discouraged by the broken glass, graffiti, and trash that litters her courtyard, explores the blocks of her neighborhood in search of "something beautiful." While the book does depict the urban realities of a littered alley, the cardboard shelter of a homeless woman, and a "garden without any flowers," there are many beautiful things in the neighborhood, too, including Mr. Lee's beautiful fruit stand, Miss Delphine's beautiful-tasting fish sandwiches, her friends' beautiful dance moves, and her baby cousin Carl's beautiful laughter.

While some teachers may be inclined to want to protect young children from some of the harshness of the urban contexts in which they reside, books like *Something Beautiful* present authentic reflections of many students' experiences and can invite important discussion about the circumstances of their lives. For example, teachers may use *Something Beautiful* as a mentor text for writing projects in which students discuss similarities and differences in their own experiences and then create their own books about "something beautiful" in their neighborhoods. In this way, urban children's literature cannot only be used to support students' literacy learning, but can also serve as a tool for engaging children in critique of social inequities, helping students begin to develop the type of "critical consciousness" that Gloria Ladson-Billings (1995, 480) describes as central to culturally relevant teaching.

Using the Criteria to Select High-Quality Literature

Table 6.1 includes a summary of the general and urban-specific review criteria outlined above, along with guiding questions to support reviews of urban children's literature and to help teachers develop high-quality, culturally relevant text collections. The sample texts presented along with the criteria above were selected for their ability to exemplify one of the six urban-specific characteristics considered when reviewing urban children's literature for quality. These examples are meant to be illustrative, rather than prescriptive. When reviewing urban children's literature, it is recommended that teachers consider all six urban criteria in combination with the general characteristics of quality realistic fiction, in order to identify urban children's books that might be most culturally relevant for children in their classrooms.

In practice, this is something of a balancing act, since it is difficult to find books that rate highly on all characteristics of quality. The goal is to identify many books that are strong in several areas, while also avoiding texts that appear to violate important nonnegotiables, such as books that privilege one cultural group over another through stereotype or attempts at humor (e.g., non-Native American characters "playing Indians"), texts with problematic translations, or books that present one-sided, negative views of city living.

By doing so, educators can develop collections that include a substantial proportion of high-quality, culturally relevant books that reflect and value our students' communities and experiences. While all children should be exposed to a wide variety of texts to support their language and literacy development, a significant representation of literature from this urban subgenre may be especially powerful for helping urban public school students and their families feel included in the life of the classroom and may serve as a critical catalyst for reading and writing development in the elementary grades.

Summing It Up: Guidelines for Selecting Literature

- Use characteristics of high-quality children's literature to identify and select books for use in the classroom
- Look for specific characteristics of high-quality urban children's literature to select books that are representative of students' lives and experiences
- Recognize and appreciate the distinct characteristics of life in an urban setting
- Identify assets while recognizing the realities of urban settings
- Consider the unique cultural, linguistic, and geographic features of urban settings in different regions or locales
- Look for books that are strong on many criteria while avoiding books that appear to violate important nonnegotiables (e.g., cultural stereotypes, problematic translations)

Notes

1. Review of criteria for assessing the quality of fiction, picture books, and multicultural literature included the following sources: Cullinan, Galda, and Sipe (2009); Hefflin and Barksdale-Ladd (2001); Huck et al. (2000); Lynch-Brown, Tomlinson, and Short (2010); Norton (2012); and Temple, Martinez, and Yakota (2011). Suggestions from Kathleen Horning (2010) on engaging young readers were also incorporated.

2. Bena Hefflin's and Mary Alice Barksdale-Ladd's (2001) guidelines for selecting African American children's literature served as a model for the development of these characteristics. Nancy Hadaway's and Terrell Young's (2010) guidance for selecting books to support English language learners was very helpful and a range of contributors to Dana Fox's and Kathy Short's (2003) discussion of cultural authenticity in children's literature were also consulted. Additional considerations for iden-

tifying high-quality multicultural literature were gleaned from Huck et al. (2000); Cullinan, Galda, and Sipe (2009); Norton (2012); Temple, Martinez, and Yakota (2011); and Lynch-Brown, Tomlinson, and Short (2010). Gloria Boutte (2002) also provided insights for avoiding stereotyping and for consideration of the background and experiences of the author and illustrator.

CHAPTER SEVEN

~

Guidelines for Text Selection

Informational Texts

> *"There's more to our history than slavery, jazz, sports, and civil rights marches."*
>
> —Mr. Mital in *What Color Is My World? The Lost History of African American Inventors* (Abdul-Jabbar and Obstfeld 2012)

The scope of informational texts is wide-ranging. This genre can include expository texts, narrative nonfiction, textbooks and encyclopedias, as well as various Internet-based materials, newspapers, magazines, brochures, and pamphlets. For purposes of this discussion, informational texts are defined as any printed materials that provide children with factual information about their world. To add to the previous discussion of literature, this chapter highlights the importance of including a diversity of representations in all genres of informational text, including books that situate mathematics, science, and social studies content in the urban context.

Informational Texts in Learning Standards

Historically there has been a tendency in the United States for classroom reading to focus more on fictional literature, especially in the early grades.[1] With the strong emphasis on the development of foundational literacy skills in the primary grades, teachers recognize the important role literature plays in emergent literacy. Listening to stories, retelling stories, and story dictation all contribute significantly to young children's understandings of story grammar, print concepts, and basic writing conventions. Regular reading of a wide range of storybooks is also important in fostering young children's interest in and love of reading.

More recently, the wide adoption of the Common Core State Standards (CCSS) has brought informational texts to the forefront of the discussion about teaching reading and writing. Several areas in the CCSS directly refer to the use of informational texts. The Reading Standards highlight the importance of teaching a distinct set of comprehension skills to develop students' understandings of main ideas and key details, as well as how to locate information efficiently using nonfiction text features such as tables of contents, headings, diagrams, captions, and glossaries.

The Language Standards emphasize the importance of vocabulary acquisition for comprehending informational texts and learning new content in social studies, science, and mathematics. Students are expected to master three tiers of vocabulary, including basic conversational vocabulary, multiple-meaning words that take on different meanings across a variety of domains (e.g., *root* in mathematics vs. science), and more domain-specific academic vocabulary of the different content areas (e.g., *isosceles* in mathematics content).

DID YOU KNOW?

It takes five to seven years to develop Cognitive Academic Language Proficiency (CALP) in a second language (Cummins 2000).

With respect to the Writing Standards, teaching with high-quality informational mentor texts is critical for developing students' skills in writing procedural, informative, and explanatory texts. Conducting research to gain new knowledge, including synthesizing information from multiple informational text sources, is also central to the Common Core Writing Standards.

It is important to include high-quality informational texts as part of the reading program for the youngest learners in order to expose readers to a wide variety of genres while they are developing their reading skills, and to support their development of comprehension skills associated with a range of text structures. As students move from the elementary grades into middle school, the stakes related to comprehension of informational text become higher and higher for academic success and advancement.

To meet the CCSS, teachers are directed to gradually increase the proportion of informational text reading as students progress through school, beginning with an equal balance of literature and informational text in kindergarten through fourth grades, increasing to 55 percent informational texts in fifth through eighth grades, and eventually 70 percent informational texts in ninth through twelfth grades (National Governors Association Center for Best Practices 2010).

DID YOU KNOW?

By sixth grade, more than 80 percent of textbook and standardized test content is informational (Thome 2013).

Where Do Pigeons Sleep?

Some teachers may be reluctant to select informational texts because they may be concerned that the material is too difficult or too dry for young children, but studies have shown that many children in the elementary grades select informational texts for their own reading in relatively equal numbers to fiction (e.g., Chapman et al. 2007; Doiron 2003). Like literature, informational texts provide many students with an entry point for reading for enjoyment (Caswell and Duke 1998; Mohr 2006). Students with an interest in a topic, such as city wildlife or how trains work, may select books on these topics and work to master decoding and comprehension skills that were not acquired through typical fiction literature (e.g., Hartman 2002).

As discussed in chapter 2, a student's motivation to learn about something that is of interest can often compensate for challenges in mastering skills. A young child coming into the classroom asking a question like, "Where *do* pigeons sleep?" provides a perfect opportunity to direct her to the classroom library shelves to locate a book on animal habitats. Carefully selected informational texts that include vibrant, informative illustrations and that are culturally and personally meaningful can be the hook to bring reluctant readers into the group.

Cultural Relevance and Understanding the World

The use of high-quality informational texts in the classroom is another opportunity for teachers to provide both windows and mirrors for their students. Research has shown that student learning in the content areas is improved when teachers connect abstract ideas to relevant experiences and situations (Pashler et al. 2007). When learning new concepts in mathematics or science, for example, children typically progress from using concrete to more abstract strategies (Bruner 1961; Carpenter 1999). When teachers use a combination of concrete examples, pictorial and graphic representations, and abstract concepts, students demonstrate a more solid understanding of new content and may be more readily able to apply their learning to new contexts (e.g., Ainsworth, Bibby, and Wood 2002; Pashler et al. 2007).

"There are so many books about carving a pumpkin, but none of my kids carve pumpkins. If you're working minimum wage, you don't have money in your budget for that. You can't work two hours to buy a $12 pumpkin. That's not reasonable."

—Jill, discussing the proliferation of books with seasonal themes that lack relevance for her students

---

For many children, much of the informational content covered in core science or social studies curricula can be far outside of their lived experience. Culturally relevant informational texts can help situate learning more solidly in the Zone of Proximal Development (ZPD), providing a familiar context for integrating this new content into existing schemas. Similarly, drawing on resources within the community and familiar experiences in children's lives can serve as an important foundation for learning new material and sparking interest in wide reading on a topic.

It Starts at Home

Consider this example of starting in the community when beginning the study of the rainforest. Many elementary-level curriculum packages cover a range of habitats, including the rainforest, deserts, and arctic regions, to address science and social studies standards, such as understanding how plants and animals rely on one another or how human decisions impact the environment. In a study of the rainforest, many students will be intrigued by the brightly colored animals and interesting vegetation, but many children who have grown up in the city have had little experience in any forest. As a result, the concept of a deeply wooded setting inhabited by a range of unusual creatures may at first seem distant and mysterious. Without much concrete experience to draw on, learning is situated at a very abstract level from the outset.

To introduce students to the concept of habitats, teachers might start with their own community and the animals and plants that are common to city settings. Students might study the squirrels and birds in the schoolyard, and perhaps take a field trip to the local park. In conjunction with hands-on, concrete experiences in the neighborhood, culturally relevant informational texts can help build content knowledge and vocabulary.

For very young children, a book like Simms Taback's *City Animals* (2009) might be used to introduce the concept of the city as a habitat. For intermediate readers, teachers can use books like Barbara Bash's *Urban Roosts: Where Birds Nest in the City* (1990) or excerpts from Nicholas Read's *City Critters: Wildlife in the Urban Jungle* (2012) to examine the ecological factors that allow wild animals to survive in urban environments.

Animals and Habitats

A typical curriculum unit for science and social studies might include the following books about animals and their habitats:

> *The ABCs of Habitats* by Bobbie Kalman
> *Animal Tracks* by Arthur Dorros
> *Biggest, Strongest, Fastest* by Steve Jenkins
> *Nature Up Close: A Salamander's Life* by John Himmelman
> *What Do You Do with a Tail Like This?* by Steve Jenkins and Robin
>   Page

These books might be good additions to the books in the curriculum set:

> *Animal Babies in Towns and Cities* by Editors of Kingfisher
> *City Critters: Wildlife in the Urban Jungle* by Nicholas Read
> *Wild Animal Neighbors: Sharing Our Urban World* by Ann Downer
> *Urban Roosts: Where Birds Nest in the City* by Barbara Bash

After developing deeper understandings about the role animals play in their community, the local climate and landscape, and the ways that local vegetation helps sustain the environment, the students are primed to apply their learning to the new context of the tropical rainforests of Central America. They have a strong foundation on which to connect new knowledge about plants and animals of the rainforest, such as the kudamundi, a raccoon-like animal, and the macaw, a member of the parrot species, both native to the rainforest. Books like *Redwoods* by Jason Chin (2009), which uses a mixture of fantasy and nonfiction to "transport" a boy from the New York City subway to the coastal redwood rainforests of Northern California, might also be used as a pictorial and contextual bridge for solidifying new vocabulary and comprehension of content.

Ensuring Diversity within Genres of Informational Text

Chapter 5 outlined the range of nonfiction genres, including informational texts, concept books, biographies, autobiographies, and memoirs. Curricular text sets and classroom library collections should include a substantial selection of books that situate information in familiar urban context and include opportunities for children to see people of color investigating, exploring, and creating knowledge. Suggestions when considering text selection in each of these genres are explored in the next sections.

Concept Books

For young children, concept books play an important role in the learning of foundational literacy, mathematics, and science knowledge by helping children learn about the alphabet, numbers, colors, and shapes. Incorporating books in which these beginning concepts are explored in an urban setting allows many children to see direct connections between the content and their communities.

For example, books like *The City ABC Book* by Zoran Milich (2003) highlight the shapes of letters of the alphabet in drain covers, brick work, and fire escapes. *Urban Animals* by Isabel Hill (2009) invites children to identify animals etched into columns and cornices of city buildings while teaching the vocabulary of architecture. Concept books can also help children explore more sophisticated concepts like community in *Quinito's Neighborhood/El vecindario de Quinito* by Ina Cumpiano (2009), or the concept of emotions illustrated so vibrantly by R. Gregory Christie in *Yesterday I Had the Blues* by Jeron Ashford Frame (2008).

Biographies, Autobiographies, and Memoirs

Teachers often do a great job of including in their instruction a diverse range of excellent biographies of high-profile figures in American history, particularly those of great Civil Rights leaders such as Martin Luther King Jr., Rosa Parks, and Cesar Chavez. It is also important, however, to include a range of less well-known biographies across a range of time periods, so children understand the contributions that historically underrepresented groups and "city kids" have made throughout our nation's history.

Examples might include *Baby Flo: Florence Mills Lights Up the Stage* by Alan Schroeder (2012), about a spunky young girl from Washington, D.C. who grew up to become one of the greatest performers of the Harlem Renaissance. Books like *Sixteen Years in Sixteen Seconds: The Sammy Lee Story* by Paula Yoo (2010), can be used to expand students' understandings of segregation while exposing them to the uplifting story of a Korean American "kid from Fresno" whose persistence and determination led to an Olympic gold medal and a medical degree. *The Storyteller's Candle/La velita de los cuentos* by Lucía González (2008), shows students how librarian Pura Belpré changed New York City through her love of literacy and pride in her Puerto Rican heritage.

"There were so many books that inspired students to be more courageous in their daily life. A great example of this was Henry's Freedom Box *(Levine 2007). My students were so amazed that Henry would risk living in a box for freedom."*

—Michael, on changes he saw in his third graders after including a diverse representation of biographies in his curriculum

---

Equally important is the inclusion of biographies of contemporary leaders, such as Jim Haskins's and Kathleen Benson's *John Lewis in the Lead* (2011), about the U.S. Congressman's prominent role in the Civil Rights movement, or *Sonia Sotomayor: A Judge Grows in the Bronx / La juez que crecio en el Bronx* by Jonah Winter (2009). Memoirs can also help students make text-to-self connections and see their experiences validated through texts. Books such as Juan Felipe Herrera's *The Upside Down Boy/El niño de cabeza* (2006) or Amada Irma Pérez's *My Diary from Here to There/ Mi diario de aquí hasta allá* (2009), in which the authors describe their experiences adjusting to life in American cities after immigrating from Mexico, may resonate with many students who may be making similar adjustments themselves.

Other Informational Texts

Many teachers report how challenging it can be to locate informational texts to teach science and mathematics that relate to urban settings. Content area instruction is all about exploring the world and learning new things, so it makes sense that all students should be engaged in wide reading of informational texts on all subjects including all kinds of contexts. When possible, teachers are encouraged to use children's understandings from familiar urban settings to ground instruction in the content areas, as in the unit of study of habitats described above.

Teachers are also urged to include diverse representations of scientists, mathematicians, and engineers in their curricula. Using primary source documents or online resources to read about heart surgery pioneer Vivien Thomas, ophthalmologist Patricia Bath, or aviators Ellen Ochoa and Katherine Cheung can help urban public-school students envision themselves as

---

Questions to ask about the depth and breadth of your informational text collection:

- Is there a strong representation of people of color as content experts, including mathematicians, scientists, social leaders, architects, artists, and musicians?
- Does the collection include books that explore science, math, and social studies content in urban contexts?
- Are children of color included as active participants in investigating, building, and creating?
- Does the collection include multiple perspectives on historical events, including the perspectives of people from historically underrepresented and/or marginalized groups?
- Are the unique perspectives of people within cultures represented through a variety of texts?
- Does the collection include illustrations of a range of artistic types?

explorers, investigators, and creators of knowledge. If teachers are not familiar with inventor Frederick McKinley Jones, chemist Dr. Percy Lavon Julian, or physicist Dr. Valerie Thomas, *What Color Is My World: The Lost History of African American Inventors* by Kareem Abdul-Jabbar and Raymond Obstfeld (2012) might be one to add to the collection. A similar compilation, *How We Are Smart* by W. Nikola-Lisa (2009), explores multiple intelligences through the accomplishments of Latin jazz musician Tito Puente, ballerina Maria Tallchief, Polar explorer Matthew Henson, and Congresswoman Patsy Mink, among others.

Characteristics of High-Quality Informational Texts

Teachers should weigh a number of factors when selecting informational texts for their classroom. Beyond the need to ensure that the material is grade-level appropriate and can be mastered by the students in the classroom, teachers should consider subject and engagement, accuracy and up-to-date information, links to current learning standards and curriculum, and the use of culturally relevant books to understand the world.

Informational Text Features That Support Children's Engagement and Understanding (Stephens 2008)

- Attractive cover
- Exciting topic
- Photographs, illustrations, and diagrams that explain and enhance content
- Well-designed organization (table of contents, headings, illustrated glossary, index)
- Developmentally appropriate font size, type, and spacing

In her book, *Exploring the Literature of Fact*, Barbara Moss (2003) describes "five A's" that should be considered by teachers when selecting informational texts: (1) Authority, (2) Accuracy, (3) Appropriateness, (4) Artistry, and (5) Attractiveness. For the purposes of this series' focus on urban children's literature, the five A's criteria from Moss (2003) have been combined

Table 7.1. The Five A's for Evaluating Multicultural and Urban Informational Texts*

Criteria	Questions to Ask
Authority	• Are the author and illustrator experts in the topic and do they know the topic because they have lived the experience? • Can they speak with cultural authority about the subject? • What research or credit do they note in preparation of the book? • Are authors or consulted experts members of the cultural groups being depicted? • Does the book avoid privileging one cultural group at the expense of another?
Accuracy	• Are the facts accurate and up to date? • Are language patterns, family relationships, cultural conventions, and values accurately depicted? • Are regional terms, captions, and labels used accurately and specifically?
Appropriateness	• Does author organize the material in a logical sequence and provide textual support such as tables of contents, chapters, headings, charts, glossaries, or other graphic aids? • Is the language level and vocabulary challenging but understandable for your students? • Does the text provide enough context or visual support for learning new academic vocabulary and content knowledge? • Does the text draw on any content that reflects your students' community and understandings? • Does the text provide concrete examples and make comparisons to content, experiences, or places that might be familiar to your students?
Artistry	• Does the book employ a variety of literary devices so the information is interesting and will capture the attention of the reader? • Is there a hook at the beginning of each chapter to keep the reader looking for more information? • Is the hook culturally relevant and developmentally appropriate?
Attractiveness	• Will the illustrations entice the reader to want to learn more about the subject? • Do a variety of visuals and graphic aids provide direct support for understanding of the text? • Are the illustrations accurate and nonbiased, avoiding tokenism or stereotyping of cultural groups or urban contexts? • Are cultural details of the time and place (architecture, dress, hairstyles) accurately depicted in illustrations, photographs, and diagrams?

*Adapted with permission from Moss (2003), 36–43.

with additional recommendations from scholars in multicultural children's literature[2] to provide a set of criteria for reviewing informational texts for cultural relevance to the urban context as well as books that contain content specific to a particular cultural group.

All classroom collections should contain an extensive range of high-quality informational text selections that will support students' development of content knowledge and academic vocabulary on a wide range of topics. When reviewing books for cultural relevance to the urban context, or books that contain culturally specific content, consider the following key questions tailored to Moss's (2003) general criteria.

Authority

Informational texts must represent content from someone of authority on the topic. Most authors are not experts in every subject, but writers of high-quality informational texts research their topics thoroughly and consult with experts whom they will typically credit on the copyright page of a book. For informational texts that are culturally specific, look for books written from the perspective of someone with lived experience inside the cultural group, as opposed to someone reporting "about" the history, cultural traditions, or perspectives of others.

Key questions about authority:

- Are the author and illustrator experts in the topic and do they know the topic because they have lived the experience?
- Can they speak with cultural authority about the subject?
- What research or credit do they note in preparation of the book?
- Are authors or consulted experts members of the cultural groups being depicted?
- Does the book avoid privileging one cultural group at the expense of another?

For example, in her book, *In My Family/En mi familia*, Carmen Lomas Garza (2000) captures elements of Mexican American culture through her paintings and recollections of her everyday experiences growing up in Texas. For historical texts, be sure to include selections that represent the perspectives of historically marginalized people, such as books about World War

II told from the perspective of Japanese Americans (e.g., Yoshiko Uchida's [2005] *Journey to Topaz*).

Accuracy

A major consideration with information texts is whether or not the scientific, historical, or mathematical material is accurate and up-to-date. Informational texts become obsolete as gains in society are accomplished. For example, a book about space travel from 1975 and one from 1999 will have vastly different information. The earlier text would include the moonwalk as the most current significant event while the latter text would note the space shuttle program. Today, of course, neither program is operating. Although all information about these space programs would be important historical content for a text set on space, it is important to make sure the collection also included the most up-to-date material as possible.

Key questions about accuracy:

- Are the facts accurate and up-to-date?
- Are the language patterns, family relationships, cultural conventions, and values depicted accurately for the time period described?
- Are regional terms, captions, and labels used accurately and specifically?

Well-respected Internet data sources are useful here. For example, *National Geographic Kids* (http://kids.nationalgeographic.com/kids) often includes topics relevant to urban settings, such as recent features on the ecology of urban rivers and urban farming. Online encyclopedias and book reviews from reference resources such as the *New York Times*, *School Library Journal*, or *Booklist* can also be of support to teachers with respect to fact checking.

Another consideration with respect to accuracy is to be sure that the author avoids overgeneralizations or misrepresentations that present people as "cultural conglomerates" (Wilkins and Gamble 1998). In any unit of study, try to locate a range of informational books that capture specific, culturally informed perspectives (e.g., cultural traditions of South Koreans, Pakistanis, or Filipinos, for example, as opposed to "Asian Americans" more generally).

For cultural specificity and accuracy, look for book reviews on the websites of organizations dedicated to children's literature featuring particular cultural groups, such as *American Indians in Children's Literature* (americanindian-sinchildrensliterature.blogspot.com) or Latin@s in Kid Lit (latinosinkidlit.com). See chapter 10 for a list of suggested resources for reviews. In addition, informational texts should, where appropriate, provide specificity in the captions and labels that provide readers with details about people and places, such as labeling a photograph of cheetahs "in the grasslands of Namibia," as opposed to more generally, "in Africa."

Another important characteristic to consider is the accuracy and specificity in the use of regional dialects in dual language texts. For example, Monica Brown's choice of *patrones* to describe the farm bosses in *Side by Side/Lado a Lado* (2009) or Rosanne Thong's use of Cantonese terms in *Gai See: What You Can See in Chinatown* (2007) are purposeful choices to reflect the language of the communities represented. These variations may or may not ring true to readers from various regions of the country. When in doubt, have a native speaker of the target language take a read through to provide recommendations about local terms that might be used for comparison and discussion. As discussed in detail in chapter 6, it also important to consider the degree to which linguistic authenticity and literary quality are preserved in interlingual texts that pepper words and phrases from a community's home language throughout a primarily English text.

Appropriateness

With informational texts, content should be well organized and sequenced appropriately for children to understand. The use of a variety of well-selected

---

Key questions about appropriateness:

- Does the author organize the material in a logical sequence and provide textual support such as tables of contents, chapters, headings, charts, glossaries, or other graphic aids?
- Is the language level and vocabulary challenging but understandable for your students?
- Does the text provide enough context or visual support for learning new academic vocabulary and content knowledge?
- Does the text draw on any content that reflects your students' community and understandings?
- Does the text provide concrete examples and make comparisons to content, experiences, or places that might be familiar to your students?

text features, such as tables of contents, headings, labeled diagrams, and glossaries provide support for comprehension and can serve as useful mentor texts for developing students' writing of informational text. The level of the book should be appropriate to the reader's age, developmental level, and reading or listening ability.

For young children, direct and concrete information is important, especially when students are first introduced to a new topic. Conceptual density—the degree to which new facts are presented and explained in basic language versus presented one after another using technical and specialized vocabulary—can significantly impact the degree of difficulty of informational text.

For urban learners, many of whom speak a home language or dialect that is substantially different from the language and vocabulary of textbooks, it is important that new academic vocabulary be presented in a meaningful context along with the visual support of illustrations, models, and real objects. Teachers should consider the extent to which students have sufficient foundational background knowledge on a topic, including whether it has been previously covered in the curriculum or at previous grade levels, when considering whether to use introductory texts or selections covering more sophisticated concepts.

Artistry
The most effective books are more than a list of facts; they employ interesting literary devices to animate the subject and "infuse it with life" (Freedman 1992, 3). Teachers should look for presentation of information with fresh elements, such as a unique voice or point of view, a nontraditional text style, or a combination of poetry, prose, and visual elements that will hook young readers and provide fodder for comparison, discussion, and debate. Consider also the range of techniques used to convey new information in a variety of

---

Key questions about artistry:

- Does the book employ a variety of literary devices so the information is interesting and will capture the attention of the reader?
- Is there a hook at the beginning of each chapter to keep the reader looking for more information?
- Is the hook culturally relevant and developmentally appropriate?

Figure 7.1. *Dreaming Up.* Copyright © 2012 by Christy Hale. Permission arranged with Lee and Low Books Inc., New York.

ways, so learners at different skill levels have multiple opportunities to access new knowledge.

One example of a unique approach to helping students connect their experiences to new content can be found in *Dreaming Up: A Celebration of Building* by Christy Hale (2012).

In order to help young children start to comprehend the often mystifying world of modern architecture, Hale illustrates complex architectural structures alongside children at play. Pillow forts become Fran Gehry's Guggenheim and LEGO® structures become Moshe Safdie's groundbreaking modular Habitat 67 housing project in Montreal. A multicultural cast of young people are engaged in building and creating new structures, complementing the images of these iconic buildings located around the world.

In a different but equally engaging informational text, *Rosa's Bus: The Ride to Civil Rights* by Jo S. Kittinger (2010) uses free-verse narrative to chronicle the "life" of Bus #2857 from the time it rolled off the General Motors assembly line in Dearborn, Michigan, to the time its now-famous passengers made history. From its opening page, *Rosa's Bus* hooks the reader with its uncommon premise: that a bus could have a biography. "When Bus #2857 rolled off the assembly line in 1948, no one cheered, no one paid attention, no one knew that one day Bus #2857 would be famous" (Kittinger 2010, 4).

Attractiveness
For informational texts, the look of the book, including the text layout, font style and size, and illustrations can be particularly important for generating interest and grabbing the reader's attention. Most importantly, illustrations and other visuals should provide additional, accurate information for supporting and extending readers' understanding of the content. In addition to accuracy, consider the visual attractiveness of the book and the degree to which visual features can help students connect their experiences to the content or can help add elements of diversity to classroom collections.

Key questions about attractiveness:

- Will the illustrations entice the reader to want to learn more about the subject?
- Do a variety of visuals and graphic aids provide direct support for understanding of the text?
- Are the illustrations accurate and nonbiased, avoiding tokenism or stereotyping of cultural groups or urban contexts?
- Are cultural details of the time and place (architecture, dress, hairstyles) accurately depicted in illustrations, photographs, and diagrams?

Consider books that have unique illustrative styles or employ special techniques, such as Duncan Tonatiuh's Mixtec codex-inspired artwork in *Dear Primo: A Letter to My Cousin* (2010), the Santiago Family's Oaxacan wood carvings in Cynthia Weill's *Opuestos: Mexican Folk Art Opposites in English and Spanish* (2009), or William Low's digital paintings in *Machines Go to Work in the City* (2012). As with all literature, informational texts that feature diverse populations in urban settings or other contexts should avoid tokenism and stereotypes in appearance, dress, or other features.

Using Informational Texts in the Classroom

As teachers make decisions about which informational texts to include, especially those with information and vocabulary that is not familiar to their students, it is important to consider instructional strategies in addition to the selection of particular books. Keep in mind that although many informational texts may be text heavy or contain language that is above the independent-reading level of students, children can still glean information from viewing photographs and diagrams or build background knowledge and vocabulary through listening to complex text read aloud. Rather than reading from cover to cover, teachers might break down a conceptually dense text into sections to be explored over several class sessions, or do close reading of a particular spread to delve more deeply into the content.

Teaching nonfiction text structures, including how to use tables of contents, indices, and glossaries or how to read diagrams, will also help children navigate more complex informational texts. As with literature, teachers should engage children in explicit instruction of comprehension strategies with informational texts, so children gain practice applying strategies to various text structures.

Examining each informational text for characteristics of quality and cultural relevance is a critical first step when choosing books for content instruction. In practice, teachers are also encouraged to think broadly in terms of the *collections* of books they select for units of instruction and the characteristics of quality each text brings to an inquiry for furthering students' understandings of the unit concepts. Examples of text sets and units of study can be found in chapter 9, which offers strategies for integrating urban children's literature with the core curriculum.

Teachers might consider pairing informational texts with literature and multimedia resources, as with the study of segregation and the era of Jim Crow laws; an example is provided in the "Try This Tomorrow" text box on the following page. Utilizing a combination of literacy sources such as these provides learners with a variety of formats for accessing the content of the unit and promotes high-level inquiry through integration of knowledge and ideas from multiple sources.

Similar to the process suggested in chapter 6 for selecting literature, educators can use the guidelines provided in table 7.1 to review informational texts in the classroom collection or provided with any packaged curriculum.

Try This Tomorrow:
Unit of study: Segregation and the era of Jim Crow
Literature: *Ruth and the Green Book* by Calvin Alexander Ramsey
<u>Informational Text</u>: *Heart and Soul: The Story of America and African Americans* by Kadir Nelson
Multimedia: Interactive Map of the Spring 1956 Edition of the *Green Book*. http://library.sc.edu/digital/collections/greenbook.html

Ask whether the current selections provide opportunities for students to draw on their current knowledge and experiences to connect with content. If not, work with colleagues to identify high-quality informational texts that can help increase the cultural relevance of the curriculum and provide a bridge to new content learning and reading and writing within the content areas.

Summing It Up: Guidelines for Selecting Informational Texts

- Understand genres of informational texts
- Identify characteristics of high-quality multicultural and urban informational texts
- Recognize the connection between current learning standards and the use of multicultural and urban children's informational texts
- Help learners connect with content by grounding instruction in familiar experiences, then expand learning to include information and understanding of the wider world
- Develop pride and understanding as students recognize the contributions of culturally diverse scholars, scientists, and others
- Compare familiar knowledge and settings to new information and contexts that expand awareness of the world, developing a global perspective
- Access high-quality information in a variety of formats, including through technology

Notes

1. Numerous studies have documented incongruence in the use of informational texts compared with literature, particularly in the elementary grades. See Nell Duke (2000), Barbara Moss and Evangeline Newton (2002), and Ruth Yopp and Hallie Yopp (2012) for examples.

2. This includes recommendations from Weimin Mo and Wenju Shen (2003) on accuracy versus authenticity in picture books and from Nancy Hadaway and Terrell Young (2010) on selecting informational text to support dual language learners. Suggestions from Jean Mendoza and Debbie Reese (2001) on avoiding "pitfalls" in selecting multicultural children's literature were also helpful.

~

CHAPTER EIGHT

Cultural and Linguistic Authenticity in Urban Children's Literature

> "[It's] not about 'highlighting' Latinos or any other ethnic group or 'teaching' readers about what makes those groups different. It's about adopting a more inclusive and authentic approach toward children's literature so that our kids can truly see themselves—and their friends—in the books they read."
>
> —Adriana Domínguez (2013)

The previous two chapters provided guidelines for selecting urban children's literature and informational texts to help students connect their experiences to content. In this chapter, we delve more deeply into considerations of cultural and linguistic authenticity, in order to help educators think deeply about what it means for a text to be authentic. In addition, this chapter discusses ways to engage children, families, and community members as expert judges of the authenticity of texts purporting to represent them.

Cultural Authenticity in Urban Children's Literature

As discussed in chapter 1, when evaluating the cultural relevance of urban children's literature, it is important to think broadly and consider the interplay of many aspects of a child's background, including race, ethnicity, social class, language, gender, family structure, and place of residence. Depictions of culture and cultural behaviors, even in texts that some might consider culturally authentic literature, are merely "approximations of reality" (Gay 2010, 12). Like all culturally specific settings, not all urban settings are the same. Dialects, landscapes, ecology, architecture, and activities can differ substantially in different cities.

Consider the Many Dimensions of Student's Lives

Books that children and family members will find most authentic will go beyond "superficial" showcasing of identity markers such as race and ethnicity to capture the multidimentionality of dynamic individuals (Gay 2010, 11). For example, in My Feet Are Laughing (Norman 2006) some students may find commonalities with Sadie's Dominican heritage and her love of the meringue, while others may readily recognize life in her grandmother's Harlem brownstone, her role as a big sister to Julie, or seeing her Pop only on weekends because he and Mami are separated (but still good friends).

As discussed in chapter 6, teachers might look for books that represent this multidimensionality without being overly instructive about it. For example, My Abuelita by Tony Johnston and Yuyi Morales (2009) captures a day in the life of a young boy and his grandmother as they race through their morning routines to get ready to go to Abuela's work. While the story focuses solidly on the loving and lively relationship between the boy and his Abuelita and the "mystery" of her very important job, other elements including the interlingual Spanish and English text, the symbols of Mexican culture and art reflected in Morales's sculptured illustrations, and the fact that Abuelita is the boy's primary caregiver all contribute to a sense of uniqueness of this family while at the same time offering various dimensions of family and cultural life in which many students might see themselves.

Other markers of cultural authenticity may be represented even more subtly. Consider the brief exchange between Lily and her mother in My Best Friend (Rodman 2007) when Lily asks for a new bathing suit. Hoping a new suit will help make second-grader Tamika like her more, first-grader Lily asks for a new two-piece suit like the one she sees Tamika wearing at the neighborhood pool. Mama quickly insists that there's "plenty of wear left" in the suit Lily has now, even though Lily feels it's too small and more worn than Mama thinks (Rodman 2007, 8).

In some communities, children are used to having several swimming suits, and this "problem" might be solved by simply buying a new suit so Lily can feel that she fits in. But in this case, Mama's insistence that Lily's current suit is fine until she outgrows it provides a subtle touchstone of socioeconomics

> *"The text-to-self connections in that one are huge. My students are used to being told, 'You can wear that for another year. It's fine.' So not only is it that they can relate to it, but it lets them know that other kids are having the same experiences that they're having. It's another way to connect."*
>
> —Jill, first-grade teacher, St. Louis, discussing My Best Friend by Mary Ann Rodman

and family practicalities that many students may recognize from their own experience.

Similar to the examples above, educators should look to integrate a wide range of texts into their collections that capture diversity in family structure, gender roles, and lifestyle combined with cultural, linguistic, and socioeconomic diversity. Consider books like *Quinito's Neighborhood*, in which "Mami is a carpenter and Papi is a nurse" (Cumpiano 2009), or *The Night Worker* (Banks 2000) in which Alex's Papa goes to work "while Mama sleeps," or *Tía Isa Wants a Car* (Medina 2011) in which a young Latina, along with her aunt and uncle, works to save "helping money" to send back home to her parents and other relatives so they might someday come to live together again. Building an extensive collection with students, their families, and communities in mind that also represents the diversity and the realities of contemporary urban life can help to ensure that there are plentiful "mirrors" that reflect the many dimensions of students' identities.

> *"You cannot take a one-size-fits-all approach. If you have a book that is geared toward a Mexican American experience near San Antonio, Texas, you can't assume that book is going to sell among Dominicans in Quisqueya Heights [New York]."*
>
> —Alisa Valdes (2013)

Start with *Your* Students *Today*

As teachers consider the degree of "cultural fit" or closeness a particular text may have to their students' experience (Hadaway and Young 2010, 41), talking with children about their day-to-day experiences will help in identifying contemporary, culturally relevant texts that spark children's interest and to which they can bring their own rich background knowledge to understand the text. It may be useful to think in terms of what Christopher Emdin (2012) calls "reality pedagogy"—teaching and learning based on the *reality* of students' experiences. Put yourself in your students' shoes: think about where they live, what their neighborhoods are like, who they spend time with, and what they do for fun. Ask children to share what their family and home is like, what happens in the neighborhood, and how their community responds to different situations.

Teachers can look to students' responses to texts to help determine the extent to which a story may or may not resonate with students. When Lauren, a second-grade teacher in Chicago, first reviewed the book *Something Beautiful* (Wyeth 2002) as a possible read-aloud text for her "Me and My Community" unit, she was initially a bit reluctant. There was a question in her mind as to whether some illustrations in the book, such as an image of a homeless person sleeping on the street, a litter-strewn alleyway, and the word "DIE" tagged on a building, would be viewed as authentic or stereotypical.

Lauren recognized that her reservations might be due to her viewing the book from her more middle-class, suburban lens. After some consultation with teachers on her grade-level team, they decided that the book's message about discovering "beautiful things" in our communities was too important not to include it in the unit. As she prepared for her read aloud, Lauren made a conscious decision to "listen to the kids first," being careful not to project her reservations into the literature discussion. After sharing *Something Beautiful* with her second-graders for the first time, Lauren had a new perspective on the text:

> You could have heard a pin drop during that read aloud. The kids were super-engaged in the discussion, making connections to their neighborhood and proposing their own solutions for beautifying the block.

As discussed in chapter 1, the topics addressed in urban children's literature sometimes reflect realistic aspects of urban life. Authentic, culturally relevant "reality pedagogy" requires a willingness to engage students—even young children—in developmentally appropriate discussions of this real life stuff. Honoring and valuing children's experiences and providing learners with opportunities to discuss and debate issues that impact their lives can serve as the basis for important and high-level discussion and critique, as well as opportunities to take action.

> *"I can't be culturally relevant if I'm teaching you based on what my perception is of your culture."*
>
> —Christopher Emdin (2013)

After making connections with *Something Beautiful*, Lauren's class wondered what they might do to beautify their environments. They wrote a persuasive letter to the school principal to help organize a "school clean-up day." As part of a science study on living things, they also created small portable flower pot plantings to deliver "something beautiful" to their neighbors at a home for the elderly down the block. Building on the connections students made with the urban children's literature in this unit, Lauren moved her instruction beyond the level of content integration to truly supporting students' construction of knowledge through meaningful engagement with their community.

Readers bring all of their experiences with them when reading a book, and these experiences will impact their responses to the book and its characters. There are those stories that enter through our minds, and then there are those that go straight to our hearts. Often, this occurs when readers encounter a text with which they can make many self-to-text connections. As educators, we can look to our students' responses to assess cultural authenticity, since they may "know it when they see it" (Bishop 2003, 27). One idea is to keep a reflective journal or recordings of the conversations evoked from reading a book. Another idea is to collect samples of students' work from response journals, drawings, and their own writing. These artifacts will allow for analysis of responses to identify the connections students are making.

How Do You Know What Is Culturally Authentic?

Teachers often wonder about being able to judge the level of cultural authenticity in texts, especially if they are not members of the cultural groups being represented. In instances when teachers find themselves as cultural "outsiders," Susan Guevera recommends that we "look to what we see ringing true" for students and families (2003, 59). For example, during a recent family literacy night at a New York City Head Start in Chinatown, a teacher presented a read aloud of the book *Chinatown* by William Low (1997). Although few of the parents spoke English, as the reader turned the pages of the book, there was a series of spontaneous gasps of delight and recognition from the listeners, all of whom lived in the neighborhood.

This collective reaction provided some evidence of the authenticity of this text for these families as they made connections to the scenes of the grocery stores and fish markets that populate their Chinatown neighborhood. Indeed, Mr. Low's story and illustrations are grounded in his own experiences living in New York and exploring Manhattan, and his resulting work in *Chinatown* seemed to serve as an authentic "mirror" for families in that Head Start's school community.

Recognize Diversity within Cultures

That is not to say that all members of a particular community will necessarily find cultural authenticity in a particular text. For example, in the book *My Steps* by Sally Derby (1996), the lead character describes a game she plays on the stoop with her two best friends called "Stone School." During a read aloud of *My Steps* at a district professional development session in Chicago, many teachers who grew up on Chicago's West Side quickly identified this game as identical to one they knew called "Rock Teacher." On the other hand, many teachers who grew up just miles away on the South Side of the city were not at all familiar with this game.

> "Even within the context of a city, there are different experiences that kids have, depending on whether they have siblings or not, or what side of town they're from, or which different family members they live with."
>
> —First-grade teacher from the west side of Chicago

As a result, their reactions to the read aloud were markedly different. Teachers who were familiar with "Rock Teacher" immediately began to relate the text to their own experiences, enthusiastically discussing how the rules of the Stone School game described in *My Steps* were similar to, or different from, the various versions of "Rock Teacher" they had played. This background knowledge enhanced their ability to connect with the text and make inferences about the characters. While everyone could understand this second-grade text at some level, the degree of engagement and connection with the text was different for each group, even though most of the teachers were of the same generation, race, and region.

Culturally Specific versus Culturally Generic Texts

The extent to which culture is incorporated as an integral part of characters' lives in children's literature varies widely. Teachers should take into account whether a book is (a) culturally *specific*, with explicit details about a group; (b) culturally *generic*, with a group featured but with less specific detail provided; or (c) culturally *neutral*, with general diversity portrayed but without a focus on a specific group (Bishop 1992, 44).

Culturally Specific Texts

Representations of all types of texts can serve useful purposes in the classroom, but culturally specific texts may provide the most authentic mirrors. Books like Jacqueline Woodson's *We Had a Picnic This Sunday Past* (1997) and *Barrio: Jose's Neighborhood* by George Ancona (2000) provide opportunities for young readers to connect with characters and families whose cultural identities play a central role in the story or informational content.

Many culturally specific texts, such as Monica Brown's (2011) *Marisol McDonald Doesn't Match/Marisol McDonald no combina* or Sun Yung Shin's *Cooper's Lesson* (2004), also provide insight about characters who may be grappling with some aspects of their cultural identities. Others, like Jan Wahl's (2004) *Candy Shop*, reflect characters facing racism or prejudice and can serve as a catalyst for rich and rigorous literature discussions. Transitional chapter books with culturally specific content, such as Nikki Grimes's *Dyamonde Daniel* series, Monica Brown's *Lola Levine* series, *or A Song for Harlem* or *Abby Takes a Stand* from Patricia McKissack's (2006) *Scraps of Time* series are rare finds among short chapter-book series and should be included in every primary and intermediate classroom collection.

Culturally Generic Texts

Culturally generic texts can also contribute to the inclusiveness of classroom collections, especially when they provide mirrors of culturally diverse characters engaged in a range of "everyday" experiences and adventures with their families and friends (Martin 2004, 52). Although they are not inclusive of much specific cultural content, books like *The Rain Stomper* (Boswell 2008) in which the fearless Jazmin "outstomps" a torrential storm on the day of her big neighborhood parade or *Redwoods* (Chin 2009) in which a young reader "explores" a California Redwood forest during a New York City subway ride help urban students of color see themselves represented in the curriculum as leaders, adventurers, and experts.

Even somewhat more culturally "generic" short chapter books like Karen English's Nikki and Deja series or Lisa Yee's *Bobby vs. Girls (Accidentally)* and *Bobby the Brave (Sometimes)* can spark student interest and increase reading frequency. Inclusion of series like these in a collection may be especially important in providing much needed "mirrors" in formats like transitional chapter book series in which urban settings and primary characters of color are scarce (Fleming and Carrillo 2011a; Hughes-Hassell, Koehler, Barkley 2010).

Culturally Neutral Texts

Even culturally neutral books that feature children of color but are "essentially about something else" (Bishop 1992, 46) can serve an important role in the classroom, provided there is also a substantial presence of culturally specific books in the collection. High-quality examples are books like Nina Crews's (2009) *The Neighborhood Sing Along*, which pairs traditional songs and finger plays with contemporary photographs of a multicultural cast of children having fun in the city, or William Low's *Machines Go to Work in the City* in which the vibrant, digitally painted illustrations depict a diverse group of city workers commanding the commuter trains, vacuum trucks, and tower cranes that help get work done. When done well, books like these paint realistic pictures of the city and its diversity, and can help promote a more general sense of inclusivity in the classroom.

Characteristics of Texts to Avoid

Teachers should keep a critical eye out for books that take a "one of each" approach to diversity, having a single, nondescript, generic character for each group: one with brown skin, one character using a wheelchair, one character with a single parent, and so on. This approach reduces people to one-dimensional characterizations with no recognition of diversity within groups. Sometimes teachers think the best way to represent the children in the classroom is to make sure they have books in their library that include "one of each," thus somehow representing everyone. Unfortunately, most of these books tend to depict no one authentically.

It is important that collections also include selections that reveal the multiple dimensions of their characters and illustrate diversity within cultures. Overrelying on a single text to represent a people with a "one-size-fits-all approach" can inadvertently lead to students narrowing their views of people from a particular subculture (Naidoo 2008), developing assumptions that all Asian Americans live in Chinatown or that American Indians always wear ceremonial regalia, for example.

Identifying high-quality selections that present realistic intersections of markers of identity is key. When readers are "surprised" to discover that the characters in *Kitchen Dance* (Manning 2008) are bilingual, or that Maizon's grandmother is a Cheyenne Indian woman who lives in a brownstone in Brooklyn (*Last Summer with Maizon*, Woodson 2002), or that Antonio has two moms (*Antonio's Card/La Tarjeta de Antonio*, González 2005), their perspectives on diversity and identity are inevitably broadened.

TRY THIS TOMORROW:
Take some time to review the books in your collection.

- Does your collection include many books that reflect the experiences of children who live in the city?
- Do many of these books contain culturally specific content, or are most culturally generic or neutral?
- Does your collection include plentiful selections that represent diversity within and across cultures?
- Are there many selections that reveal multiple dimensions of characters' cultural identities?

The Language of Authenticity

Another issue that arises in the discussion of urban children's literature is that of linguistic authenticity. Many teachers are reluctant to include books in which characters speak various dialects of English or that employ discourse that might be more typical of everyday conversations heard within urban neighborhoods. Teachers sometime face skepticism from administrators or other colleagues when including books in their collection that do not adhere strictly to grammatical conventions of what is commonly accepted as standard English.

Interestingly, some educators who recognize the value in including dual language texts for English language learners in their classrooms inadvertently employ a "double standard" when it comes to books that incorporate African American English, for example. Books like Ruth Forman's (2007a) *Young Cornrows Callin Out the Moon* or Melrose Cooper's (1998) *Gettin' Through Thursday* are mistakenly viewed by some educators as counterproductive to students' mastery of grade-level learning standards when they incorporate linguistic features written to capture the meaning, structure, and spirit of the dialect. Consider a few lines from the picture book poem, *Young Cornrows Callin Out the Moon:*[*]

> So you know, we don really want no backyard/frontyard neither/cuz we got to call out the moon/ wit black magic n brownstone steps (Forman 2007b, p. 30–31.)

In reality, the ability to code-switch in different contexts, or even use two languages in the same conversation, is a sign of mastery of both languages, not a sign of confusion or lack of understanding (Cummins 2000). Writers like Jacqueline Woodson recognize the value in student code switching, comparing her use of "Standard" English to "putting on a nice suit—one that you feel good in in the outside world but wouldn't choose for a lazy Sunday afternoon" (2003, 41).

Fluency and literacy in more than one language or dialect is an asset, and students should be encouraged to "harness the power" of more than one language in thinking, communicating, and expressing themselves creatively in reading and writing (Moll and Dworin 1996). Children can learn a great deal from books that are representative of the language they use in their homes and neighborhoods. It is beneficial for students to read and write in dialect, as this is a tool of writing as a craft that authors employ in order to best capture their intended meaning, tone, and characterization in their writing. Writers make important decisions about how their characters will speak and what they will say, depending on who they are interacting with or what the setting is. These are important decisions for young writers to consider in their own works.

"There's no way that I could accurately represent that experience with standard English."

—Ruth Forman (2007b), discussing her decision to write *Young Cornrows Callin Out the Moon* in African American English (AAE)

NPR (2007a). Used with permission.

This is not to suggest that children do not require formal instruction in the spoken and written forms of different languages and dialects; certainly explicit oral and written language instruction is a critical component of all literacy programs. The distance between children's oral language and the

---

[*]*Young Cornrows Callin Out the Moon*. Text copyright © 2007 by Ruth Foreman. Permission arranged with Lee & Low Books Inc., New York, NY 10016.

conventional written language of many texts will help determine how much explicit instruction in the vocabulary, morphology, and syntax of different types of writing children will need.

Teachers should ground this instruction in students' understandings of their home language or dialect, using techniques such as contrastive analysis, vocabulary instruction, and identification of cognates to support children's recognition of similarities and differences in the use of language in different contexts (see Beeman and Urow [2012] for details). In these ways, urban children's literature can play an active, supportive role in developing and maintaining students' positive identities as bilingual or bidialectal learners while serving as excellent mentor texts for language and writing instruction.

Unfortunately, rather than being viewed as assets, the cultural knowledge and home language of urban youth are too often viewed by educators as liabilities, or even justification for the learning challenges that many urban public school students face. "Who can talk, about what, with whom, when, and using what language" can provide either opportunities or constraints for how students are able to negotiate meaning in school (Lee and Smagorinsky 2000, 2). It is critical to understand the importance of language as a foundation for literacy learning and that it can be used as a resource to ensure students' access to the curriculum.

Developing a Sense for Authenticity

The challenge becomes, "How do you assess cultural authenticity in children's literature if you are not a member of that particular group?" The search for cultural authenticity is complicated and may lead to some occasional missteps along the way, but it should not be a deterrent for creating a literary space in the classroom that represents the rich lives of our students (see Dudley-Marling [2003] for discussion). It may involve teachers taking the stance of a *learner of culture* and allowing time to observe and ask questions about the resources at hand.

To develop a sense of what constitutes cultural authenticity, Sims Bishop (2007) recommends that educators engage in the "close reading of texts by highly respected writers from the cultural group," to help readers recognize recurring themes and text features that constitute distinctive features of a body of a subgenre of multicultural literature (Bishop 1992, 44). For urban children's literature, teachers might do careful reading of works by writers featured in chapter 5, such as Coe Booth, Sandra Cisneros, Sharon Draper, Matt de la Peña, Sharon G. Flake, Nikki Grimes, Tony Medina, Walter Dean Myers, G. Neri, Rita Williams-Garcia, and Jacqueline Woodson. For examples of illustrations that integrate culturally authentic artistic elements in conjunction with urban literature, look to artists such as Adjoa Burrowes, R. Gregory Christie, Bryan Collier, Maya Christina Gonzalez, Yuyi Morales, Frank Morrison, Christopher Myers, Duncan Tonatiuh, and Javaka Steptoe.

Cultural Insiders versus Outsiders

The debate over who should write and/or illustrate culturally reflective children's literature is not new and elicits strong emotion among authors, illustrators, editors, publishers, teachers, librarians, and researchers (see Fox and Short [2003] for an excellent discussion). The debate goes beyond whether or not characters and their lives can be written about in an authentic voice. It reaches the heart of the matter of how we view cultural diversity as a society.

If authors and illustrators write about or depict the lives of people they have limited knowledge about, how can it be authentic? Attempts by cultural outsiders to portray a people in very broad strokes often discounts the nuanced understandings one gains when living within a cultural or ethnic group: the critical knowledge about history, geography, shared triumphs and challenges, and common expectations and assumptions.

There is substantial evidence that demonstrates that authors residing within a cultural group tend to more fully capture the essence of a cultural experience and create more authentic depictions than those outside the culture (e.g., Naidoo 2010; Noll 2003; Mendoza and Reese 2001). While an author's or illustrator's cultural background is certainly no guarantee of authenticity, it definitely can help, particularly when writers draw on culturally specific content from their own lives, the experiences of people they've known, or situations they've encountered. Readers should look to the text selection guidelines outlines in chapters 6 and 7, while also considering writers' and illustrators' cultural backgrounds and life experiences.

Writing across Cultures: How to Know When Authors and Illustrators Get It Right

There are examples of high-quality urban children's literature that have been written cross-culturally. The best of these tend to be written as a result of an author's extensive experience living in a particular social or cultural context, or in some cases in collaboration with a cultural insider. For example, the characters and events in Alice Mead's *Junebug* trilogy emerged, in part, from her experience as a young teacher in a Boston housing project. The boy who

> *"It is easy to tell who has and who has not been inside 'my house.'"*
>
> —Jacqueline Woodson (2003, 45)

inspired *Junebug*'s character was one of Mead's students. In many ways, it was, in part, *her* story and, as a result, Junebug reflects authentic elements of her lived experience.

Similarly, Jacqueline Woodson describes having "stepped inside the house of my partner's experience" [being Jewish] in order to capture elements of Ellie's character in *If You Come Softly* (2003, 44). To Mead, the Auburn Housing Project in *Junebug* was not "her house" but there were elements of those experiences that she and the boy who inspired *Junebug* shared (personal communication, May 2009).

Perhaps the most convincing assessment of an authors' success in capturing cultural authenticity in their characters' lives can come from the students who read their books. When Mead joined a Skype-based author talk with a group of fourth graders in St. Louis, the children were shocked to discover that Ms. Mead was a white, middle-aged woman, when most of the primary characters in *Junebug* are young, African American boys. Judi Moreillon describes this as the true test of cross-cultural authenticity: "when an author who writes from an outsider perspective shows up at a school for a visit, students should be surprised to learn that the author isn't a member of the culture depicted in the book" (2003, 75).

Selecting Cross-Cultural Literature: Questions to Ask
In "Who Can Tell My Story?" writer Jacqueline Woodson suggests some questions to ask about authors who try to write cross-culturally (2003, 44):

1. Why did the author need to tell this story?
2. Does the author bring themselves to the story in some way, or are they solely writing "about" others? Are there any characters that share the author's background and/or experiences?
3. Does the author have significant lived experience with the cultural group being represented, or are they simply trying to "tell someone else's story"?

Engaging Families and Communities
as Partners in Assessing Cultural Authenticity

In addition to observing and discussing students' reactions to texts, participating in conversations with family and community members can provide excellent insider perspectives in helping teachers examine cultural authenticity in children's books. One way this can be done is through school-based literacy activities.

Clarena Larotta and Jesse Gainer (2008) described an after-school literacy project they did with families from Mexico living in the United States. In this project, family members were given culturally relevant books they could use to support practice of reading comprehension strategies with their children at home. Using Spanish language and dual language books that were reflective of caregivers' cultural and linguistic identities affirmed their beliefs about the importance of supporting bilingualism for their children and generated interest and energy around reading books in Spanish at home. They also reported that reading the books together inspired conversations between themselves and their children as they connected with a text.

Consider the similar scenario in Sandy's story below:

Sandy's Story:

I think about an event at our school where Latino families, mostly from Mexico, were invited to their children's school for a family literacy night. One of the activities was to share a reading of Amada Irma. Pérez's My Very Own Room/Mi propio cuartitio. Afterward, some of the teachers involved the children in an extension activity, while others stayed and talked with family members. A conversation ensued about some of the reading strategies used by the teacher who read the story, but more importantly, families were encouraged to share their own stories about living with extended family when they came from their native countries and/or letting family live with them when they first arrived to the United States. There was some laughter when one family member pointed out the picture, from the book, of the long line of people waiting to use the bathroom. Many families asked where they could find more books like the one shared. This experience helped validate the cultural authenticity of the book for these families. In another example, a family member read through Quinito's Neighborhood, by Ina Cumpiano, and noted the dialect of the Spanish in the book did not match the dialect that was spoken in her home. The book is culturally authentic for some Latino families, yet not all.

The community can offer a wealth of resources to help assess cultural authenticity in books. Using selection criteria outlined in chapters 6 and 7, teachers should seek partners in reviewing texts for cultural authenticity. Family members are usually receptive and supportive when they see teachers' genuine desire to include books that authentically represent children's experiences. In addition, educators can partner with cultural centers, places of worship, and local colleges that might have staff that can provide an "insider" perspective. Many times, these partnerships are mutually beneficial in helping community members find books of interest to share with their own children or learn about books that they can use within their own organizations.

No Book Is Perfect

Chapters 6, 7, and 8 have outlined many criteria for evaluating the quality of urban children's literature. In reality, it is rare to find texts that meet all of the proposed criteria; in fact, many of the texts featured in these chapters don't necessarily meet them all. The intention in setting the bar high: start

---

Summing It Up: Cultural and Linguistic Authenticity in Urban Children's Literature

- Teaching and learning based on the *reality* of students' experiences allows students to apply prior knowledge to new learning
- Authentic depictions of multicultural families and communities capture diversity in family structure, gender roles, and lifestyle while also affirming cultural, linguistic, and socioeconomic diversity
- Using literature that provides opportunities for code-switching between home and school languages builds linguistic fluency and biliteracy while affirming the linguistic assets children bring to the classroom
- Cultural authenticity can serve as the basis for high-level discussion and critique, as well as opportunities to take action
- Review texts critically for authenticity of themes, situations, characters, language, and cultural specificity
- Draw on children's knowledge as well as people and resources in your community to help assess cultural authenticity in books

with books of quality that may meet multiple criteria, or even some that meet one so well that it seems to be a standout for its use as a mentor text (e.g., quality of language, accuracy of characters or context). This really is a balancing act. As teachers, we use many different books for different purposes, and often use the same book for multiple purposes.

Children pay careful attention to what we hold up as important. It is critical that we be very intentional about the messages we are sending to children every day, both in our choices of individual books for instruction as well as in the entirety of our classroom library and curriculum collections.

CHAPTER NINE

Transforming Your Curriculum with Urban Children's Literature

> *"All instruction is culturally responsive.*
> *The question is: to which culture is it currently oriented?"*
>
> —Gloria Ladson-Billings
> (National Equity Project 2012)

Educators in urban schools must think seriously and intentionally about se-lecting materials and designing learning opportunities that allow students to rely on their cultural knowledge and experiences. As discussed in chapter 1, culturally relevant teaching (CRT) draws purposefully from students' home and community knowledge to make meaningful and relevant connections to school curriculum and culture. Although the theoretical framework for CRT emerged as a response to the disproportionate and historical underachieve-ment of ethnically and linguistically diverse children in schools across the United States, its student-centered approach and emphasis on curriculum and teaching grounded in the everyday lives of students make CRT ap-proaches suitable for all students.

Previous chapters have provided guidelines for the selection of high-quality urban literature and informational texts, with a focus on examining characteristics of individual books for quality and cultural relevance. This chapter focuses on strategies for building *text sets* that incorporate urban children's literature in order to increase cultural relevance in the core curriculum. Text sets are collections of books related to a theme or topic under study. They typically include an assortment of books of different formats, genres, and reading levels to allow readers with varied interests and skills to participate collectively in exploring a common topic.

Many educators work from district-mandated, nationally distributed curricula in which the text sets recommended for instruction may include few selections that are relevant to their students. This chapter highlights strategies for integrating urban children's literature with these core curricula and developing units that connect students' experiences to content while addressing a range of learning standards.

Middle-Class Teachers in Lower-Income Schools: Recognizing Mismatches in Experience

Teachers working in high-poverty communities sometimes express concern about their perceptions of a "lack of experience" or "limited background knowledge" amongst their students. But ask any Chicago second-grader to explain the rules and contingencies of a game of Rock Teacher (a game of chance played with stones, on a stoop), or to generate possible solutions to beautifying their block, or to estimate how much certain foods and other necessities cost (e.g., Ensign 2003), and it is not hard to discover that students have an abundance of background knowledge and experience to help them connect with content. The challenge is that this is not often the type of knowledge or experience that gets represented in the published curricula that are typically utilized in urban districts.

Jill's Story:

Where are the books about going to the play park? What about the church parties [our families] have for holidays? My kids don't really go trick-or-treating in the neighborhood, but they go to their church or they go to the mall for trick-or-treating. There are so many things that are real staples in urban life. Even going to the library to use the computers—everybody [in our school community] does that. I mean everybody! Where are these books, these experiences?

In addition, middle-class teachers in lower-income schools do not always share this same knowledge and experience. As a result, teachers may not readily know how to help students make connections to school curricula. Indeed, educators may not always immediately recognize when their instruction is grounded in *their* experience, not that of their students. Consider the following example of how several teacher education students discovered this while doing their fieldwork in an urban school.

Susan's Story:

Two student teachers were given the opportunity to plan a life science unit on living things. One lesson they planned within the curriculum unit was to give the first-graders experience with different types of fruit, including fruits that have seeds that are typically eaten and fruits that have seeds that are not eaten. They collected six fruits from their suburban superstore: cantaloupe, banana, star fruit, pomegranate, kiwi, and apple. During the lesson, they held up each fruit to activate learning, asking the students to identify the fruit. Their plan was to cut open each one, have the children taste the fruit, and examine the seeds. They would extend this lesson by planting some seeds and measuring the growth of the plants over several months.

As they held up the fruit, they were surprised to learn that the students could only identify the apple and banana. Also, most students were reluctant to try tasting the kiwi, star fruit, or pomegranate. During their supervisory debriefing, the student teachers were dumbfounded to discover that the closest grocery store that would have the types of fruits they brought in would be more than ten miles outside the perimeter of the school and would require transportation beyond the local bus service to get to the store. In addition, the cost of these fruits—in the winter, in the Midwest—would likely be prohibitive for families living in their school community.

At this point, the experience for the student teachers could have gone a number of ways. It could result in their indictment of the shortage of healthy foods in low-income areas, forcing families to purchase their groceries from corner stores or convenient marts where packaged, preserved foods are dominant. It could become a judgmental discussion about families or about the limited knowledge of the students. Or, it could be the opportunity for these teachers to learn more about the lives of their students from a positive, supportive perspective.

> *First, these student teachers went back and asked the children what types of fruit they liked and usually ate. The answer included oranges, pears, peaches, applesauce, and bananas—things they usually got from the breakfast or lunch served at the school, and many times these items were canned. This was the starting point. The teachers went back to the superstore and bought fresh items that the children could identify with some prompting and were willing to taste. Then, they revisited the other fruits that the students were not familiar with, such as kiwi, star fruit, different types of melons, and different varieties of apples. This lesson became a rich, diverse discussion on fruits from around the world, comparisons with what was readily available, with opportunities to graph preferences, not only in the first-grade classroom but also across the school when the project expanded into the lunchroom.*

When asked *"To which culture is your instruction currently oriented?"* these teachers had to acknowledge that they were working and planning through a middle-class, suburban lens. The children's inability to recognize a pomegranate or their reluctance to try the kiwi fruit at the introduction to this unit could have easily been interpreted by these teachers as disinterest or disengagement, when in reality it was due to a cultural mismatch between the teachers' experience and that of their students.

It is important that urban educators begin to recognize these mismatches by taking time to examine content from students' perspectives and actively "question the curriculum" and its relevance to their students' lives (Irvine 2010, 60). When mismatches are revealed, teachers must work to find relevant examples from their students' experiences to help make connections between new content and their current understandings.

Urban Children's Literature as a Bridge

Teachers who do not share their students' cultural background, language, or life experiences can sometimes feel intimidated or unprepared about ways to make instruction more culturally and personally relevant for their students. In these cases, urban children's literature can serve as an instructional "bridge" (Lee 2000), providing opportunities for making connections and engaging in literature discussion that helps develop shared understandings among students and teachers.

In addition, as discussed in chapter 3, urban children's literature may provide a relevant context for beginning or struggling readers to practice application of various comprehension strategies. For example, students may draw on their experiences to infer the mix of feelings Andre experiences in Melrose Cooper's *Gettin' Through Thursday* (1998). Others may compare and contrast their journeys to the United States from Thailand or Colombia or Senegal with those of Amada in *My Diary from Here to There* (Pérez 2009). When given the opportunity to build on what they know, students will begin

---

Jill's Story:

A fourth grade class was reading Alice Mead's Junebug in Trouble *(2002), the story of a ten-year-old boy with big dreams, navigating life with friends and family in and around the Auburn Street housing project. One day the class was discussing what life might be like for Robert, the title character's best friend, after Junebug and his family moved out of Auburn. Partway through the discussion, one student spontaneously began to relate a text-to-text connection with Scott O'Dell's* The Island of the Blue Dolphins *(1960), a classic tale of a twelve-year-old girl who lives alone on an island in the Pacific.*

Teacher: What did [the book] say about what things are like at home for Robert?

Several students respond: It's trashy. Lots of things are broken at the projects.

Teacher: Ok. What do you think Robert's life is like at Auburn Street? What are some words we can use to describe it?

Students: Dirty. Trashy. Crazy. Sad. He feels sad. Angry. He's mad at people 'cause nobody ever wants to be around him. He's lonely.

Khalil (spontaneously): I remember in *Island of the Blue Dolphins*, the girl, she got left behind and she was lonely. She was the only girl on the island. (Other students begin to relate additional details.)

Teacher: Tell me what you think is similar about Karana and Robert.

Several students respond: They both are lonely. Sad. Tired.

Khalil: They both always gotta stay alone somewhere.

Teacher: Right. They're stuck there. Can you imagine what Robert feels like?

to apply these comprehension skills to all kinds of texts, including those that may not be especially relevant or contemporary.

Consider Jill's Story in which students make connections between the experiences of Robert in Alice Mead's *Junebug* (2009) to those of Karana in Scott O'Dell's classic *Island of the Blue Dolphins* (1988).

Not only can urban children's literature support meaning-making and application of comprehension skills, it also can provide familiar grounding for the teaching of literary elements (setting, plot, theme, tone) or informational text structure. Once students are familiar with a book, it can be used as a mentor text for teaching more complex literary devices, such as the "SLAP, clatter, clatter, SLAP!" of onomatopoeia to describe the intensity of the storm in *The Rain Stomper* (Boswell 2008, 8) or the use of metaphor ("My tongue is a rock") to describe Juanito's challenge to communicate in English in *The Upside Down Boy* (Herrera 2006, 10). The key is that educators be intentional in their efforts to select texts that draw on students' prior knowledge and lived experience to better situate literacy learning in the Zone of Proximal Development (ZPD) (Vygotsky 1978) and support students in making connections to new content.

"When students have a story they really connect with, they remember those stories, they internalize those stories. Then it's easier to teach other 'big' concepts, such as setting or resolution. If they love this book, they'll remember specific aspects of it, like that the setting was in the park or on the block. Other things you want to teach become easier, because they have a reference."

—First-grade teacher, Chicago

Developing Text Sets for Instructional Units

Text sets are collections of books related to a common topic, theme, or type of text (Opitz 1998). For units organized around a theme or topic, a text set will typically include a mixture of books of different formats and genres and at a range of reading levels, each with content related to that topic or theme. For units that engage students in the study of a particular genre (e.g., contemporary realistic fiction, traditional literature, fantasy, etc.), a text set will include an assortment of texts within that genre, allowing for an exploration of a range of books that supports students in identifying the characteristics of the genre, the various forms it might take, and the range of content represented within the genre.

Utilizing Urban Children's Literature in Genre Study

When teachers have the freedom to develop units of study, including a rich representation of culturally relevant urban children's literature is relatively straightforward. Consider, for example, the text set outlined in Table 9.1 which was developed "from scratch" for a fifth-grade genre study of poetry.

The range of titles includes many different types of poetry, such as rhyme-and-meter, free verse, ballads, haikus, rebuses, and riddles. There are classic and contemporary selections to engage students in comparing writers' varied approaches to a range of topics or events, to study changes in poetic form over time, and to explore the ways in which language can capture the essence of an era. The selected texts present the poems in a variety of formats, including picture books by a single author, illustrated collections on a common theme, or anthologies with historical or cultural significance.

Multiple Points of Access

The text set includes numerous options written at a variety of reading levels to provide access to the unit to all students, including challenging selections for read aloud or for those who may be excelling at reading (e.g., *The 100 Best African American Poems*, Giovanni 2010) and high interest, but accessible selections for students who may be working toward grade-level reading (e.g., *You Don't Even Know Me*, Flake 2010). CDs included with some selections provide additional support for meaning making, as well as opportunities for students to compare and contrast what they envision when reading versus what they hear when they listen to a poet's reading of his or her writing.

Multiple text selections by poets such as Nikki Grimes, Tony Medina, and Pat Mora allow for some author study within this unit, and representation of illustrators who use a wide variety of techniques and styles, such as Jamel Akib's pastel illustrations in *Tan to Tamarind* (2009) or Javaka Steptoe's multimedia collage in *In Daddy's Arms I Am Tall* (1997), provide excellent models for students to consider when illustrating their own poems. Author websites (e.g., sharongflake.com) and YouTube poetry jams provide additional video and audio resources to compliment the unit, support comprehension, and provide models against which students might fashion their own writing and performing. All in all, the unit plan allows for many opportunities to explore the genre in rigorous ways.

Amidst this diversity, there is a strong representation of urban children's literature, intentionally selected to provide these fifth graders with texts in

Table 9.1. Text Set for a Fifth-Grade Poetry Unit

Title	Author/Illustrator	Format	Reading Level	Time Period	Context
The 100 Best African American Poems	Nikki Giovanni (Ed.)	Anthology	6.0+	Classic and Contemporary	Varies
100 Essential American Poems	Leslie M. Pokell (Ed.)	Anthology	6.0+	Classic	Varies
The Black Poets	Dudley Randall	Anthology	6.1	Classic and Contemporary	Varies
Confetti: Poems for Children	Pat Mora/ Enrique O. Sanchez	Illustrated Collection	3.7	Contemporary	Southwest
DeShawn Days	Tony Medina/ R. Gregory Christie	Picture Book	4.2	Contemporary	Urban
Falling Up	Shel Silverstein	Illustrated Collection	3.5	Contemporary	Varies
Harlem	Walter Dean Meyers/ Christopher Myers	Picture Book	3.6	Contemporary	Urban
In Daddy's Arms I Am Tall	Javaka Steptoe	Illustrated Collection	3.1	Contemporary	Varies
Love to Langston	Tony Medina/ R. Gregory Christie	Illustrated Collection	4.5	Contemporary/ Biographical	Varies
Love to Mamá: A Tribute to Mothers	Pat Mora (Ed.)	Illustrated Collection	4.5	Contemporary	Varies
Meet Danitra Brown	Nikki Grimes/ Floyd Cooper	Picture Book	3.4	Contemporary	Urban

Title	Author/Illustrator	Format	Level	Type	Setting
My Feet Are Laughing	Lissette Norman/ Frank Morrison	Picture Book	4.0	Contemporary	Urban
My Man Blue	Nikki Grimes/ Jerome Lagarrigue	Picture Book	3.9	Contemporary	Urban
The Neighborhood Mother Goose	Nina Crews	Illustrated Collection	3.8	Classic	Urban
The Palm of My Heart: Poetry by African American Children	D. Adedjouma (Ed.)/ R. Gregory Christie	Illustrated Collection	2.8	Contemporary	Varies
Poetry in Motion: 100 Poems from the Subways and Buses	N. Peacock, E. Paschen, and P. Neches (Eds.)	Anthology	5.0+	Classic and Contemporary	Varies
Poetry Speaks Who I Am	Elise Paschen (Ed.)	Anthology	6.0+	Classic and Contemporary	Varies
Sky Scrape/City Scape: Poems of City Life	Jane Yolen/ Ken Condon	Picture Book	4.9	Contemporary	Urban
Speak to Me (And I Will Listen between the Lines)	Karen English/ Amy June Bates	Picture Book	3.6	Contemporary	Urban
Tan to Tamarind	Malathi M. Iyengar/Jamel Akib	Picture Book	3.5	Contemporary	Varies
Thanks a Million	Nikki Grimes/ Cozbi A. Cabrera	Picture Book	3.0	Contemporary	Varies
You Don't Even Know Me: Stories and Poems about Boys	Sharon G. Flake	Poetry Collection	3.6	Contemporary	Urban

Table 9.2. Fifth-Grade Poetry Unit: Activities and Goals

Intro/Activation/Large Group	Activities/Small Group	Explorations/Extensions
What Is a poem? Review of the Elements of Poetry	Exploration of poems and poets. Review text set. Find examples of the elements in the published poetry. Compare and contrast poems and poets. Learn about poets; why did they write that? What is context? Who is the author?	• Select a favorite poem to share by reading it aloud. • Use technology to develop definitions and examples of key poetry elements, terms, and forms. • Share thoughts on the meaning of a poem. • Plan periodic poetry breaks for individuals to share favorite poems.
Imagery	Find examples of poems that paint pictures with words. Review text set—interpret meanings of poems from the illustrated texts. Writing exercises that create imagery. Using pictures to help create imagery in poems. Use of white space and line breaks.	• Select a favorite poem to share by reading it aloud. • Illustrate a poem with original drawings. • Illustrate a poem through interpretative movement/performance. • Plan periodic poetry breaks for individuals to share themed original and favorite poems.
Rhythm	Find examples of poems with a variety of rhythms. Review text set—interpret role of rhythm and music in different poems. Writing exercises that apply rhythm, imagery, and original writing. Use of instruments (bells, chimes, whistles, percussion).	• Select a favorite poem to share by reading it aloud. • Use a favorite piece/style of music and create an original poem to share. • Use instruments to create rhythm, mood, and tone in selected or original poems. • Plan periodic poetry breaks for individuals to share themed original and favorite poems.
Choosing Words	Identifying poems with powerful words. Identifying metaphors and similes. Writing and revision of original poetry. Identifying favorite poets and discussing their work; creating poetry anthologies.	• Select a favorite poem to share by reading it aloud. • Develop/play games using metaphors and similes made up in small groups. • Plan periodic poetry breaks for individuals to share and perform favorite poems. • Start to share original writing.

| Poetry Slam | Preparing original poetry to deliver to the group. Use of technology to enhance and practice poetry. | • Share original poetry.
• Watch slam poets on YouTube and have mini-slam performances.
• Include imagery, music, or movement in poetry performance. |

Content Learning Goals/Outcomes

Common Core State Standards for English Language Arts:

CCSS.ELA-Literature.5.1 Quote accurately from a text when explaining what the text says explicitly and when drawing inferences from the text.

CCSS.ELA-Literature.5.2 Determine a theme of a story, drama, or poem from details in the text, including how characters in a story or drama respond to challenges or how the speaker in a poem reflects upon a topic; summarize the text.

CCSS.ELA-Literature.5.3 Compare and contrast two or more characters, settings, or events in a story or drama, drawing on specific details in the text (e.g., how characters interact).

CCSS.ELA-Literature.5.4 Determine the meaning of words and phrases as they are used in a text, including figurative language such as metaphors and similes.

CCSS.ELA-Literature.5.6 Describe how a narrator or speaker's point of view influences how events are described.

CCSS.ELA-Literature.5.7 Analyze how visual and multimedia elements contribute to the meaning, tone, or beauty of a text.

CCSS.ELA-Writing.5.4 Produce clear, coherent writing in which the development and organization are appropriate to the task, purpose, and audience.

CCSS.ELA-Writing.5.5 With guidance and support from peers and adults, develop and strengthen writing as needed by planning, revising, editing, rewriting, or trying a different approach.

CCSS.ELA-Writing.5.6 With some guidance and support from adults, use technology to produce and publish writing as well as to interact and collaborate with others.

CCSS.ELA-Writing.5.10 Write routinely over extended and shorter time frames for a range of discipline-specific tasks, purposes, and audiences.

which they can see their experiences reflected. There are poems (and poets) that might remind students of themselves or of people they know (e.g., *My Man Blue*, Grimes 1999), poems that capture life in the neighborhood or their block (e.g., *DeShawn Days*, Medina 2003), poems that employ language that is familiar and feels like home (e.g., *Young Cornrows Callin Out the Moon*, Forman 2007b; *Love to Mamá*, Mora 2001). In addition, there are works written by distinguished poets (e.g., *100 Essential American Poems*, Pockell 2009) as well as by children their own age (e.g., *The Palm of My Heart*, Adedjouma 1996).

This text set was specifically designed to support students in making personal connections to the genre, while also capturing a diversity of cultural representations, experiences, places, and time periods. Notice that there are many "mirrors" as well as "windows" among the selections. By grounding instruction in a varied and culturally relevant collection, these teachers first established a familiar context for engaging students with the genre. Then the goal was to lead students in studying the elements of poetry, examining the use of imagery and rhythm, and exploring word choice to establish mood and tone.

Exposure to a wide variety of poets with diverse forms of expression provided plenty of literary mentors to inspire ideas for students' own poetry writing and performance. The unit culminated in a student-led poetry jam that allowed for students to express their excitement, interest, and love of the genre while demonstrating mastery of the content using their original poems.

Engaging children in culturally relevant instruction with urban literature had the added benefit of conveying a strong, positive message to parents and other caregivers that teachers valued their experiences and were carefully crafting instruction that was inclusive of their children and families. Family members of many of the children involved attended the poetry jam, demonstrating how welcoming and valuing the community can contribute to adults' engagement as well.

Beyond a "Contributions" Approach

James Banks (1995) describes five dimensions of multicultural education ranging from content integration, which involves adding content about historically underrepresented groups to an existing curriculum, to school-wide approaches that alter structures or policies to make the overall school culture more equitable for all students.

This sample poetry unit goes beyond what Banks (1995) would call a "contributions" or "additive" approach to multicultural education in which special lessons or units are merely "added on" to the standard curriculum. In-

Table 9.3. Banks's Dimensions of Multicultural Education

Dimensions of Multicultural Education	Key Activities	Example
Dimension 1: Content Integration	Adding content about people of color or historically underrepresented groups into the curriculum.	Adding a unit on Latin American culture during National Hispanic Heritage Month.
Dimension 2: Knowledge Construction	Helping students recognize cultural assumptions and frames of reference implicit in content being taught.	Breaking down terms like "westward expansion" to consider from whose perspective (Anglo-American settlers) content is being presented in texts.
Dimension 3: Equity Pedagogy	Changing teaching methods to enable all students to achieve.	Providing opportunities for students to explore content in cooperative groups.
Dimension 4: Prejudice Reduction	Helping students develop positive attitudes toward different racial, ethnic, and cultural groups.	Examining the contributions of Benjamin Banneker, Ron McNair, and Mae Jamison in the study of astronomy.
Dimension 5: Empowering School Culture and Social Structure	Working to make the overall school culture more equitable.	Eliminating gate keeping policies and providing social supports to allow more students of color access to Advanced Placement coursework.

Note: Drawn from Banks (1995, 3–24).

stead, this unit incorporates multiple dimensions of multicultural education, including knowledge construction, equity pedagogy, and prejudice reduction.

Specifically, these teachers worked to transform the curriculum, using urban children's literature as tools for drawing on students' lived experiences and supporting their construction of new knowledge about poetry. In addition to engaging students in reading and writing poetry, they used music, graphic arts, performance, and technology to provide students with opportunities to tap into a wide range of talents to demonstrate what they had learned.

These teachers purposefully included classic and contemporary poetry written by artists from a range of time periods and cultural perspectives so students could examine various forms of poetry from different perspectives and points of view. Poets such as Sonia Sanchez, Tony Medina, and Tupac Shakur shared equal footing with Emily Dickenson, Robert Frost, and Langston Hughes in this unit, making these poets' contributions integral to the unit and placing equal value on the content captured in their works.

Planning Integrated Units That Incorporate Urban Children's Literature

In contrast to genre study, integrated units organize content by theme, taking a multidisciplinary approach designed to help students make connections across subject areas. One example of CRT in an integrated unit is in the kindergarten "Wheels Project" outlined below. This type of curriculum unit may be familiar to many preschool and primary grade teachers who use a Project Approach to designing curriculum (Chard 2013).

In this multidisciplinary inquiry project, children worked collaboratively with classmates and teachers to explore wheels in their various forms and uses. It covers many content standards through natural exploration with social studies (transportation and community resources), science (physical science—motion, energy, force), mathematics (geometry—shapes, size), and of course, language arts (exploring literature and informational texts on a range of subjects).

Urban settings provide opportunities to study a rich array of transportation methods and the role that wheels play as part of transportation. The unit supports the expansion of students' content knowledge and vocabulary (e.g., traffic, tunnels, harbor, ferry, passengers, turnstiles, gridlock, commute). The text set covers both literature and informational texts about shapes (round, wheels) and modes of transportation (taxis, subways, buses, trains). Activities were designed to provide opportunities for students to explore the unit theme across disciplines and in the context of their daily lives.

Students' number sense and understanding of probability was developed by counting the number of wheels children identified in a neighborhood walk with their teachers and by graphing the frequency of various modes of transportation used by everyone in the class to get to school. Model vehicles and ramps were used to investigate the relationship between force and motion in science. Students experimented with architectural features, using a variety of recycled materials to build tunnels and bridges that replicated the ones they crossed or saw each morning. Students' concepts about wheels and modes of transportation were expanded with discussions of ferries, trucks, and other methods to move cargo around an urban landscape.

Table 9.4. Integrated Unit Plan for Kindergarten: Wheels Project—How Can Wheels Help Us in Our Everyday Lives?

Content	Intro/Activation/Large Group	Activities/Small Group	Explorations/Extensions
Language Arts	Introduce the topic of Wheels. Wheels are round objects. They are also called spheres. Can you think of things that are round or spherical? Discuss the essential question: how do these wheels help us in our everyday lives? Make a list on chart paper. Add to the list as more things are discovered and children deepen their understandings. Plan a community walk and count the number of wheels there are on different things. Make sure children have paper/pencils to record their findings and a camera for pictures to document the experience. Engage children in read alouds and literature discussion of selections from Wheels text set. Be intentional about selections and how each new read aloud will contribute to deepening children's understandings around the essential question. Continue to chart learning as children discuss new ideas.	Display books read at the rug in the library attractively so children will want to revisit them. Add additional text selections to the classroom library and center areas. Check current selection to include culturally relevant books, familiar scenes, and characters that reflect the children in the classroom. Make books available for checkout for home reading. Develop a unit-specific word wall for content vocabulary as new words are learned. Refer to the wall regularly during unit activities. Encourage frequent use of new vocabulary in discussions and encourage children to incorporate in their writing.	Have materials available for pretend play "on the bus," in a cab, building or repairing vehicles, and for dramatization of storybooks read. Include tools, work clothes, and so on. Extend stories with puppet materials in the writing area. Have paper and a variety of writing tools available to draw and write own stories or concept books about wheels, transportation. Ask students to bring something round to school each day—look for small round items at home.
Science	Collect a variety of round objects and objects with wheels for children to explore. Ask them to identify similarities and differences. What do they notice about the objects? How are round objects used as tools? How do they make life easier?	Collect round items and blocks for building. Add a flat board so things can be moved with round items and flat board. Include a variety of vehicles, wheeled toys, and balls. Cooking: Engage children and families in making round items such as tortillas, roti, pizza, cookies. Note shapes of various tools used (rolling pin, pizza cutter) and how they help.	Include a variety of games that use balls or round items: marbles, jacks, pick-up sticks.

(continued)

Table 9.4. *(continued)*

Content	Intro/Activation/Large Group	Activities/Small Group	Explorations/Extensions
Mathematics	Graph data collected for each activity (e.g., neighborhood walk, counts of wheels and modes of transportation, ways children get to school, number of wheels on different modes of transportation, etc.)	Exploring with String Shapes—Lay out strands of string and cut-out shapes. Have children wrap the string around the perimeter of shapes. Remove the shapes to see the outlines.	Wheel bingo. Sorting and matching different wheels by shape, size, and use.
Social Studies	Explore how people get from place to place. Brainstorm types of transportation and transportation systems children use or see in their environments, including bridges, roads, subway trains, airplanes, helicopters, bicycles, and so on. Discuss the value and limitations of different modes of transportation. Which are best for different purposes?	Have students identify a mode of transportation they want to explore in depth. Engage children in projects, representing their learning by creating 3-D objects (model, diorama), collage, or uses of media to represent what they've learned.	Take neighborhood field trips or engage family and community members at school to explore a fire truck, police car, taxi, subway, delivery truck, and so on. Prepare children to ask questions and share their learning with community members.
Art		Marble Paint Patterns—Take a shallow box, put a piece of construction paper in the bottom, use marbles, small bowl, paint, and spoon. Dip marbles in paint with spoon, drop on paper and have children move marble around by shifting the box. Display creations and discuss shapes of patterns.	Use newspaper as molding material with masking tape to build wheels and representations of modes of transportation. Add materials to a discovery center to explore uses of wheels and round items. Include magazines and scissors for identifying wheels and round items for class collage to provide visual compliment to concept chart and word wall.

Technology	
Look for educational apps for children that feature round shapes, wheels, and transportation (e.g., ChuggaBugga, Cars in the Sandbox: Construction).	Use cameras to document field trips and support research of transportation modes.

Learning Standards Addressed

Language Arts (Common Core State Standards)
Listening and Speaking: Comprehension and Collaboration. Participate in collaborative conversations about kindergarten topics and texts in small and large groups; presentation of knowledge and ideas though drawings and other visual displays.
Reading Literature: Key Ideas and Details. With prompting and support, ask and answer questions about key details in a text; Retell familiar stories, including key details.
Reading Informational Texts: Key Ideas and Details. With prompting and support, identify the main idea and retell key details of a text; craft and structure. Ask and answer questions about unknown words in a text. Integration of Knowledge: identify similarities and differences between two texts on the same topic.
Writing: Text Types and Purposes. Use a combination of drawing, dictating, and writing to compose informative texts; research to build and present knowledge. Participate in shared research and writing projects.

Mathematics (Common Core State Standards)
Counting and Cardinality (K.CC)—Know counting sequence, count to tell number of objects, compare numbers, solve problems.
Measurement and Data (K.MD)—Describe and measure attributes; classify objects; reason with shapes and their attributes; represent and interpret data.
Geometry (K.G)—Identify and describe shapes; analyze, compare, create, and compose shapes.

Science (National Academy of Science)
Properties of objects and materials; position and motion of objects.

Social Studies (National Council for the Social Studies)
Study of people, places, and environments for the purpose of understanding the relationship between humans and the physical world, evolving cultures, and changing relationships with the environment.

Table 9.5. Wheels Unit Text Set

Title	Author	Illustrator	Genre
The Adventures of Taxi Dog	Debra and Sal Barracca	Mark Buehner	Animal Fantasy
Bicycle Race	Donald Crews	Donald Crews	Informational
The Bus for Us	Suzanne Boom	Suzanne Bloom	Concept
Don't Let the Pigeon Drive the Bus	Mo Willems	Mo Willems	Animal Fantasy
Hot, Hot Roti for Dada-ji	F. Zia	Ken Min	Realistic Fiction/Elements of Fantasy
Fire! ¡Fuego! Brave Bomberos	Susan Middleton Elya	Dan Santat	Poetry/Realistic Fiction
Flying	Donald Crews	Donald Crews	Informational
Freight Train	Donald Crews	Donald Crews	Informational
Last Stop on Market Street	Matt de la Peña	Christian Robinson	Realistic Fiction
Listen to the City	Rachel Isadora	Rachel Isadora	Concept
Machines Go to Work in the City	William Low	William Low	Informational
One Afternoon	Yumi Heo	Yumi Heo	Realistic Fiction
Round Is a Mooncake: A Book of Shapes	Roseanne Thong	Grace Lin	Concept
Round Is a Tortilla: A Book of Shapes	Roseanne Greenfield Thong	John Parra	Concept
School Bus	Donald Crews	Donald Crews	Informational
Subway	Anastasia Suen	Karen Katz	Poetry/Informational
Subway	Christoph Niemann	Christoph Niemann	Poetry/Informational
Subway Sparrow	Leyla Torres	Leyla Torres	Realistic Fiction
Tía Isa Wants a Car	Meg Medina	Claudio Muñoz	Realistic Fiction
Truck	Donald Crews	Donald Crews	Informational
Trucks: Whizz, Zoom, Rumble	Patricia Hubbell	Megan Halsey	Informational
Whose Vehicle Is This? A Look at Vehicles Workers Drive	Sharon Katz Cooper	Amy Bailey Muehlenhardt	Informational

The critical feature of this unit is that it draws on the urban setting, providing students with familiar landscapes and vocabulary on which to begin to build the investigation. In Banks's (1995) first dimension of multiculturalism, teachers purposefully and intentionally build bridges in the curriculum through content integration, selecting materials and developing activities that will support students in connecting their prior knowledge with new material to be learned.

In this example, teachers in New York City developed a text set with this in mind, including books like *Subway* by Christoph Niemann (2010) and *My Subway Ride* by Paul DuBois Jacobs, Jennifer Swender, and Selina Alko (2004). Both books include vivid illustrations of the subway system in New York, a typical method of transportation for students. *My Subway Ride* includes illustrations depicting a diverse community of children and adults riding and experiencing life using the subway. As part of an inquiry project on wheels, these books help students living in this New York City school community see themselves in the curriculum and draw on familiar experiences to support new learning.

Integrating Urban Children's Literature with Published Curricula

Supporting students' construction of knowledge with urban children's literature is facilitated when educators are given responsibility and autonomy in the design of their curriculum. While many educators would relish the professional freedoms inherent in the "build it from scratch" examples above, it is important to recognize that many teachers face constraints in the liberties they are able take with their districts' mandated curricula. Many urban school districts have identified published language arts curricula that teachers are expected to implement with fidelity, potentially limiting their opportunities for fully infusing culturally responsive texts and instructional strategies.

Still, as discussed in chapter 3, blending a rich collection of urban children's literature with selections from a mandated curriculum is a critical step toward creating a more culturally relevant curriculum. While learning to read and write, children must see themselves, their families, and their communities represented in literature to support them in activating their prior knowledge and making meaningful connections between what they are reading and what they are experiencing in their everyday lives. While many major publishers have significantly improved the diversity of text selections in their language arts basal series with respect to *multicultural* children's literature, urban educators tend to find only a few selections representing authentic urban experiences in curricula intended for a broad, national audience.

With the majority of states adopting the Common Core State Standards (CCSS) in recent years, there has also been a great deal of renewed attention to the selection of literature and informational texts of sufficient complexity for meeting grade level standards. As a result, many schools are reexamining the reading selections in their core curricula for text complexity in relation to the CCSS Appendix B text exemplars (National Governors Association Center for Best Practices, Council of Chief State School Officers 2010).

Although the CCSS exemplar texts are presented primarily as comparative targets for assessing text difficulty and quality, there is significant concern in the field about the lack of multicultural, contemporary selections among texts listed in the CCSS's exemplar list (e.g., Chiariello 2013; Cunningham 2013; Short 2013). As schools and districts undertake this work, it is essential for educators to consider a much broader range of literature and informational texts, in order to identify relevant, contemporary selections that can foster engagement and facilitate the use of family, community, and cultural knowledge in literacy learning.

An Important First Step: Content Integration
Table 9.6 presents an example of how one team of primary grades teachers in a racially and linguistically diverse, urban elementary school approached the first step of content integration in order to identify more "mirrors" for their core literacy curriculum. This team started by examining the range of themes already covered in the language arts curriculum used at their school. The teachers then worked together to identify developmentally appropriate urban literature and informational texts to integrate with the core curriculum, using a range of resources to locate texts that might draw on their students' knowledge and experiences (see chapter 10 for resources for getting started).

Selected supplemental texts are well aligned with each curricular theme and include a range of fiction and nonfiction texts aimed at helping a wide array of students connect their experiences to this language arts content. Developing diverse text sets allows students with a range of interests, backgrounds, and reading levels to explore common themes through a variety of sources. In order to provide both "mirrors" and "windows" in each unit, teachers planned to weave many of these culturally relevant literature selections into the curriculum in conjunction with some of the publisher's recommended texts.

Exploring themes from multiple perspectives with a variety of carefully selected texts like these can help expand students' understandings of concepts such as *kindness* and *cooperation*. It also provides many opportunities to engage students in applying high-level comprehension strategies such as making connections, synthesizing information from multiple sources, and comparing and contrasting content across texts. The result is a curriculum that intentionally supports students in integrating knowledge and ideas from their lived experience with new content, while at the same time maintaining the integrity of the district's framework for literacy instruction.

The same process could be used with any core curriculum, such as identifying urban children's literature to use with Stephanie Harvey's and Anne Goudvis's (2008) *Primary Comprehension Toolkit* or Lucy Calkins's (2013) *Units of Study in Opinion, Information, and Narrative Writing*. As discussed in chapter 3, the goal is to identify culturally relevant texts that help better situate instruction in the ZPD so students can focus more of their attention and mental energy on application of strategies or identifying features of writing craft.

Text Sets and Teaching Sequence

Many published curricula suggest a range of options for mentor texts for teaching comprehension strategies or writing craft. For example, a second-grade unit on narrative writing in Calkins's (2013) Units of Study includes the mentor texts *Owl Moon* by Jane Yolen (1987) and *The Leaving Morning* by Angela Johnson (1992) to explore the authors' craft in writing stories about small moments in their characters' lives.

Owl Moon describes a late-night adventure a young girl and her father take through the country on a moonlit night. *The Leaving Morning* captures a day in the life of a young boy as he and his family prepare to move from their apartment in the city to a new home. One goal of the unit is to have students identify small moments in their own lives to come up with ideas for their stories. While these are both excellent mentor texts for modeling how writers capture particular moments or experiences in their stories, one may be more culturally relevant for some students than another selection.

In these cases, teachers should use their professional judgment to determine the order in which mentor texts are presented in the unit. Introducing the unit with a book like *The Leaving Morning* may help situate the initial discussion of small moments in a familiar context, providing fertile ground for students to make connections with their experiences and begin generating ideas for their own small moment stories.

Table 9.6. Blending Culturally Relevant Literature with the Core Curriculum

	Kindergarten	First Grade	Second Grade
UNIT 1	**Families Same and Different**	**Me, Myself, and Others**	**Exploring Relationships**
Possible Supplemental Texts	*Dear Primo: A Letter to My Cousin* by Duncan Tonatiuh (I) *Gracias/Thanks* by Pat Mora (P) *Kitchen Dance* by Maurie J. Manning (RF) *My Abuelita* by Tony Johnston (RF) *One Family* by George Shannon (C)	*Marisol McDonald and the Clash Bash/Marisol McDonald y la fiesta sin igual* by Monica Brown (RF) *My Best Friend* by Mary Ann Rodman (RF) *The Other Side* by Jacqueline Woodson (HF) *Subway Sparrow* by Leyla Torres (RF) *Yesterday I Had the Blues* by Jeron Ashfors Frame (C)	*Jones Family Express* by Javaka Steptoe (RF) *My Feet Are Laughing* by Lisette Norman (P) *Nana's Big Surprise/¡Qué Sorpresa!* by Amada Irma Pérez (M) *Pink and Say* by Patricia Polacco (B) *Tía Isa Wants a Car* by Meg Medina (RF)
UNIT 2	**Making Friends**	**Me and My Community**	**Identity and Personal Growth**
Possible Supplemental Texts	*Hot Day on Abbott Avenue* by Javaka Steptoe (RF) *Join Hands!* by Pat Mora (P) *Mis amigos/My Friends* by George Ancona (B) *Moony Luna/Luna, Lunita, Lunera* by Jorge Argueta (RF) *Rain!* by Linda Ashman (RF)	*Jazzy Miz Mozetta* by Brenda C. Roberts (RF) *Machines Go to Work in the City* by William Low (I) *Mi Barrio/My Neighborhood* by George Ancona (B) *Quinito's Neighborhood/El vecindario de Quinito* by I. Cumpiano (C) *Something Beautiful* by Sharon Dennis Wyeth (RF)	*My Very Own Room* by Amada Irma Pérez (M) *My Feet Are Laughing* by Lisette Norman (P) *She Come Bringing Me That Little Baby Girl* by Eloise Greenfield (RF) *Tan to Tamarind* by Malathi Michelle Iyengar (P) *Teammates* by Peter Goldenbock (B)

UNIT 3 Possible Supplemental Texts	Getting Around Town	Family and Cultural Traditions	Working Together to Solve Problems
	The Adventures of Taxi Dog by Debra Barracca (AF)	*Grandma's Records* by Eric Velasquez (M)	*Estela's Swap* by Alexis O'Neill (RF)
	The Bicycle Race, Flying, Harbor and others by Donald Crews (I)	*How My Family Lives in America* by Susan Kuklin (I)	*Gettin' Through Thursday* by Melrose Cooper (RF)
	The Bus for Us by Suzanne Bloom (C)	*Henry's First Moon Birthday* by Lenore Look (RF)	*Side by Side/Lado a Lado* by Monica Brown (B)
	Last Stop on Market Street by Matt de la Peña (RF)	*In My Family/En mi familia* by Carmen Lomas Garza (A)	*Sit-In: How Four Friends Stood Up by Sitting Down* by Andrea Davis Pinkney (B/I)
	Subway by Anastasia Suen (P)	*We Had a Picnic This Sunday Past* by Jacqueline Woodson (RF)	*Uncle Rain Cloud* by Tony Johnston (RF)

Genre Key: AF—Animal Fantasy; B—Biography; C—Concept; I—Informational; M—Memoir; P—Poetry; RF—Realistic Fiction.

In subsequent mini-lessons, a range of mentor texts, including *Owl Moon*, can be used to further students' thinking about the possibilities for their small-moment stories, providing examples of how writers sometimes tell stories they've experienced themselves, and sometimes tell stories they've heard from others, researched, or even just imagined. For upper primary and intermediate students, this type of wide reading of narrative texts lends itself well to explorations of genre, as students examine similarities and differences among realistic fiction, historical fiction, fantasy, and science fiction and explore these in their own writing.

Beyond Integration: Teaching for Social Justice

In addition to increasing the cultural relevance of the curriculum with a stronger presence of urban children's literature, it is equally important that teachers develop competence in effectively utilizing these in instruction. While each of Banks's dimensions of multicultural education is important, in itself, content integration is only a first step. Culturally relevant instruction involves more than materials—it is about the way teachers engage children with them, drawing on students' experiences and using that knowledge as foundational "bridges" on which to develop sophisticated reading and writing skills and deeper understandings about content. As well as supporting students' academic success, culturally relevant instruction can help nurture a "critical consciousness" among students (Ladson-Billings 1995) and help them to develop an orientation toward engagement and action. As James Banks describes, we want children "to know, to care, and to act" (Banks and Tucker 2003, 7).

This level of culturally relevant teaching is sometimes more challenging for teachers, moving from simply using multicultural literature for inclusionary purposes to carefully crafting learning opportunities and leading students to higher level, critical conversations that help them develop new "ways of looking at the world" (Nieto 1994). When given the chance, even primary-grades students can participate thoughtfully in "real world" discussions in developmentally appropriate ways.

For example, urban children's literature can be an excellent tool for engaging students in examining issues that affect their lives, such as encounters with bigotry and discrimination (*The Candy Shop*, Wahl 2004), enduring economic challenges (*Getting' Through Thursday*, Cooper 1998), negotiating gender roles (*Allie's Basketball Dream*, Barber 1996), and experiencing loss or separation (*Bird*, Elliott 2008; *From North to South/Del Norte al Sur*, Laínez 2010). Book 3 in this series provides examples from classrooms in

TRY THIS TOMORROW:

Take a few minutes to reexamine the text set for a current or upcoming unit of study in language arts or another content area.

- How many of the current text selections will support your students in connecting their experiences and cultural knowledge to learning new content?

which teachers have used urban children's literature to engage their students in projects focused on this kind of knowledge construction and prejudice reduction.

Building a culturally relevant curriculum and engaging in teaching for social justice takes time and collaboration with colleagues. For some educators, taking on this task may seem overwhelming. An important first step to take is to revisit your curriculum with a critical eye, asking yourself, *"to whose*

Summing It Up: Transforming Your Curriculum with Urban Children's Literature

- View your curricula with a critical lens in considering to whose culture your instruction is currently oriented
- Use urban children's literature as a bridge to connect relevant examples from children's lives to new content to solidify and expand concepts
- Support mastery of learning standards by integrating culturally relevant children's literature and information texts with texts recommended in your core curriculum
- Develop multigenre text sets that incorporate high-quality urban children's literature and informational texts to support connections to content
- Recognize opportunities to explore issues that affect your students' lives and to take action to create change in your school or community

culture is it currently oriented?" Where you recognize potential mismatches in cultural relevance, work to intentionally build in more connections to your students' experiences using urban children's literature as a tool. As one teacher-colleague recommended, "start one book at a time." Chapter 10 provides a practical step-by-step guide for getting started in adding more urban children's literature to your curriculum to better capitalize on students' knowledge and create stronger links to learning new content.

CHAPTER TEN

~

Getting Started

Adding More Mirrors in the Classroom

> *"Because he looks like me."*
>
> —Amari, age eleven, on why he selected *Ron's Big Mission* from among many books being given away at an after-school literacy event

We could present ten more chapters full of research-based justifications and teaching examples to make the case for inclusion of more urban children's literature in the classroom. But Amari's reason for his text selection speaks a simple and powerful truth: children should have access to books in which they see themselves, their communities, and their worlds represented and valued.

Classroom libraries and school curricula should be filled with high-quality multicultural children's literature and informational texts of a wide variety of topics, formats, and genres. All children should have access to a wide range of texts that represent the many "windows" of the world: a diversity of characters, settings, stories, and information reflective of our broader society. But the importance of books that are mirrors cannot be overlooked.

More "mirrors" help children and their families see that school is for them, about them, and open to them. Mirrors make the curriculum more relevant to students' lives, providing a foundation for meaningful and effective instruction. Mirrors can increase student engagement and help activate

the background knowledge, linguistic awareness, and cultural understandings that can be such critical assets in the development of word recognition,
reading fluency, and comprehension skills. And mirrors can open doors to
conversations, helping teachers and students get to know each other better
and understand each other more.

This chapter provides a summary of steps that new and experienced educators can take to get started in using urban children's literature to increase
literacy and support students in making connections to content. As you work
to add more mirrors to your collection, consult each of the previous chapters
more detailed support in making the case, selecting texts, and integrating
more urban children's literature into your curricula.

You've Got the Power

Classroom teachers, librarians, and school leaders play a crucial role in ensuring that high-quality urban children's literature is included as a central
component of the curriculum in literacy instruction. Teachers can select
books for their classroom library collections and work together to identify
culturally relevant selections to supplement the curriculum. Librarians and
media specialists can bring expertise in urban children's literature to their
teaching teams and provide resources and recommendations for making the
curriculum more relevant.

School administrators can make this a priority, raising awareness among
their teaching staff about the importance of urban children's literature and
supporting teachers in making decisions about how to modify curricula to
best meet the needs of their students. Urban teacher educators can ensure
that the next generation of teacher candidates is exposed to the wealth of
urban children's literature that is available and methods for using these
resources in the classroom. Educators make decisions every day about how
to design learning experiences and explore content with students in their
classrooms. Materials matter, but it is *educators* who determine whether or
not a student connects with the curriculum we use for instruction and learning experiences we design.

Developing greater cultural competence may take intentional study,
purposeful practice, and a willingness to make mistakes. Even teachers who
share a common ethnic background, language, and locale with students may
have very different experiences and cultural knowledge in terms of socioeconomics, family structure, education, and life experience. Educators should
adopt a stance of humility in their practice, acknowledging that they may
not have all the answers and that they likely need the support of families

and other teachers to navigate these cultural complexities, making sure the curriculum is appropriately reflective of the students in the classroom.

Ten Steps for Getting Started

1. Evaluate and Supplement Your Current Collection

The first step in making your curriculum more culturally relevant is to evaluate the contents of your current collection as well as the texts typically used for instruction in your curriculum. Work with your colleagues to examine your collection from the perspective of the students in your classroom or school. Can students find themselves represented amongst the texts in the classroom library and the curriculum? Is there a strong representation of urban children's literature across formats, topics, and genres in your collection? Ask yourself the guiding questions in the textbox below to start to identify gaps in your collection or in units in your curriculum. Where might the cultural relevance of instruction be improved with the addition of urban children's literature?

Key Questions to Ask about Your Curriculum and Collection

- Does your core literacy curriculum include many literature and informational text selections in which your students can see themselves, their families, and their communities reflected and valued?
- What proportion of books in your classroom or school library include characters in urban settings that share your students' culture, language, and community context?
- Does your collection reflect your students in realistic family, community, and friendship stories, or are the majority of multicultural selections limited to the study of history, holidays, or world cultures?
- Does your collection include many informational texts in which people of color are featured as content experts and inventors, developers, and creators of new knowledge?
- Does your curriculum include many text selections that can support your students in connecting their lived experiences with language arts, mathematics, science, and social studies content?

Where you find gaps, consult the resources suggested in step 2 to help identify high-quality urban children's literature and informational texts to add to your collection or supplement your curriculum.

2. Explore Resources for High-Quality Urban Children's Literature

High-quality urban children's literature can often be difficult to find since publishers' and distributors' catalogs and websites don't consistently identify this subgenre in marketing materials or with search terms. The recommended children's literature reference list included in this book is a good place to start in identifying many titles that might be appropriate for your collection.

A number of literacy organizations and children's book publishers are working to raise awareness among educators about the depth and breadth of high-quality multicultural and urban children's literature currently available, while also working to increase representations of diversity within and across genres. Educators should take the time to locate books that are available through these sources.

Kids Like Us

Kids Like Us is a nonprofit organization dedicated to raising awareness about high-quality multicultural and urban children's literature and providing teachers with training and support for integrating cultural relevant literature into their instruction. The children's literature featured in this book can be found on the Kids Like Us website, www.kidslikeus.org, along with many other high-quality selections, teaching resources, and links to author and illustrator websites.

We understand that searching for individual titles across so many publishers' sites, using random key words to try to land on potentially culturally relevant texts, is prohibitively time consuming for teachers. The Kids Like Us website is designed to help focus your search, providing educators with a one-stop resource for locating high-quality multicultural and urban children's books and text sets aligned with common curricular themes.

Books featured on the Kids Like Us website have been reviewed according to the characteristics of quality discussed in chapters 6 and 7 of this book. While it is up to educators to determine which books might be the most appropriate additions for their curricula or most culturally relevant to their students, the Kids Like Us website is a good place to start in identifying books that have met many of the criteria for quality recommended here.

Publishers Committed to Diversity in Children's Literature

Many quality urban children's literature selections are published by the "Big 5" U.S. trade book publishers (Hatchette Book Group, HarperCollins, Macmillan, Penguin Random House, and Simon and Schuster). In general, however, multicultural and urban children's literature still represents a very small proportion of these publishers' vast inventories.

Alternatively, there are a number of smaller, independent publishers that focus specifically on producing multicultural children's literature. We strongly recommend that educators support these publishing houses that work to increase diversity in children's literature as part of their unique missions. Ordering from them directly, whenever possible, can keep more of these books available and in print. Examples of publishing houses we recommend are listed below.

- *Arte Público Press*, and its imprint for children and young adults, *Piñata Books*, is dedicated to the realistic and authentic portrayal of the themes, languages, characters, and customs of Hispanic culture in the United States. artepublicopress.com
- *Cinco Puntos Press*, with its roots on the US/Mexico border, publishes books to make a difference in the way we see the world. cincopuntos. com
- *Just Us Books* was founded in 1987 by two parents who grew tired of the lack of positive, vibrant Black-interest books available to their children. Just Us Books publishes children's books that celebrate the diversity of Black history, culture, and experience. justusbooks.com
- *Groundwood Books* is an independent children's publisher based in Toronto that is particularly committed to publishing books for and about children by people whose voices are not always heard, including writers of Latin American origin and works by the First Peoples of the Western Hemisphere. groundwoodbooks.com.
- *Lee and Low* is an independent publisher of stories that children of color can identify with and that all children can enjoy. Lee and Low has several outstanding imprints: *Children's Book Press*, literature for children by and about people from the Latino, African American, Asian/ Pacific Islander, and Native American communities; *Shen's Books*, multicultural children's literature that emphasizes cultural diversity and tolerance with a focus on introducing children to the cultures of Asia; and *Tu Books*, a one-of-a-kind imprint featuring multicultural science fiction, fantasy, and mysteries for middle-grades students and young adults. leeandlow.com

Distributors Focused on Cultural and Linguistic Diversity

In order to simplify and consolidate their purchasing power, school districts frequently look to larger distributors who supply books drawn from many different publishing houses. This is particularly true when teachers are seeking books written in languages other than English, which can still be very challenging in the United States. Below is a starting list of U.S. distributors that carry titles in a variety of world languages.

- *Del Sol Books*, includes Spanish, English, and bilingual children's books and music. delsolbooks.com
- *East West Discovery Press* is an independent publisher and distributor of multicultural and bilingual books in more than fifty languages. eastwestdiscovery.com
- *First Book* distributes new books and educational resources at drastically reduced prices to educators in schools and community organizations serving students from low-income communities through its First Book Marketplace. In recent years, First Book has intensified its commitment to increasing the range of culturally and linguistically diverse titles available in the First Book Marketplace through its Stories for All Project. fbmarketplace.org
- *Lectorum* is the largest distributor of Spanish-language books in the country. lectorum.com
- *Mantra Lingua* produces dual language and culturally specific books in more than fifty languages. mantralingua.com
- *One Moore Book* publishes and distributes culturally sensitive stories for children of countries with low literacy rates and underrepresented cultures. One Moore Book is a potentially good source for representations of children whose families have recently immigrated to the United States. onemoorebook.com
- *Santillana USA* is a division of the largest Spanish educational publisher in the world. santillanausa.com
- *Star Bright Books* publishes dual language picture books and early readers in more than twenty languages. starbrightbooks.org

Keep in mind that not all publishers' and distributors' selections have been evaluated for quality, cultural authenticity, and linguistic accuracy. As a result, the range of quality in texts supplied by a single distributor can sometimes vary greatly. It is important to consider the guidelines in chapters 6, 7, and 8 on selecting high-quality, culturally relevant texts. Also, be sure to consult book jackets, author notes, and author, illustrator, and publisher websites for information about the writers' backgrounds and any research done for the book.

Social Media, Blogs, and Websites

In addition to seeking titles through publishers and distributors, there are many excellent social media sources for learning about new releases and for perusing reviews of existing and new titles. Social media also provide a platform for a strong community of writers, illustrators, and educators advocating for more diversity in children's literature to engage in discussion and raise awareness about trends in research and publishing. For Twitter, Tumbler, and Facebook users, join the conversation at Kids Like Us (@KLUBooks), Lee and Low (@LeeandLow), We Need Diverse Books (@diversebooks), L4LL (@Latinas4LatLit), and Rich in Color (@Rich_In_Color), among many others.

Many of these handles link to websites on which to find book reviews, blogs, and other great resources related to teaching with culturally relevant texts. A number of children's book authors also have websites that provide links to a wealth of resources related to multicultural children's literature. Look for Cynthia Leitich Smith's website and Cynsations blog (cynthialeitichsmith.com), Pat Mora's Bookjoy (patmora.com), and Mitali Perkins's Fire Escape (mitaliperkins.com) for a great start.

Other excellent resources include the Brown Bookshelf (brownbookshelf.com), which features the 28 Days Later series, a Black History Month celebration of children's literature, and I'm Your Neighbor (imyourneighborbooks.org), which promotes the use of children's literature featuring "new arrival" cultures and provides lists of books including protagonists from groups that are typically underrepresented in the world of children's literature (e.g., Bangladeshi Americans, Haitian Americans, Kosovar Americans, etc.). Look for "resources" pages on these and other websites for leads on additional sources for finding high-quality multicultural and urban children's literature.

3. Consider Strength in Numbers

While all classroom collections should include a balance of texts that can serve as both "mirrors" and "windows" for students, it is important to have a significant number of urban children's books in the classroom library that might serve as potential mirrors. Because of the complexity of cultural relevance and diversity of experiences of people within cultures, educators should be careful not to assume that a particular text is representative of students. Rather than trying to identify a single text that might best match teachers' perceptions of students' identities (e.g., Dudley-Marling 2003), having access to a wealth of options opens the door for students to decide.

Having plentiful selections that represent urban diversity allows all students to read about and experience a variety of representations of children, families, settings, and languages, increasing the likelihood that they might make meaningful connections to texts and see various aspects of their lives reflected in the curriculum. This will also provide ample opportunities for students to compare and contrast themes, settings, and plots with their own experiences and identify similarities and differences between texts on a common topic or of similar types (e.g., memoirs).

4. Engage Readers in Text Selection and Review

One way to check for relevance and authenticity of urban children's literature is to ask students to determine what resonates with them and why. Making time for regular read alouds, regardless of students' ages, and engaging in rich discussions about literature can give teachers a more multifaceted view of children's identities, which characters they relate to, what experiences they identify and make connections with, and which elements of the setting or context "ring true." Students will lead the way, making connections with texts and noting where the characters or content reflect their own lives.

Opportunities for teachers to learn from their students grounds the classroom culture in a mutual learning experience for both adults and children. Like "Carter's Story" about reading the book *My Steps* in chapter 2, teachers and children learn from each other and decide together if the book is truly reflective of their experiences. This can also lead to critical discussions about potential stereotypes or misrepresentations of people in children's books and may spark ideas for student advocacy for authenticity in the depiction of urban communities in children's books and other media (e.g., writing persuasive letters to book publishers).

Including brief rating scales or child-friendly rubrics for book reviews in the classroom library is another strategy for gaining insight into how students are thinking about literacy and what topics interest them (sample review forms are available at www.kidslikeus.org). Use student reviews as discussion starters or feature them in the classroom library and solicit votes from the rest of the class to get many students reading, sharing, and defending their opinions about various texts.

Inclusion in social activities related to reading and writing, such as sharing and reviewing books, may be of particular importance for reluctant readers. When given the opportunity to offer their expertise in evaluating the authenticity of a book or to offer their critique of a book, many reluctant readers will be more enthusiastic and engaged in reading. Making the literacy experience more personally relevant and working toward collective, rather than solely individual, goals may help motivate readers to persist even when reading is challenging.

5. Take Action When Mirrors Are Missing

Teachers working in school districts facing budget cuts and other financial challenges may have limited options for purchasing supplemental texts to add to the classroom library or core curriculum. To get around this, many teachers have been successful in funding projects through organizations such as Donors Choose (www.donorschoose.org) or the Ezra Jack Keats Foundation (www.ezra-jack-keats.org). Associations like the American Library Association (www.ala.org) and the National Education Association (www.nea.org) also have a variety of grant opportunities available to teachers, librarians, and media specialists each year.

Corporate and family foundations often make literacy a priority in their missions (e.g., Target Foundation, Dollar General Literacy Foundation, Barbara Bush Foundation for Family Literacy, etc.). Oftentimes corporate foundations prioritize efforts in the geographic regions surrounding their corporate headquarters, so look first to grant opportunities that may be available through companies operating in your city.

Consider collaborating with colleagues to develop a grant proposal that will help fund a grade-level project or school-wide initiative around culturally relevant teaching that can include funds for purchasing urban children's literature for your collection. Use the research reviewed in the early chapters of this book to strengthen your proposal.

> "If you can't find something you're looking for in a book, write it yourself
> . . . You have stories that other kids might need to read.
> You have stories that should be heard."
>
> —Walter Dean Myers (2012)

Even with the availability of some discretionary funds, teachers may sometimes struggle to identify many selections that provide truly authentic "mirrors" for all of the students in their classroom due to limitations in the availability and diversity of urban children's literature as described in chapter

5. When teachers find this is the case, another option is to make books yourselves.

Providing space and time for students to create their own books, telling their own family, friendship, and neighborhood stories, writing about topics of interest on which they are "experts," or interviewing family or residents of the community for a class magazine can help to dramatically increase the cultural relevance of your collection. These can become instant additions to the classroom library that can be reread and shared with others, and will likely have a dramatic impact on student engagement and reading frequency.

6. Integrate Urban Children's Literature into Your Core Curriculum

Intentionally integrating urban children's literature with each unit of study can help engage students in learning and make the curriculum more relevant while maintaining consistency with the learning objectives set forth in the core curricula. Teachers should review units in their published curricula and consider the extent to which the recommended text selections provide op-portunities for students to connect their experiences with content.

Refer to examples provided in chapters 3 and 9, and consider opportuni-ties to supplement or swap-in urban literature and informational texts that may be more culturally relevant for students in your classroom. For example, books like *The Rain Stomper* (Boswell 2008) and *Redwoods* (Chin 2009) make for great additions to units related to nature, while *Destiny's Gift* (Tarpley 2002), ¡*Si, Se Puede!/Yes, We Can! Janitor Strike in L.A.* (Cohn 2005), or *Farmer Will Allen and the Growing Table* (Martin 2013) can tie nicely to a study of community and citizenship.

Begin the unit with text selections that may best resonate with your stu-dents, providing the groundwork for meaningful and effective instruction that allows students to use their experiences, their language, and their cul-tural understandings about the world as a foundation for literacy learning and a springboard for learning new content. Then add in curriculum-required texts, engaging students in intentional discussions and comparisons that con-nect and integrate content from both sets of text. During the course of the unit, teachers should make these culturally relevant text selections available to students in the classroom library, referring to them regularly throughout the unit and displaying covers facing outward to showcase their centrality to the unit of study.

7. Use Urban Children's Literature in Teaching for Social Justice

Achieving a real curriculum transformation requires not just the availability of materials, but purposeful and intentional planning in how they are used.

Instruction should go beyond the sharing of individual books, extending learning opportunities through integrated units and inquiry projects like those described in chapter 9. Moreover, effective teaching for social justice requires that teachers move beyond content integration, engaging students in projects that encourage prejudice reduction and result in student empowerment toward action (Banks 2007).

Even young children can participate in action-oriented projects that engage them in thinking critically about issues that impact their lives. For example, in inquiry projects like the "Me and My Community" project described in chapter 8, students' exploration and discussion of "What Makes a Community?" resulted in a "school clean-up day" and an outreach effort to connect with members of their community, including delivering beautiful spring plantings to their elderly neighbors.

Similarly, the poetry unit described in chapter 9 culminated in students hosting a Poetry Jam that was open to the community. Through their public performances, students were able to demonstrate what they had learned about the genre as well as create a forum through which their original poetry and young voices could be heard. When students are engaged in co-constructing learning opportunities such as these and are invited to incorporate their firsthand knowledge and experiences as resources in the process, the possibilities for engagement and depth of learning are endless.

8. Don't Shy Away from Books with Strong Themes

When reviewing urban children's literature, teachers sometimes express concerns about some books that take on what they perceive as difficult subject matter, such as economic challenges, homelessness or housing insecurity, or separation due to deportation or incarceration. While it is understandable that this content might raise some red flags for teachers of young children, the fact is that these issues are present in the day-to-day realities of many of our students. As discussed in chapter 2, when learning is connected with students' lives and they are invited to bring their "whole selves" to school, there is a strong positive effect on motivation and students' sense of themselves as learners. In addition, urban children's literature can often be an effective tool for helping children work through their thoughts about challenging situations through the safe distance of a character's experiences.

Some teachers express reluctance in allowing children to share too much personal information in the classroom because it may lead to conversations that are too unpredictable. Having the courage to take this leap of faith can often lead to rich discussions and authentic opportunities for instruction. Being confident about having these conversations in many ways depends on the

> "I should never assume what children can or can't handle."
>
> —Michelle Martin (2004, 149), after witnessing kindergarteners' understanding and engagement while reading *Martin's Big Words*

quality of relationships and sense of community teachers have established in the classroom. Getting to know students and building strong, trusting, positive relationships with learners and their families is key.

When teachers have questions about potentially using texts with serious themes, we recommend consulting with colleagues and seeking advice from family members about when and how they might best be shared (e.g., whole group, small group, with individual students, with a caregiver). Try not to dismiss books out of hand just because they contain content that might strike you as "challenging." Like Lauren's experience with sharing *Something Beautiful* in chapter 8, you may just find that they can help open the door to a whole new kind of learning experience for you and your students.

9. Find Your Voice as an Advocate for Equity

In our experience, once educators become aware of the availability of high-quality urban children's literature and its potential as a tool for increasing literacy and supporting content learning, they are eager to begin to integrate new titles into their instruction. Occasionally, though, teachers may face resistance from colleagues or administrators when proposing changes to the curriculum or when making recommendations of texts that represent cultural, socioeconomic, and linguistic diversity.

> *"Equity is hearing someone's voice about what they need and providing them with that."*
>
> —Christopher Emdin (2012)

Culturally competent teachers understand that making cultural connections between home and school can significantly improve the quality and effectiveness of children's learning experiences. If you encounter push-back from colleagues who may not be comfortable with this, use the early chapters of this book to help "make the case" for inclusion of more urban children's literature in the classroom. Backing your reasoning with some of the research may help colleagues understand how urban children's literature can promote students' academic self-concept, increase literacy learning, and help expand vocabulary and support language development.

Don't go it alone; connect with like-minded colleagues invested in increasing cultural relevance in your curriculum, and work together to make it happen. Above all, be persistent, keep your students' learning at the forefront, and give them what they need.

10. Enjoy the Exploration

This book, along with the Kids Like Us website, is designed to showcase the wealth of high-quality urban children's literature available to you and your students right now. These beautiful stories and remarkable informational texts can help build bridges between urban students' experiences and the world of the classroom.

The interest that is generated when teachers and students get their hands on these books is palpable. Give some of these books a try, and see how urban children's literature can change the dynamic in your classroom. Notice the changes in your students' participation and productivity in literature discussions, look for differences in students' intrinsic motivation for reading and writing, and listen for applications of sophisticated comprehension strategies as students draw on their experiences in making inferences about characters' actions or making connections to content.

In addition, use your expertise and creativity to engage students in multidisciplinary inquiry projects that draw on text sets infused with urban children's literature. Use collections of texts in author and illustrator studies to help students envision themselves as writers and artists with stories to tell. Connect with authors and illustrators through their websites or with school-based or virtual visits; it can be incredibly powerful for students to meet the real people who have written "their" stories. Use urban children's literature to connect with families and help them feel welcomed and valued in your school community. The possibilities are endless. Most of all, take time to explore and enjoy these books, and savor these experiences with your students.

Summing It Up

There is sufficient evidence that urban children's literature holds great potential for increasing student interest and engagement and supporting students' acquisition and development of reading and writing skills. The cultural relevance of a text influences what students attend to when they read, how much they comprehend, and what knowledge and skills they retain. A significant representation from this urban subgenre can be especially powerful for helping urban public school students and their families feel included in the life of the classroom and may serve as a critical catalyst for reading and writing development. The role that culturally relevant text selection can play in reducing cognitive overload during strategy instruction may be particularly important for beginning readers, struggling readers, and children learning to read and write in a new language.

We hope that this book helps educators make the case for a critical examination of the texts used for reading and writing instruction in urban schools, and that it leads to more intentional text selection to support children in better utilizing their cultural and linguistic assets as tools in literacy learning. We also hope it can serve as a resource to teachers everywhere for considering the role that culturally relevant texts play in reading and writing development for children in any setting. We can do this. Let's get more mirrors in the classroom.

Reference List of Recommended Children's Literature

Abdul-Jabbar, Kareem, and Raymond Obstfeld. 2012. *What Color Is My World: The Lost History of African American Inventors.* Illus. Ben Boos and A. G. Ford. Somerville: Candlewick Press.

Adedjouma, Davida. 1996. *The Palm of My Heart: Poetry by African American Children.* Illus. R. Gregory Christie. New York: Lee and Low Books.

Ancona, George. 2000. *Barrio: Jose's Neighborhood.* San Diego: Harcourt Paperbacks.

Ancona, George, F. Isabel Campoy, and Alma Flor Ada. 2004. *Mi Barrio/My Neighborhood.* New York: Children's Press.

———. 2005. *Mis Amigos/My Friends.* New York: Children's Press.

Anzaldúa, Gloria. 1993. *Friends from the Other Side/Amigos del otro lado.* Illus. Consuelo Méndez. San Francisco: Children's Book Press.

Argueta, Jorge. 2007. *A Movie in My Pillow/Una pelicula en mi almohada.* Illus. Elizabeth Gomez. San Francisco: Children's Book Press.

———. 2008. *Xóchitl and the Flowers/Xóchitl, la Niña de las flores.* Illus. Carl Angel. New York: Children's Book Press.

———. 2013. *Moony Luna/Luna, Lunita, Lunera.* New York: Children's Book Press.

Ashman, Linda. 2013. *Rain!* Illus. Christian Robinson. New York: HMH Books for Young Readers.

Bahk, Jane. 2015. *Juna's Jar.* Illus. Felicia Hoshino. New York: Lee & Row Books.

Banks, Kate. 2000. *The Night Worker.* Illus. Georg Hallensleben. New York: Farrar, Straus and Giroux.

Barnett, Marc. 2010. *Oh No! Or How My Science Project Destroyed the World.* Illus. Dan Santat. New York: Disney-Hyperion.

Bash, Barbara. 1990. *Urban Roosts: Where Birds Nest in the City.* New York: Little, Brown and Company.

Beaty, Daniel. 2013. *Knock Knock: My Dad's Dream for Me*. Illus. Bryan Collier. New York: Little, Brown and Company.

Bloom, Suzanne. 2001. *The Bus for Us*. Honesdale, PA: Boyds Mills Press.

Boswell, Addie K. 2008. *The Rain Stomper*. Illus. Eric Velasquez. New York: Marshall Cavendish Children.

Brooks, Gwendolyn. 2006. *Bronzeville Boys and Girls*. Illus. Faith Ringgold. Amistad.

Brown, Monica. 2007. *Butterflies on Carmen Street/Mariposas en la calle Carmen*. Illus. April Ward. Houston, TX: Piñata Books.

———. 2009. *Side by Side/Lado a Lado*. Illus. Joe Cepeda. New York: HarperCollins.

———. 2011. *Marisol McDonald Doesn't Match/Marisol McDonald no combina*. Illus. Sara Palacios. New York: Children's Book Press.

———. 2013. *Marisol McDonald and the Clash Bash/Marisol McDonald y la fiesta sin igual*. Illus. Sara Palacios. New York: Children's Book Press.

Budhos, Marina. 2006. *Ask Me No Questions*. New York: Simon and Schuster.

Chin, Jason. 2009. *Redwoods*. New York: Flashpoint.

Chinn, Karen. 1997. *Sam and the Lucky Money*. Illus. Cornelius Van Wright and Ying-Hwa Hu. New York: Lee and Low Books.

Chocolate, Debbi. 2009. *El Barrio*. Illus. David Diaz. New York: Henry Holt and Company.

Cisneros, Sandra. 1991. *The House on Mango Street*. New York: Vintage.

———. 1997. *Hairs/Pelitos*. Dragonfly Books.

Cohn, Diana. 2005. *¡Si, Se Puede!/Yes, We Can! Janitor Strike In L.A.* Illus. Francisco Delgado. El Paso, TX: Cinco Puntos Press.

Collier, Bryan. 2000. *Uptown*. New York: Henry Holt.

Cooper, Melrose. 1998. *Gettin' Through Thursday*. Illus. Nneka Bennett. New York: Lee and Low Books.

Cotten, Cynthia. 2008. *Rain Play*. Illus. Javaka Steptoe. New York: Henry Holt.

Crews, Donald. 1985. *Bicycle Race*. New York: Greenwillow Books.

———. 1987. *Harbor*. New York: Greenwillow Books.

———. 1989. *Flying*. New York: Greenwillow Books.

———. 1996. *Freight Train*. New York: Greenwillow Books.

———. 1993. *School Bus*. New York: Greenwillow Books.

———. 1991. *Truck*. New York: Greenwillow Books.

Crews, Nina. 1995. *One Hot Summer Day*. New York: Greenwillow Books.

———. 2004. *The Neighborhood Mother Goose*. New York: Greenwillow Books.

———. 2009. *The Neighborhood Sing Along*. New York: Greenwillow Books.

———. 2011. *Jack and the Beanstalk*. New York: Henry Holt.

Cumpiano, Ina. 2005. *Quinito's Neighborhood*. Illus. José Ramírez. San Francisco: Children's Book Press.

———. 2008. *Quinito, Day and Night*. Illus. José Ramírez. San Francisco: Children's Book Press.

de la Peña, Matt. 2015. *Last Stop on Market Street*. Illus. Christian Robinson. New York: G. P. Putnam's Sons.

Derby, Sally. 1999. *My Steps*. Illus. Adjoa J. Burrowes New York: Lee and Low Books.

Downer, Ann. 2013. *Wild Animal Neighbors: Sharing Our Urban World*. Minneapolis: Twenty-First Century Books.

Dugan, Joanne. 2007. *123 NYC: A Counting Book of New York City*. New York: Abrams.

English, Karen. 2007. *Nikki and Deja*. Illus. Laura Freeman. New York: Clarion Books.

———. 2013. *Dog Days: The Carver Chronicles, Book 1*. Illus. Laura Freeman. New York: Clarion Books.

Elliott, Zetta. 2008. *Bird*. Illus. Shadra Strickland. New York: Lee and Low Books.

———. 2012. *Ship of Souls*. Las Vegas: Skyscape.

Elya, Susan Middleton. 2006. *Bebé Goes Shopping*. Illus. Steven Salerno. Orlando: Harcourt.

———. 2012. *Fire!¡Fuego! Brave Bomberos*. Illus. Dan Santat. New York: Bloomsbury.

Farris, Christine King. 2008. *March On! The Day My Brother Martin Changed the World*. Illus. London Ladd. New York: Scholastic.

Flake, Sharon. 2007. *The Broken Bike Boy and the Queen of 33rd Street*. Illus. Colin Bootman. New York: Jump at the Sun.

———. 2010. *You Don't Even Know Me*. New York: Disney Jump.

———. 2012. *Pinned*. New York: Scholastic.

Forman, Ruth. 2007. *Young Cornrows Callin Out the Moon*. Illus. Cbabi Bayoc. New York: Children's Book Press.

Frame, Jeron Ashford. 2008. *Yesterday I Had the Blues*. Illus. R. Gregory Christie. Berkley, CA: Tricycle Press.

Garza, Carmen Lomas. 2000. *In My Family/En mi familia*. New York: Children's Book Press.

Giovanni, Nikki. 2010. *The 100 Best African American Poems*. Naperville, IL: Sourcebooks MediaFusion.

González, Lucía. 2008. *The Storyteller's Candle/La velita de los cuentos*. Illus. Lula Delacre. New York: Lee and Low Books.

González, Rigoberto. 2005. *Antonio's Card/La Tarjeta de Antonio*. Illus. Cecilia Álvarez. New York: Children's Book Press.

Greenfield, Eloise. 1974. *She Come Bringing Me That Little Baby Girl*. Illus. John Steptoe. New York: HarperCollins Press.

Grimes, Nikki. 1994. *Meet Danitra Brown*. Illus. Floyd Cooper. New York: Lothrop, Lee and Shepard.

———. 1999. *My Man Blue*. Illus. Jerome Lagarrigue. New York: Dial Books for Young Readers.

———. 2005. *Danitra Brown, Class Clown*. Illus. E. B. Lewis. New York: HarperCollins Press.

———. 2006. *Thanks a Million*. Illus. Cozbi A. Cabrera. New York: Amistad.

———. 2010. *Make Way for Dyamonde Daniel*. New York: Puffin.

———. 2013. *Words with Wings*. Honesdale, PA: WordSong.

Gunning, Monica. 2004. *America, My New Home*. Illus. Ken Condon. Honesdale, PA: WordSong.

———. *A Shelter in Our Car*. Illus. Elaine Pedlar. San Francisco: Children's Book Press.

Hale, Christy. 2012. *Dreaming Up: A Celebration of Building*. New York: Lee and Low Books.

Haskins, Jim, and Kathleen Benson. 2011. *John Lewis in the Lead*. Illus. Benny Andrews. New York: Lee and Low Books.

Heo, Yumi. 1994. *One Afternoon*. London: Orchard Books.

Herrera, Juan Felipe. 2006. *The Upside Down Boy/El niño de cabeza*. Illus. Elizabeth Gómez. New York: Lee and Low Books.

Hesse, Karen. 1999. *Come on Rain*. Illus. Jon J. Muth. New York: Scholastic.

Hill, Isabel. 2009. *Urban Animals*. Long Island City: Star Bright Books.

Hill, Laban Carrick. 2013. *When the Beat Was Born: DJ Kool Herc and the Creation of Hip Hop*. Illus. Theodore Taylor. Roaring Brook Press.

Iyengar, Malathi Michelle. 2009. *Tan to Tamarind: Poems about the Color Brown*. Illus. Jamel Akib. New York: Children's Book Press.

Jiménez, Francisco. 1997. *The Circuit: Stories from the Life of a Migrant Child*. New York: Houghton Mifflin.

Johnson, Angela. 1992. *The Leaving Morning*. Illus. David Soman. New York: Orchard Books.

———. 1995. *One of Three*. Illus. David Soman. New York: Orchard Books.

———. 2007. *A Sweet Smell of Roses*. Illus. Eric Velasquez. New York: Simon and Schuster Children's Publishing.

Johnston, Tony. 2003. *Any Small Goodness*. New York: Scholastic.

———. 2003. *Uncle Rain Cloud*. Illus. Fabricio Vanden Broeck. Watertown, MA: Charlesbridge.

———. 2009. *My Abuelita*. Illus. Yuyi Morales. Orlando: Houghton Mifflin.

Joosse, Barbara. 2001. *Stars in the Darkness*. Illus. R. Gregory Christie. San Francisco: Chronicle Books.

———. 2004. *Hot City*. Illus. R. Gregory Christie. New York: Philomel.

Jules, Jacqueline. 2013. *Freddie Ramos Takes Off (Zapato Power)*. Illus. Miguel Benítez. New York: Albert Whitman and Company.

Keats, Ezra Jack. 1960. *My Dog Is Lost!* New York: Viking.

———. 1964. *Whistle for Willie*. New York: Viking.

———. 1972. *Pet Show!* New York: Viking.

———. 1976. *The Snowy Day*. New York: Viking Press.

———. 1998. *A Letter to Amy*. New York: Puffin.

———. 1998. *Goggles*. New York: Puffin.

———. 1998. *Peter's Chair*. New York: Puffin.

———. 1999. *Apt. 3*. New York: Puffin.

———. 2001. *Louie's Search*. New York: Puffin.

Khan, Rukhsana. 2010. *Big Red Lollipop*. Illus. Sophie Blackall. New York: Viking Juvenile.

Kittinger, Jo S. 2010. *Rosa's Bus: The Ride to Civil Rights*. Illus. Steven Walker. Honesdale: Boyds Mills Press.

Krull, Kathleen. 2003. *Harvesting Hope: The Story of Cesar Chavez*. Illus. Yuyi Morales. Boston: Harcourt.

Laínez, René Colato. 2010. *From North to South*. Illus. Joe Cepeda. San Francisco: Children's Book Press.

Levine, Ellen. 2007. *Henry's Freedom Box: A True Story from the Underground Railroad*. Illus. Kadir Nelson. New York: Scholastic.

Liao, Jimmy. 2006. *The Sound of Colors: A Journey of the Imagination*. New York: Little, Brown and Company.

Look, Lenore. 2001. *Henry's First Moon Birthday*. New York: Atheneum Books for Yound Readers.

Lopez, Loretta. 1997. *The Birthday Swap*. New York: Lee and Low Books.

Low, William. 1997. *Chinatown*. New York: Henry Holt.

———. 2012. *Machines Go to Work in the City*. New York: Henry Holt.

Mak, Kam. 2001. *My Chinatown: A Year in Poems*. New York: HarperCollins.

Manning, Maurie J. 2008. *Kitchen Dance*. New York: Clarion Books.

Martin, Jacqueline Briggs. 2013. *Farmer Will Allen and the Growing Table*. Illus. Eric Larkin. Bellevue, WA: Readers to Eaters.

Mathis, Sharon Bell. 1971. *Sidewalk Story*. New York: Penguin.

———. 2001. *Ray Charles*. New York: Lee and Low Books.

McKissack, Patricia. 2006. *Abby Takes a Stand*. Illus. Gordon James. New York: Puffin.

———. 2008. *A Song for Harlem*. Illus. Gordon James. New York: Puffin.

Mead, Alice. 1995. *Junebug*. New York: Farrar, Straus and Giroux.

———. 2002. *Junebug in Trouble*. New York: Farrar, Straus and Giroux.

Medina, Meg. 2011. *Tía Isa Wants a Car*. Illus. Claudio Muñoz. Somerville, MA: Candlewick Press.

———. 2013. *Yaqui Delgado Wants to Kick Your Ass*. Somerville, MA: Candlewick Press.

———. 2015. *Mango, Abuela, and Me*. Somerville, MA: Candlewick Press.

Medina, Tony. 2001. *Deshawn Days*. Illus. R. Gregory Christie. New York: Lee and Low Books.

Michelson, Richard. 2006. *Across the Alley*. Illus. E. B. Lewis. New York: G. P. Putnam's Sons.

Milich, Zoran. 2003. *The City ABC Book*. Toronto: Kids Can Press.

Montes, Marisa. 2003. *Get Ready for Gabí: A Crazy Mixed-Up Spanglish Day*. Illus. Joe Cepeda. New York: Scholastic.

Mora, Pat. 2001. *The Bakery Lady/La Señora de la Panadería*. Illus. Pablo Torrecilla. Houston, TX: Piñata Books.

———. 2001. *Love to Mamá: A Tribute to Mothers*. Illus. Paula Barragán. New York: Lee and Low Books.

———. 2005. *Gracias Thanks*. New York: Lee and Low Books.

———. 2008. *Join Hands!* Illus. George Ancona. Watertown, MA: Charlesbridge.

Morales, Yuyi. 2013. *Niño Wrestles the World.* New York: Roaring Brook Press.

Myers, Christopher. 1999. *Black Cat.* New York: Scholastic.

———. 2000. *Wings.* New York: Scholastic.

———. 2001. *Fly.* New York: Jump at the Sun.

———. 2012. *H.O.R.S.E.: A Game of Basketball and Imagination.* New York: Egmont USA.

Myers, Walter Dean. 1997. *Harlem.* Illus. Christopher Myers. New York: Scholastic.

———. 2003. *Malcolm X: A Fire Burning Brightly.* Illus. Leonard Jenkins. New York: Amistad.

———. 2009. *Looking Like Me.* Illus. Christopher Myers. New York: Egmont USA.

———. 2010. *The Cruisers.* New York: Scholastic.

———. 2012. *Just Write: Here's How.* New York: HarperTeen.

Nelson, Kadir. 2011. *Heart and Soul: The Story of America and African Americans.* New York: Balzer and Bray.

Neri, G. 2007. *Chess Rumble.* Illus. Jesse Joshua Watson. New York: Lee and Low Books.

———. 2013. *Ghetto Cowboy.* Illus. Jesse Joshua Watson. New York: Candlewick.

Niemann, Christoph. 2010. *Subway.* New York: HarperCollins.

Nikola-Lisa, W. 2009. *How We Are Smart.* Illus. Sean Qualls. New York: Lee and Low Books.

Nolen, Jerdine. 2002. *Raising Dragons.* Illus. Elise Primavera. Orlando: Harcourt Books.

Norman, Lissette. 2006. *My Feet Are Laughing.* Illus. Frank Morrison. New York: Farrar, Straus and Giroux.

Nye, Naomi Shihab. 1997. *Sitti's Secrets.* Illus. Nancy Carpenter. New York: Simon and Schuster.

O'Neill, Alexis. 2007. *Estela's Swap.* Illus. Enrique O. Sanchez. New York: Lee and Low Books.

Park, Frances, and Ginger Park. 2008. *The Have a Good Day Café.* Illus. Katherine Potter. New York: Lee and Low Books.

Paschen, Elise, and Dominique Raccah. 2010. *Poetry Speaks Who I Am.* Naperville, IL: Sourcebooks Jabberwocky.

Pérez, Amada Irma. 2007. *Nana's Big Surprise/Nana, ¡Qué Sorpresa!* Illus. Maya Christina Gonzalez. New York: Children's Book Press.

———. 2008. *My Very Own Room/Mi Propio Cuartito.* Illus. Maya Christina Gonzalez. New York: Lee and Low Books.

———. 2009. *My Diary from Here to There/Mi diario de aqui hasta allá.* Illus. Maya Christina Gonzalez. New York: Children's Book Press.

Pinkney, Andrea Davis. 2010. *Sit-In: How Four Friends Stood Up by Sitting Down.* Illus. Brian Pinkney. New York: Little, Brown Books for Young Readers.

Pockell, Leslie. 2009. *100 Essential American Poems.* New York: Thomas Dunne Books.

Polacco, Patricia. 1994. *Pink and Say*. New York: Philomel.

———. 2001. *The Keeping Quilt*. New York: Simon and Schuster.

Ramsey, Calvin Alexander, and Gwen Strauss. 2013. *Ruth and the Green Book*. Illus. Floyd Cooper. New York: Scholastic.

Read, Nicholas. 2012. *City Critters: Wildlife in the Urban Jungle*. Custer, Washington: Orca Book Publishing.

Ringgold, Faith. 1991. *Tar Beach*. New York: Dragonfly Books.

———. 2002. *Cassie's Word Quilt*. New York: Dragonfly Books.

Roberts, Brenda C. 2004. *Jazzy Miz Mozetta*. Illus. Frank Morrison. New York: Farrar, Straus and Giroux.

Robles, Anthony D. 2006. *Lakas and the Makibaka Hotel*. Illus. Carl Angel. San Francisco: Children's Book Press.

Rodman, Mary Ann. 2007. *My Best Friend*. Illus. E. B. Lewis. New York: Puffin.

Schofield-Morrison, Connie. 2014. *I Got the Rhythm*. Illus. Frank Morrison. New York: Bloomsbury, USA.

Schroeder, Alan. 2012. *Baby Flo: Florence Mills Lights Up the Stage*. Illus. Cornelius Van Wright and Ying-Hwa Hu. New York: Lee and Low Books.

Schulman, Janet. 2008. *Pale Male: Citizen Hawk of New York City*. Illus. Meilo So. New York: Knopf Books for Young Readers.

Shannon, George. 2015. *One Family*. Illus. Blanca Gomez. New York: Farrar, Straus and Giroux.

Shin, Sun Yung. 2004. *Cooper's Lesson*. Illus. Kim Cogan. San Francisco: Children's Book Press.

Siegel, Siena Cherson. 2006. *To Dance: A Ballerina's Graphic Novel*. Illus. Mark Siegel. New York: Antheneum Books for Young Readers.

Sís, Peter. 2000. *Madlenka*. New York: Farrar, Straus and Giroux.

———. 2010. *Madlenka Soccer Star*. New York: Farrar, Straus and Giroux.

———. 2010. *The Wall*. New York: Farrar, Straus and Giroux.

Smith, Cynthia Leitich. 2002. *Indian Shoes*. New York: HarperCollins.

Smith, Hope Anita. 2003. *The Way a Door Closes*. Illus. Shane W. Evans. New York: Henry Holt.

———. 2008. *Keeping the Night Watch*. Illus. E. B. Lewis. New York: Henry Holt.

Smothers, Ethel F. 2003. *The Hard-Times Jar*. Illus. John Holyfield. New York: Farrar, Straus, and Giroux.

Soto, Gary. 1991. *Taking Sides*. Orlando: Harcourt.

———. 2005. *Neighborhood Odes*. Illus. David Diaz. Orlando: HMH Books for Young Readers.

Spinelli, Eileen. 2000. *Night Shift Daddy*. Illus. Melissa Iwai. New York: Hyperion Books.

Stead, Rebecca. 2009. *When You Reach Me*. New York: Yearling.

Steptoe, Javaka. 1997. *In Daddy's Arms I Am Tall*. New York: Lee and Low Books.

———. 2003. *The Jones Family Express*. New York: Lee and Low Books.

———. 2004. *Hot Day on Abbott Avenue*. New York: Clarion Books.

Steptoe, John. 1971. *Train Ride*. New York: HarperCollins.
———. 1986. *Stevie*. New York: HarperCollins.
———. 2003. *Creativity*. Illus. E. B. Lewis. Boston: HMH Books for Young Readers.
Suen, Anastasia. 2008. *Subway*. Illus. Karen Katz. New York: Viking.
Taback, Simms. 2009. *City Animals*. Maplewood: Blue Apple Books.
Tarpley, Natasha. 2002. *Bippity Bop Barbershop*. Illus. E. B. Lewis. New York: Little, Brown and Company.
———. 2004. *Destiny's Gift*. Illus. Adjoa J. Burrowes. New York: Lee and Low Books.
Taylor, Debbie. 2004. *Sweet Music in Harlem*. Illus. Frank Morrison. New York: Lee and Low Books.
Teachers and Writers Collaborative. 2012. *A Poem as Big as New York City: Little Kids Write about the Big Apple*. Illus. Masha D'yans. New York: Universe Publishing.
Thong, Roseanne. 2000. *Round Is a Mooncake: A Book of Shapes*. Illus. Grace Lin. San Francisco: Chronicle Books.
———. 2007. *Gai See: What You Can See in Chinatown*. Illus. Yangsook Choi. New York: Abrams.
———. 2013. *Round Is a Tortilla: A Book of Shapes*. Illus. John Parra. San Francisco: Chronicle Books.
Tonatiuh, Duncan. 2010. *Dear Primo: A Letter to My Cousin*. New York: Abrams.
Torres, Leyla. 1997. *Subway Sparrow*. New York: Square Fish Publishing.
Uchida, Yoshiko. 1995. *The Invisible Thread*. New York: Beech Tree Books.
———. 2005. *Journey to Topaz*. Berkeley, CA: Heyday Books.
Uegaki, Chieri. 2005. *Suki's Kimono*. Illus. Stephanie Jorisch. Toronto: Kids Can Press.
Velasquez, Eric. 2001. *Grandma's Records*. New York: Walker and Company.
———. 2010. *Grandma's Gift*. Walker and Company.
Wahl, Jan. 2004. *Candy Shop*. Illus. Nicole Wong. Watertown, MA: Charlesbridge.
Wakim Dennis, Yvonne, and Arlene B. Hirschfelder. 2003. *Children of Native America Today*. Watertown, MA: Charlesbridge.
Weatherford, Carole Boston. 2006. *Sidewalk Chalk*. Illus. Dimitrea Tokunbo. Word-Song.
———. 2014. *Sugar Hill: Harlem's Historic Neighborhood*. Illus. R. Gregory Christie. Park Ridge, IL: Albert Whitman Company.
Weill, Cynthia. 2009. *Opuestos: Mexican Folk Art Opposites in English and Spanish*. Illus. Martin Santiago and Quirino Santiago. El Paso, TX: Cinco Puntos Press.
Williams-Garcia, Rita. 2010. *One Crazy Summer*. New York: HarperCollins.
———. 2013. *P.S. Be Eleven*. New York: HarperCollins.
Willems, Mo. 2003. *Don't Let the Pigeon Drive the Bus!* New York: Hyperion Books for Children.
———. 2004. *Knuffle Bunny: A Cautionary Tale*. New York: Hyperion Books.
Winter, Jonah. 2009. *Sonia Sotomayor: A Judge Grows in the Bronx /La juez que crecio en el Bronx*. Illus. Edel Rodriguez. New York: Atheneum Books for Young Readers.
Witte, Anna. 2011. *Lola's Fandango*. Illus. Micha Archer. Cambridge, MA Barefoot Books.

Wolf, Bernard. 2003. *Coming to America: A Muslim Family's Story*. New York: Lee and Low Books.

Wong, Janet S. 2006. *Apple Pie 4th of July*. Illus. Margaret Chodos-Irvine. Boston: HMH Books for Young Readers.

———. 2006. *Minn and Jake's Almost Terrible Summer*. Illus. Genevieve Cote. New York: Farrar, Straus and Giroux.

Woodson, Jacqueline. 1997. *We Had a Picnic This Sunday Past*. Illus. Diane Greenseid. New York: Hyperion Books for Children.

———. 2001. *The Other Side*. Illus. E. B. Lewis. New York: Putnam.

———. 2002. *Last Summer with Maizon*. New York: Puffin.

———. 2002. *Visiting Day*. Illus. James Ransome. New York: Scholastic.

———. 2003. *If You Come Softly*. New York: Penguin.

———. 2013. *This Is the Rope*. Illus. James Ransome. New York: Nancy Paulsen Books.

Wyeth, Sharon D. 2002. *Something Beautiful*. Illus. Chris K. Soentpiet. New York: Dragonfly Books.

Yee, Lisa. 2010. *Bobby vs. Girls (Accidentally)*. New York: Scholastic.

———. 2012. *Bobby the Brave (Sometimes)*. New York: Scholastic.

Yep, Laurence. 2000. *The Magic Paintbrush*. Illus. Suling Wang. New York: HarperCollins.

Yezerski, Thomas F. 2011. *Meadowlands: A Wetlands Survival Story*. New York: Farrar, Straus and Giroux.

Yoo, Paula. 2010. *Sixteen Years in Sixteen Seconds: The Sammy Lee Story*. Illus. Dom Lee. New York: Lee and Low Books.

Zia, F. 2011. *Hot, Hot Roti for Dada-ji*. Illus. Ken Min. New York: Lee and Low Books.

References

Abdul-Jabbar, Kareem, and Raymond Obstfeld. 2012. *What Color Is My World: The Lost History of African American Inventors*. Illus. Ben Boos and A.G. Ford. Somerville: Candlewick Press.

Adams, Beverly, Laura Bell, and Charles Perfetti. 1995. "A Trading Relationship Between Reading Skill and Domain Knowledge in Children's Text Comprehension." *Discourse Processes* 20 (3): 307–23.

Adedjouma, Davida. 1996. *The Palm of My Heart: Poetry by African American Children*. Illus. and R. Gregory Christie. New York: Lee and Low Books.

Agosto, Denise E. 2007. "Building a Multicultural School Library: Issues and Challenges." *Teacher Librarian* 34 (3): 27–31.

Ahn, Hey Jun. 2005. "Child Care Teachers' Strategies in Children's Socialization of Emotion." *Early Child Development and Care* 175 (1): 49–61.

Ainsworth, Shaaron E., Peter A. Bibby, and David J. Wood. 2002. "Examining the Effects of Different Multiple Representational Systems in Learning Primary Mathematics." *Journal of the Learning Sciences* 11 (1): 25–62.

Akil, Mara Brock. 2013. "Black Girls Rock: Mara Brock Is a Shot Caller." BET Black Girls Rock. http://www.bet.com/video/blackgirlsrock/2013/acceptance-speeches/shot-caller-mara-brock-akil.html.

Alalou, Elizabeth, and Ali Alalou. 2008. *The Butter Man*. Illus. Julie Klear Essakalli. Charlesbridge Publishing.

Alanis, Illiana. 2007. "Developing Literacy through Culturally Relevant Texts." *Social Studies and the Young Learner* 20 (1): 29–32.

Al-Hazza, Tami Craft. 2010. "Motivating Disengaged Readers Through Multicultural Children's Literature." *New England Reading Association Journal* 45 (2): 63.

Altieri, Jennifer L. 1993. "African-American Stories and Literary Responses: Does a Child's Ethnicity Affect the Focus of a Response?" *Reading Horizons* 33 (3): 236–44.

Amanti, Cathy. 2005. "Beyond the Beads and Feathers Approach." In *Funds of Knowledge: Theorizing Practices in Households, Communities, and Classrooms*, edited by Norma González, Luis C. Moll, and Cathy Amanti, 131–41. Mahwah, NJ: Erlbaum.

Ancona, George. 2000. *Barrio: Jose's Neighborhood*. San Diego: Harcourt Paperbacks.

Ancona, George, F. Isabel Campoy, and Alam Flor Ada. 2004. *Mi Barrio/My Neighborhood*. New York: Children's Press.

———. 2005. *Mis Amigos/My Friends*. New York: Children's Press.

Anderson, Elaine S. 1986. "The Acquisition of Register Variation by Anglo American Children." In *Language Socialization Across Cultures*, edited by Bambi B. Schieffelin and Elinor Ochs, 153–64. New York: Cambridge University Press.

Anderson, Laurie H. 2010. *Chains (Seeds of America)*. New York: Atheneum Books for Young Readers.

Anderson, Neil J. 1999. *Exploring Second Language Reading*. Boston: Heinle and Heinle.

Anderson, Richard C., and David P. Pearson. 1984. "A Shema-Theoretic View of Reading Comprehension." In *Handbook of Reading Research*, edited by David P. Pearson, 255–91. New York: Longman.

Anzaldúa, Gloria. 1993. *Friends from the Other Side/Amigos del otro lado*. Illus. Consuelo Méndez. San Francisco: Children's Book Press.

Argueta, Jorge. 2007. *A Movie in My Pillow/Una pelicula en mi almohada*. Illus. Elizabeth Gomez. San Francisco: Children's Book Press.

———. 2008. *Xóchitl and the Flowers/Xóchitl, la Niña de las flores*. Illus. Carl Angel. San Francisco: Children's Book Press.

———. 2013. *Moony Luna/Luna, Lunita, Lunera*. New York: Children's Book Press.

Arnosky, Jim. 2001. *Rabbits and Raindrops*. New York: Puffin.

Atherton, James S. 2013. *Learning and Teaching: Constructivism in Learning*. http://www.learningandteaching.info/learning/constructivism.htm.

Ashman, Linda. 2013. *Rain!* Illus. Christian Robinson. New York: HMH Books for Young Readers.

Au, Kathryn. 2001. "Culturally Responsive Instruction as a Dimension of New Literacies." *Reading Online* 5 (1). DOI: 10.1080/15544800701343562.

Aud, Susan, Sidney Wilkinson-Flicker, Paul Kristapovich, Amy Rathbun, Xiaolei Wang, and Jijun Zhang. 2013. *The Condition of Education 2013* (NCES 2013-037). U.S. Department of Education, National Center for Education Statistics. Washington, DC. http://nces.ed.gov/pubsearch.

Baghban, Marcia. 2007. "Immigration in Childhood: Using Picture Books to Cope." *Social Studies* 98 (2): 71–76.

Baker, Linda, and Allan Wigfield. 1999. "Dimensions of Children's Motivation for Reading and Their Relations to Reading Activity and Reading Achievement." *Reading Research Quarterly* 34 (4): 452–77.

Bahk, Jane. 2015. *Juna's Jar*. Illus. Felicia Hoshino. New York: Lee & Row Books.

Baldwin, James. 1965. "Sonny's Blues." In *Going to Meet the Man*. New York: Dial Press.

Banks, Cherry, A. McGee, and James Banks. 1995. "Equity Pedagogy: An Essential Component of Multicultural Education." *Theory into Practice* 34 (3): 152–58.

Banks, James. 1993. "Approaches to Multicultural Curriculum Reform." In *Multicultural Education: Issues and Perspectives*, edited by James Banks and Cherry Banks. Boston: Allyn and Bacon.

———. 1995. "Multicultural Education: Historical Development, Dimensions, and Practice." In *Handbook of Research on Multicultural Education*, edited by J. A. Banks and C. A. M. Banks, 3–24. New York: Macmillan.

———. 2007. *Educating Citizens in a Multicultural Society*, second edition. New York: Teachers College Press.

Banks, James A., and Michelle Tucker. 2003. "Multiculturalism's Five Dimensions." *NEA Today Online*. http://www.learner.org/workshops/socialstudies/session3/explore.html.

Banks, Kate. 2000. *The Night Worker*. Illus. Georg Hallensleben. New York: Farrar, Straus and Giroux.

Banks, Lynne Reid. 2010. *The Indian in the Cupboard*. New York: Yearling Press.

Barber, Barbara E. 1996. *Allie's Basketball Dream*. Illus. Darryl Ligasan. New York: Lee and Low Books.

Barnett, Marc. 2010. *Oh No! Or How My Science Project Destroyed the World*. Illus. Dan Santat. New York: Disney-Hyperion.

Barracca, Debra, Sal Barracca, and Mark Buehner. 1990. *The Adventures of Taxi Dog*. New York: Dial Books for Young Readers.

Barrera, Rosalinda B. and Ruth E. Quiroa. 2003. "The Use of Spanish in Latino Children's Literature in English: What Makes for Cultural Authenticity?" *In Stories Matter: The Complexity of Cultural Authenticity in Children's Literature*, edited by D.L. Fox and K.G. Short, 247-265. Urban, IL: National Council of Teachers of English."

Bash, Barbara, and Sierra Club Books. 1990. *Urban Roosts: Where Birds Nest in the City*. New York: Little, Brown and Company.

Beach, Richard. 1993. "Cultural Theories of Response." In *A Teacher's Introduction to Reader-Response Theories*, edited by Richard Beach, 133–52. Urbana: National Council of Teachers of English.

Beaty, Daniel. 2013. *Knock Knock: My Dad's Dream for Me*. Illus. Bryan Collier. New York: Little, Brown and Company.

Becker, Michael, Nele McElvany, and Marthe Kortenbruck. 2010. "Intrinsic and Extrinsic Reading Motivation as Predictors of Reading Literacy: A Longitudinal Study." *Journal of Educational Psychology* 102 (4): 773–85.

Beeman, Karen, and Cheryl Urow. 2012. *Teaching for Biliteracy: Strengthening Bridges Between Languages*. Philadelphia: Caslon Publishing.

Berns, Carol. F. 2004. "Bibliotherapy: Using books to help bereaved children." *OMEGA—Journal of Death and Dying* 48 (4): 321–36. DOI: 10.2190/361D-JHD8-RNJT-RYJV.

Bishop, Rudine Sims. 1990. "Mirrors, Windows, and Sliding Glass Doors." *Perspectives: Choosing and Using Books for the Classroom* 6 (3): ix–xi. http://www.rif.org/us/literacy-resources/multicultural/mirrors-windows-and-sliding-glass-doors.htm.

———. 1992. "Multicultural Literature for Children: Making Informed Choices." In *Teaching Multicultural Literature in Grades K–8*, edited by Violet J. Harris, 37–54. Norwood, MA: Christopher Gordon.

———. 1997. "Selecting Literature for a Multicultural Curriculum." In *Using Multiethnic Literature in the K–8 Classroom*, edited by Violet Harris, 1–20. Norwood, MA: Christopher-Gordon Publishers.

———. 2003. "Reframing the Debate About Cultural Authenticity." In *Stories Matter: The Complexity of Cultural Authenticity in Children's Literature*, edited by Dana L. Fox and Kathy G. Short, 25–40. Urbana, IL: National Council of Teachers of English.

———. 2007. *Free within Ourselves: The Development of African American Children's Literature*. Portsmouth: Heinemann.

Bloom, Suzanne. 2001. *The Bus for Us*. Honesdale, PA: Boyds Mills Press.

Boggs, Stephen T. 1985. "The Meaning of Questions and Narratives to Hawaiian Children." In *Functions of Language in the Classroom*, edited by Courtney Cazden, Vera John, and Dell Hymes, 299–327. Prospect Heights, IL: Waveland Press.

Bontemps, Arna, and Virginia Lee Burton. 1937. *Sad-Faced Boy*. New York: Houghton Mifflin.

Boston, Genyne H., and Traci Baxley. 2007. "Living the Literature: Race, Gender Construction, and Black Female Adolescents." *Urban Education* 42: 560–81. DOI: 10.1177/0042085907305186.

Boswell, Addie K. 2008. *The Rain Stomper*. Illus. Eric Velasquez. New York: Marshall Cavendish Children.

Boutte, Gloria S. 2002. "The Critical Literacy Process: Guidelines for Examining Books." *Childhood Education* 78:147–52.

Boyd, Candy D. 1997. "I See Myself There: Experiencing Self and Others in Multiethnic Children's Literature." In *The New Press Guide to Multicultural Resources for Young Readers*, edited by Daphne Muse, 106–14. New York: The New Press.

Brassell, Danny. 1999. "Creating a Culturally Sensitive Classroom Library." *Teaching Reading* 52 (6): 651–52.

Bredekamp, Sue. 2004. "Play and School Readiness." In *Children's Play: The Roots of Reading*, edited by Edward F. Zigler, Dorothy G. Singer, and Sandra J. Bishop-Josef, 159–74. Washington, DC: Zero to Three.

Brisk, Marja E., and Margaret Harrington. 2000. *Literacy and Bilingualism: A Handbook for ALL Teachers*. Mahwah, NJ: Erlbaum.

Brooks, Gwendolyn. 2006/1955. *Bronzeville Boys and Girls*. Illus. Faith Ringgold. New York: Amistad.

Brooks, Wanda. 2006. "Reading Representations of Themselves: Urban Youth Use Culture and African American Textual Features to Develop Literacy Understandings." *Reading Research Quarterly* 41 (3): 372–92.

Brophy, Jere. 2008. "Developing Students' Appreciation for What Is Taught in School." *Educational Psychologist* 43 (3): 132–41. DOI: 10.1080/00461520701756511.

Brown, Christia Spears, and Hui Chu. 2012. "Discrimination, Ethnic Identity, and Academic Outcomes of Mexican Immigrant Children: The Importance of School Context." *Child Development* 83:1477–85.

Brown, Monica. 2007. *Butterflies on Carmen Street/Mariposas en la calle Carmen*. Illus. April Ward. Houston, TX: Piñata Books.

———. 2009. *Side by Side/Lado a Lado*. Illus. Joe Cepeda. New York: HarperCollins.

———. 2011. *Marisol McDonald Doesn't Match/Marisol McDonald no combina*. Illus. Sara Palacios. New York: Children's Book Press.

———. 2013. *Marisol McDonald and the Clash Bash/Marisol McDonald y la fiesta sin igual*. Illus. Sara Palacios. New York: Children's Book Press.

Bruner, Jerome S. 1961. "The Act of Discovery." *Harvard Educational Review* 31:21–32.

———. 1975. "The Ontogenesis of Speech Acts." *Journal of Child Language* 2:1–40.

Bryan, Lynn A., and Mary M. Atwater. 2002. "Teacher Beliefs and Cultural Models: A Challenge for Science Teacher Preparation Programs." *Science Teacher Education* 86:821–39.

Budhos, Marina. 2007. *Ask Me No Questions*. New York: Simon and Schuster.

Bunting, Eve. 1994. *Flower Garden*. Illus. Kathryn Hewitt. Orlando, FL: Harcourt.

———. 1997. *A Day's Work*. Illus. Ronald Himler. New York: Houghton Mifflin.

———. 1999. *Smoky Night*. Illus. David Diaz. Orlando: Harcourt.

Calkins, Lucy. 2013. *Units of Study in Opinion, Information, and Narrative Writing*. Portsmouth, NH: Heinemann.

Calo, Kristine M. 2011. "Incorporating Informational Texts in the Primary Grades: A Research-Based Rationale, Practical Strategies, and Two Teachers' Experiences." *Early Childhood Education Journal* 39:291–95.

Carpenter, Thomas, Elizabeth Fennema, Megan Loef Franke, Linda Levi, and Susan B. Empson. 1999. *Children's Mathematics: Cognitively Guided Instruction*. Portsmouth, NH: Heinemann.

Carrillo, Sandy. 2012. "Using Multicultural Books to Support the Writing of English Language Learners." Presentation at the annual conference of the American Association for Colleges of Teacher Education (AACTE), Chicago, IL, February 17–19.

Caswell, Linda J., and Nell K. Duke. 1998. "Non-Narrative as a Catalyst for Literacy Development." *Language Arts* 75:108–17.

Catapano, Susan, and Jane Fleming. 2009. "Supporting New Teachers with Transformative Professional Development." Paper presented at the annual conference of the American Education Research Association (AERA), San Diego, CA, April 13–17.

Celic, Christina M. 2009. *English Language Learners Day by Day K–6: A Complete Guide to Literacy, Content-Area, and Language Instruction*. Portsmouth, NH: Heinemann.

Chapman, Marilyn, Margot Filipenko, Marianne McTavish, and Jon Shapiro. 2007. "First Graders' Preferences for Narrative and/or Information Books and Perceptions of Other Boys' and Girls' Book Preferences. *Canadian Journal of Education* 30 (2): 531–53.

Chandler, Daniel. 1997. An Introduction to Genre Theory. http://www.aber.ac.uk/~mcswww/Documents/intgenre/chandler_genre_theory.pdf.

Chard, Sylvia C. 2013. *The Project Approach Study Guide.* http://www.projectapproach.org/ProjectApproachStudyGuide.pdf.

Chavous, Tabbye M., Debra H. Bernat, Karen Schmeelk-Cone, Cleopatra Caldwell, Laura Kohn-Wood, and Marc Zimmerman. 2003. "Racial Identity and Academic Attainment among African American Adolescents." *Child Development* 74:1076–90.

Chiariello, Emily. 2013. "Building Diversity into the Common Core." http://www.tolerance.org/blog/building-diversity-common-core.

Chin, Jason. 2009. *Redwoods.* New York: Flashpoint.

Chinn, Karen. 1997. *Sam and the Lucky Money.* Illus. Cornelius Van Wright and Ying-Hwa Hu. New York: Lee and Low Books.

Chocolate, Debbi. 2009. *El Barrio.* Illus. David Diaz. New York: Henry Holt.

Cisneros, Sandra. 1984. *The House on Mango Street.* Houston, TX: Arte Público Press.

———. 1997. *Hairs/Pelitos.* Decorah, IA: Dragonfly Books.

Clay, Marie. 2000. *Concepts about Print: What Have Children Learned about the Way We Print Language?* Portsmouth, NH: Heinemann.

Clifton, Lucille. 1970. *Some of the Days of Everett Anderson.* Illus. Evaline Ness. New York: Holt, Rinehart and Winston.

———. 1973. *The Boy Who Didn't Believe in Spring.* Illus. Brinton Turkle. New York: Dutton Children's Books.

———. 1983. *Everett Anderson's Goodbye.* Illus. Ann Grifalconi. Markham, ON: Fitzhenry and Whiteside.

Cohn, Diana. 2005. *Si, Se Puede!/Yes, We Can! Janitor Strike in L.A.* Illus. Francisco Delgado. El Paso, TX: Cinco Puntos Press.

Collier, Bryan. 2000. *Uptown.* New York: Henry Holt.

Cooper, Melrose. 1998. *Gettin' Through Thursday.* Illus. Nneka Bennett. New York: Lee and Low Books.

Cooper, Sharon Katz. 2006. *Whose Vehicle Is This? A Look at Vehicles Workers Drive.* Illus. Amy Bailey Muehlenhardt. Mankato, MN: Picture Window Books.

Cooperative Children's Book Center. 2012. *50 Multicultural Books Every Child Should Know.* Madison, WI. http://www.education.wisc.edu/ccbc/books/detailListBooks.asp?idBookLists=42.

———. 2013. *Choices 2013.* Madison, WI: Friends of the CCBC.

———. 2015. *Multicultural Literature 2014: Statistics Gathered by the Cooperative Children's Book Center.* Madison: University of Wisconsin-Madison. http://ccbc.education.wisc.edu/books/2014statistics.asp.

Copenhaver, Jeane. 2001. "Listening to Their Voices Connect Literary and Cultural Understandings: Responses to Small Group Read-Alouds of Malcolm X: A Fire." *New Advocate* 14 (4): 343–59.

Cotten, Cynthia 2008. *Rain Play*. Illus. Javaka Steptoe. New York: Henry Holt.

Crews, Donald. 1985. *Bicycle Race*. New York: Greenwillow Books.

———. 1987. *Harbor*. New York: Greenwillow Books.

———. 1989. *Flying*. New York: Greenwillow Books.

———. 1996. *Freight Train*. New York: Greenwillow Books.

———. 1993. *School Bus*. New York: Greenwillow Books.

———. 1991. *Trucks*. New York: Greenwillow Books.

Crews, Nina. 1995. *One Hot Summer Day*. New York: Greenwillow Books.

———. 2004. *The Neighborhood Mother Goose*. New York: Greenwillow Books.

———. 2009. *The Neighborhood Sing Along*. New York: Greenwillow Books.

———. 2011. *Jack and the Beanstalk*. New York: Henry Holt.

Crouch, Ron. 2012. "The United States of Education: The Changing Demographics of the United States and Their Schools." *The Center for Public Education*. http://www.centerforpubliceducation.org/You-May-Also-Be-Interested-In-landing-page-level/Organizing-a-School-YMABI/The-United-States-of-education-The-changing-demographics-of-the-United-States-and-their-schools.html.

Cullinan, Bernice E., Lee Galda, and Lawrence Sipe. 2009. *Literature and the Child*. New York: Wadsworth Publishing.

Cummins, Jim. 2000. "Biliteracy, Empowerment, and Transformative Pedagogy." In *The Power of Two Languages: Effective Dual Language Use across the Curriculum*, edited by J. V. Tinajero and R. A. DeVillar, 9–19. New York: McGraw-Hill.

———. 2001. *Negotiating Identities: Education for Empowerment in a Diverse Society*, second edition. Ontario, CA: California Association for Bilingual Education.

Cummins, Jim. 2000. *Language, Power, and Pedagogy: Bilingual Children in the Crossfire*. Tonawanda, NY: Multilingual Matters.

Cumpiano, Ina. 2009. *Quinito's Neighborhood*. Illus. José Ramírez. San Francisco: Children's Book Press.

———. 2008. *Quinito, Day and Night*. Illus. José Ramírez. San Francisco: Children's Book Press.

Cunningham, Anne E., and Keith E. Stanovich. 1991. "Tracking the Unique Effects of Print Exposure in Children: Associations with Vocabulary, General Knowledge, and Spelling." *Journal of Educational Psychology* 83 (2): 264–74.

Cunningham, Katie. 2013. "What's in Your Classroom Library? Rethinking Common Core Recommended Texts." *Lee and Low*. http://blog.leeandlow.com/2013/01/07/whats-in-your-classroom-library-rethinking-common-core-recommended-texts/.

Darling-Hammond, Linda. 2010. *The Flat World and Education: How America's Commitment to Equity Will Determine Our Future*. New York: Teachers College Press.

Davies, Nicola. 2001. *Bat Loves the Night*. Illus. Sarah Fox-Davies. Somerville: Candlewick Press.

Davis, Rachel. 2000. "African American Females' Voices in the Classroom: Young Sisters Making Connections through Literature." *The New Advocate* 13 (3): 259–71.

Davis, Sampson, George Jenkins, Rameck Hunt, and Sharon Draper. 2005. *We Beat the Street: How a Friendship Pact Led to Success*. New York: Penguin.

de la Peña, Matt. 2015. *Last Stop on Market Street*. Illus. Christian Robinson. New York: G. P. Putnam's Sons.

Delpit, Lisa. 2012. *Multiplication Is for White People: Raising Expectations for Other People's Children*. New York: The New Press.

Derby, Sally. 1996. *My Steps*. New York: Lee and Low Books.

Derman-Sparks, Louise. 2013. "An Updated Guide to Choosing Anti-Bias Texts." *Teaching for Change*. http://bbpbooks.teachingforchange.org/2013-guide-anti-bias-childrens-books.

Dewey, John. 1938. *Experience and Education*. New York: Kappa Delta Pi. Kindle Edition.

Dickinson, David K., and Patton O. Tabors. 2001. *Beginning Literacy with Language: Young Children Learning at Home and School*. Baltimore, MD: Brookes Publishing.

DiSalvo-Ryan, DyAnne. 1994. *City Green*. New York: HarperCollins.

Donovan, Carol A., and Laura B. Smolkin. 2001. "Genre and Other Factors Influencing Teachers' Book Selections for Science Instruction." *Reading Research Quarterly* 36 (4): 412–40.

Doiron, Ray. 2003. "Boy Books, Girl Books: Should We Re-Organize Our School Library Collections?" *Teacher Librarian* 30 (3): 14–17.

Dorros, Arthur. 1996. *Animal Tracks*. New York: Houghton Mifflin.

———. 1997. *Abuela*. New York: Penguin.

Downer, Ann. 2013. *Wild Animal Neighbors: Sharing Our Urban World*. Minneapolis, MN: Twenty-First Century Books.

Doyle, Anna Beth, and Frances E. Aboud. 1995. "A Longitudinal Study of White Children's Racial Prejudice as a Social-Cognitive Development." *Merrill-Palmer Quarterly* 41: 209–28.

Droop, Mienke, and Ludo Verhoeven. 1998. "Background Knowledge, Linguistic Complexity, and Second-Language Reading Comprehension." *Journal of Literacy Research* 30 (2): 253–71.

Dudley-Marling, Curt. 2003. "I'm Not from Pakistan": Multicultural Literature and the Problem of Representation." In *Stories Matter: The Complexity of Cultural Authenticity in Children's Literature*, edited by Dana L. Fox and Kathy G. Short, 304–18. Urbana, IL: National Council of Teachers of English.

Dugan, Joanne. 2007. *123 NYC: A Counting Book of New York City*. New York: Abrams.

Duke, Nell K. 2000. "3.6 Minutes Per Day: The Scarcity of Informational Texts in First Grade." *Reading Research Quarterly* 35 (2): 202–24.

———. 2004. "The Case for Information Text." *Educational Leadership* 61 (6): 40–44.

Duke, Nell, Samantha Caughlan, Mary Juzwik, and Nicole Martin. 2011. *Reading and Writing Genre with Purpose in K–8 Classrooms*. Portsmouth, NH: Heinemann.

Dwyer, Julie, and Susan B. Neuman. 2008. "Selecting Books for Children Birth through Four: A Developmental Approach." *Early Childhood Education Journal* 35:489–94.

Dyson, Anne H. 1994. "'I'm Gonna Express Myself': The Politics of Story in the Children's Worlds." In *The Need for Story: Cultural Diversity in Classroom and Community*, edited by Anne Dyson and Celia Genishi. Urbana, IL: National Council of Teachers of English.

Eastman, Charles A. 1902. *Indian Boyhood*. Illus. E.L. Blumenschein. New York: McClure, Phillips & Co.

Ebe, Ann E. 2010. "Culturally Relevant Texts and Reading Assessment for English Language Learners." *Reading Horizons* 50 (3): 193–210.

———. 2012. "Supporting the Reading Development of Middle School English Language Learners Through Culturally Relevant Texts." *Reading and Writing Quarterly* 28:179–98.

Eccles, Jacquelynne S. 2006. "A Motivational Perspective on School Achievement: Taking Responsibility for Learning, Teaching, and Supporting." In *Optimizing Student Success in School with the Other Three Rs*, edited by Robert J. Sternberg and Rena F. Subontnik, 199–224. Greenwich, CT: Information Age Publishing.

Eccles, Jacquelynne S., and Robert W. Roesner. 2011. "Schools as Developmental Contexts during Adolescence." *Journal of Research on Adolescence* 21 (1): 225–41.

Eccles, Jacquelynne S., Carol A. Wong, C., and Steven C. Peck. 2006. "Ethnicity as a Social Context for the Development of African-American Adolescents." *Journal of School Psychology* 44 (5): 407–26.

Echols, Laura, Richard West, Keith E. Stanovich, and Kathleen Zehr. 1996. "Using Children's Literacy Activities to Predict Growth in Verbal Cognitive Skills: A Longitudinal Investigation." *Journal of Educational Psychology* 88 (2): 296–304.

Editors of Kingfisher. 2005. *Animals Babies in Towns and Cities*. Boston: Houghton Mifflin.

Elya, Susan Middleton. 2006. *Bebé Goes Shopping*. Illus. Steven Salerno. Orlando: Harcourt.

———. 2012. *Fire! ¡Fuego! Brave Bomberos*. Illus. Dan Santat. New York: Bloomsbury.

Emdin, Christopher. 2012. Reality Pedagogy: Christopher Emdin at TEDxTeachersCollege. http://www.youtube.com/watch?v=2Y9tVf_8fqo.

Enciso, Patricia. 1997. "Negotiating the Meaning of Difference: Talking Back to Multicultural Literature." In *Reading Across Cultures: Teaching Literature in a Diverse Society*, edited by Theresa Rogers and Anna Soter. New York: Teachers College Press.

English, Karen. 2007. *Nikki and Deja*. Illus. Laura Freeman. New York: Clarion Books.

———. 2013. *Dog Days: The Carver Chronicles, Book 1*. Illus. Laura Freeman. New York: Clarion Books.

Ensign, Jacque. 2003. "Including Culturally Relevant Math in an Urban School." *Educational Studies*, 34 (4): 414-423.

Elliott, Zetta. 2008. *Bird*. Illus. Shadra Strickland. New York: Lee and Low Books.

———. 2012. *Ship of Souls*. Las Vegas, NV: Skyscape.

Erdrich, Louise. 2012. *Chickadee*. New York: HarperCollins.

Erten, Ismail H., and Salim Razi. 2009. "The Effects of Cultural Familiarity on Reading Comprehension." *Reading in a Foreign Language* 21 (1): 60–77.

Esteban-Guitart, Moisès, and Luis C. Moll. 2014. "Funds of Identity: A New Concept Based on the Funds of Knowledge Approach." *Culture and Psychology* 20 (1): 31–48.

Ezra Jack Keats Foundation. 2014. "Ezra's Characters." http://www.ezra-jack-keats.org/ezras-books-characters/ezras-characters/.

Fairbanks, Colleen M., and Mary Ariail. 2006. "The Role of Social and Cultural Resources in Literacy and Schooling: Three Contrasting Cases." *Research in the Teaching of English* 40 (3): 310–54.

Faircloth, Beverly S. 2012. "'Wearing a Mask' vs. Connecting Identity with Learning." *Contemporary Educational Psychology* 37:186–94.

Farris, Christine King. 2008. *March On! The Day My Brother Martin Changed the World*. Illus. London Ladd. New York: Scholastic.

Feger, Mary-Virginia. 2006. "'I Want to Read'": How Culturally Relevant Texts Increase Student Engagement in Reading." *Multicultural Education* 13 (3): 18–19.

Fishbone, Greg R. 2011. *Galaxy Games: The Challengers*. New York: Lee and Low Books.

Flake, Sharon. 2007. *The Broken Bike Boy and the Queen of 33rd Street*. Illus. Colin Bootman. New York: Jump at the Sun.

———. 2010. *You Don't Even Know Me*. New York: Disney Jump.

———. 2012. *Pinned*. New York: Scholastic.

Fleming, Jane, and Sandy Carrillo. 2011a. "A Missing Link in Closing Reading · Achievement Gaps: Transitional Chapter Book Series with Primary Characters of Color." Paper presented at annual conference for the National Association for the Education of Young Children (NAEYC), Orlando, Florida, November 2–5.

———. 2011b. "No 'Mirrors' in My Teacher's Classroom: Restrictions in Access to Culturally Relevant Literature for Children in City Schools." National Black Child Development Institute, Nashville, TN, October 9–11.

Fleming, Jane, and Amy Clark. 2014. "'You Could Have Heard a Pin Drop': Case Studies of Beginning Teachers' Attempts at Culturally Relevant Instruction." Presentation at the National Association for the Education of Young Children (NAEYC) Annual Conference and Expo, Dallas, TX, November 5–8.

Fleming, Jane and Iara Fuenmayor. 2013. *A Review of Ethnic, Linguistic, and Thematic Characteristics of Picture Books Featuring Latino Protagonists*. KLU Research Brief. Chicago: Kids Like Us.

Fleming, Jane, Lisa Jordan, Tracy Reynolds, and Ashley Smith. 2007. "Selecting High-Quality, Urban-Themed Literature to Engage Beginning Readers." Paper presented at the annual conference of the American Education Research Association (AERA), Chicago, IL, April 9–13.

Forman, Ruth. 2007a. April 18. Interview. *NPR*. http://www.ruthforman.com/press/.

———. 2007b. *Young Cornrows Callin Out the Moon*. Illus. Cbabi Bayoc. San Francisco: Children's Book Press.

Fountas, Irene, and Gay Su Pinnell. 2012. *Genre Study: Teaching with Fiction and Nonfiction Books*. Portsmouth, NH: Heinemann.

Fox, Dana L., and Kathy G. Short. 2003. *Stories Matter: The Complexity of Cultural Authenticity in Children's Literature*. Urbana, IL: National Council of Teachers of English. www.uacoe.arizona.edu/short/Publications/Cultural%20Authenticity.pdf.

Fox, Dana L., and Kathy Short. 2004. "The Complexity of Cultural Authenticity in Children's Literature: A Critical Review." In *53rd Yearbook of the National Reading Conference*, edited by Jo Worthy, Beth Maloch, James V. Hoffman, Diane L. Schallert, and Colleen M. Fairbanks, 373–84. Oak Creek, WI: National Reading Conference, Inc.

Frame, Jeron Ashford. 2008. *Yesterday I Had the Blues*. Illus. R. Gregory Christie. Berkley, CA: Tricycle Press.

Francois, Chantal. 2013. "Reading Is about Relating: Urban Youths Give Voice to the Possibilities for School Literacy." *Journal of Adolescent and Adult Literacy* 57 (2): 141–49.

Freedman, Russell. 1992. "Fact or Fiction?" In *Using Nonfiction Trade Books in the Elementary Classroom: From Ants to Zeppelins*, edited by Evelyn B. Freeman and Diane G. Person, 2–10. Urbana, IL: National Council of Teachers of English.

Freeman, Yvonne, and David Freeman. 2004. "Connecting Students to Culturally Relevant Texts." *NCTE Talking Points* 15:7–11.

Galda, Lee, and Bernice Cullinan. 2006. *Literature and the Child*. Belmont, CA: Wadsworth/Thomson Learning.

García Coll, Cynthia, and Amy K. Marks. 2009. *Immigrant Stories: Ethnicity and Academics in Middle Childhood*. New York: Oxford University Press.

Gardner, Howard. 1991. *The Unschooled Mind: How Children Think and How Schools Should Teach*. New York: Basic Books.

Garth McCullough, Ruanda. 2013. "The Relationship Between Reader Response and Prior Knowledge on African American Students' Reading Comprehension Performance Using Multicultural Literature." *Reading Psychology* 34:397–435.

Garza, Carmen Lomas. 2000. *In My Family/En mi familia*. San Francisco: Children's Book Press.

Gay, Geneva. 1990. "Achieving Educational Equality through Curriculum Desegregation." *Phi Delta Kappan* 72 (1): 56–62.

———. 2010. *Culturally Responsive Teaching: Theory, Research, and Practice*, second edition New York: Teachers College Press.

Gee, James P. 2004. *Situated Language and Learning: A Critique of Traditional Schooling*. New York: Routledge.

Gilton, Donna L. 2007. *Multicultural and Ethnic Children's Literature in the United States*. Lanham, MD: Scarecrow Press.

Giovanni, Nikki. 2010. *The 100 Best African American Poems*. Naperville, IL: Sourcebooks MediaFusion.

Gledhill, Christina. 2000. "Rethinking Genre." In *Reinventing Film Studies*, edited by Christina Gledhill and Linda Williams. London: Edward Arnold.

Goble, Paul. 1993. *Iktomi and the Ducks. A Plains Indian Story*. New York: Orchard Books.

———. 2001. *Storm Maker's Tipi*. New York: Orchard Books.

González, Lucía. 2008. *The Storyteller's Candle/La velita de los cuentos*. Illus. Lula Delacre. New York: Lee and Low Books.

Gonzalez, Maya C. 2010. "I Am All That I See . . . The Power of Reflection, Inside and Out." www.reflectionpress.com.

González, Rigoberto. 2005. *Antonio's Card/La Tarjeta de Antonio*. Illus. Cecilia Álvarez. New York: Children's Book Press.

Gorski, Paul. 2012. "Stages of Multicultural Curriculum Transformation." http://www.edchange.org/multicultural/curriculum/steps.html.

Graff, Jennifer M. 2010. "'Books Can Hurt or Help You': A Case Study of a Reader's Relationship with Books and the World." *Journal of Education* 190 (3): 13–25.

Graham, Lorenz. 1965. *North Town*. New York: Crowell.

Greenfield, Eloise. 1972. *Bubbles*. Washington, DC: Drum and Spear Press.

———. 1974. *She Come Bringing Me That Little Baby Girl*. Illus. John Steptoe. New York: HarperCollins.

———. 2011. In-depth written interview with TeachingBooks.net. Washington, DC. April 26, 2011. http://www.teachingbooks.net/interview.cgi?id=94anda=1.

Greenfield, Eloise, and Pat Cummings. 1977. *Good News*. New York: Putnam.

Grimes, Nikki. 1994. *Meet Danitra Brown*. Illus. Floyd Cooper. New York: Lothrop, Lee and Shepard.

———. 1999. *My Man Blue*. Illus. Jerome Lagarrigue. New York: Dial Books for Young Readers.

———. 2005. *Danitra Brown, Class Clown*. Illus. E. B. Lewis. New York: HarperCollins.

———. 2006. *Thanks a Million*. Illus. Cozbi A. Cabrera. New York: Amistad.

———. 2010. *Make Way for Dyamonde Daniel*. New York: Puffin.

———. 2013. *Words with Wings*. Honesdale, PA: WordSong.

Guevera, Susan. 2003. "Authentic Enough: Am I? Are You? Interpreting Culture for Children's Literature." In *Stories Matter: The Complexity of Cultural Authenticity in Children's Literature*, edited by Dana L. Fox and Kathy G. Short, 50–60. Urbana, IL: National Council of Teachers of English.

Gunning, Monica. 2004. *America, My New Home*. Illus. Ken Condon. Honesdale, PA: WordSong.

———. *A Shelter in Our Car*. 2004. Illus. Elaine Pedlar. San Francisco: Children's Book Press.

Guthrie, John T., and Allan Wigfield. 2000. "Engagement and Motivation in Reading." In *Reading Research Handbook, Vol. III*, edited by Michael L. Kamil, Peter B. Mosenthal, P. David Pearson, and Rebecca Barr, 403–24. Mahwah, NJ: Erlbaum.

Guthrie, John, William Schafer, and Chun-Wei Huang. 2001. "Benefits of Opportunity to Read and Balanced Instruction on the NAEP." *Journal of Educational Research* 94 (3): 145–62.

Hadaway, Nancy L. 2009. "A Narrow Bridge to Academic Reading." *Educational Leadership* 66 (7): 38–41.

Hadaway, Nancy L., and Terrell Young. 2010. *Matching Books and Readers: Helping English Language Learners in Grades K–6*. New York: Guilford Press.

Hale, Christy. 2012. *Dreaming Up: A Celebration of Building*. New York: Lee and Low Books.

Hammond, Zaretta. 2015. *Culturally Responsive Teaching and the Brain: Promoting Authentic Engagement and Rigor among Culturally and Linguistically Diverse Students*. Thousand Oaks, CA: Corwin.

Harcourt Publishers. 2011. *StoryTown*. Orlando, FL.

Hartman, Douglas K. 2002. "Using Informational Books in the Classroom: Letting the Facts (and Research) Speak for Themselves." *Redbrick Learning*. http://www.capstonepub.com/CAP/downloads/misc/LNCB_HartmanPaper.pdf.

Harvey, Stephanie, and Anne Goudvis. 2008. *The Primary Comprehension Toolkit*. Portsmouth, NH: Heinemann.

Haskins, Jim, and Kathleen Benson. 2011. *John Lewis in the Lead*. Illus. Benny Andrews. New York: Lee and Low Books.

Hawley, Willis D., and Sonia Nieto. 2010, November. "Another Inconvenient Truth: Race and Ethnicity." *Educational Leadership*. http://wlbuss.files.wordpress.com/2012/07hawley-and-nieto-race-and-ethnicity-matter.pdf.

Hayes, Joe. 2004. *La Llorona/The Weeping Woman*. Illus. Vicki Trego Hill and Mona Pennypacker. El Paso, TX: Cinco Puntos Press.

Haynes, Judie, and Debbie Zacharin. 2010. *Teaching English Language Learners across the Content Areas*. Alexandria: ASCD.

Heath, Shirley B. 1983. *Ways with Words: Language, Life, and Work in Communities and Classrooms*. New York: Cambridge University Press.

———. 1993. "Building Identities for Inner-City Youth." In *Identity and Inner-City Youth: Beyond Ethnicity and Gender*, edited by Shirley Heath and Milbrey W. McLaughlin, 1–12. New York: Teachers College Press.

Hefflin, Bena R., and Mary Alice Barksdale-Ladd. 2001. "African American Children's Literature That Helps Students Find Themselves: Selection Guidelines for Grades K–3." *The Reading Teacher* 54:810–19.

Heo, Yumi. 1994. *One Afternoon*. London: Orchard Books.

Herrera, Juan Felipe. 2006. *The Upside Down Boy/El niño de cabeza*. Illus. Elizabeth Gómez. New York: Lee and Low Books.

Hesse, Karen. 1999. *Come on Rain*. Illus. Jon J. Muth. New York: Scholastic.

Hill, K. Dara. 2012. "We're Actually Comfortable with Diversity: Affirming Teacher Candidates for Culturally Relevant Reading Pedagogy in Urban Practicum." *Action in Teacher Education* 3:420–32.

Hill, Isabel. 2009. *Urban Animals*. New York: Star Bright Books.

Hill, Laban Carrick. 2013. *When the Beat Was Born: DJ Kool Herc and the Creation of Hip Hop*. Illus. Theodore Taylor. New York: Roaring Brook Press.

Himmelman, John. 1998. *A Salamander's Life: Nature Up Close.* New York: Children's Press.

Hines, Mary Beth. 1997. "Multiplicity and Difference in Literary Inquiry: Toward a Conceptual Framework for Reader-Centered Cultural Criticism." In *Reading across Cultures: Teaching Literacy in a Diverse Society,* edited by Theresa Rogers and Anna Soter, 116–34. New York: Teachers College Press.

Hopkins, Lee Bennett. 2009. *City I Love.* Illus. Marcellus Hall. New York: Abrams Books for Young Readers.

Hopkinson, Deborah. 1995. *Sweet Clara and the Freedom Quilt.* Illus. James Ransome. New York: Dragonfly Books.

Horning, Kathleen T. 2010. *From Cover to Cover: Evaluating and Reviewing Children's Books.* New York: HarperCollins.

Howard, Elizabeth Fitzgerald. 1991a. "Authentic Multicultural Literature for Children: An Author's Perspective." In *The Multicolored Mirror: Cultural Substance in Literature for Children and Young Adults,* edited by Merri Lindgren, 91–99. Fort Atkinson, WI: Highsmith.

———. 1991b. *Aunt Flossie's Hats (and Crab Cakes Later).* Illus. James Ransome. New York: Clarion Books.

Howes, Carollee, and Catherine Matheson. 1992a. "Contextual Constraints on the Concordance of Mother–Child and Teacher–Child Relationships." In *Beyond the Parent: The Role of Other Adults in Children's Lives,* edited by Robert Pianta, 25–40. San Francisco, CA: Jossey-Bass.

———. 1992b. "Sequences in the Development of Competent Play with Peers: Social and Social Pretend Play." *Developmental Psychology* 28 (5): 961–74.

Howes, Carollee, and Alison G. Wishard. 2004. "Revisiting Shared Meaning: Looking through the Lens of Culture and Linking Shared Pretend Play through Proto-Narrative Development to Emergent Literacy." In *Children's Play: The Roots of Reading,* edited by Edward Zigler, Dorothy Singer, and Sandra J. Bishop-Josef, 143–58. Washington, DC: Zero to Three.

Hubbell, Patricia. 2006. *Trucks: Whizz! Zoom! Rumble!* Las Vegas, NV: Amazon Publishing.

Huck, Charlotte S., Susan Hepler, Janet Hickman, and Barbara Kiefer. 2000. *Children's Literature in the Elementary School,* seventh edition. New York: McGraw-Hill.

Hughes-Hassell, Sandra, Heather A. Barkley, and E. Koehler. 2009. "Promoting Equity in Children's Literacy Instruction: Using a Critical Race Theory Framework to Examine Transitional Books." *School Library Media Research* 12 (online). http://www.ala.org/ala/mgrps/divs/aasl/aaslpubsandjournals/slmrb/slmrcontents/volume12/hughes_hassell.cfm.

Hughes-Hassell, Sandra, E. Koehler, and Heather A. Barkley. 2010. "Supporting the Literacy Needs of African American Transitional Readers." *Teacher Librarian* (online). http://www.teacherlibrarian.com/2010/10/26/supporting-the-literacy-needs-of-african-american-transitional-readers/.

Hunsberger, P. 2007. "Where Am I? A Call for Connectedness in Literacy." *Reading Research Quarterly* 42 (3), 420–24.

Hurley, Eric A., Brenda A. Allen, and A. Wade Boykin. 2005. "Communal vs. Individual Learning of a Math-Estimation Task: African American Children and the Culture of Learning Contexts." *Journal of Psychology: Interdisciplinary and Applied* 139 (6): 513–27.

Igoa, Cristina. 1995. *The Inner World of the Immigrant Child*. Mahwah, NJ: Lawrence Erlbaum.

Irvine, Jacqueline. 1990. *Black Student and School Failure*. Westport, CT: Westport Greenwood Press.

———. 2010. "Culturally Relevant Pedagogy." *Education Digest* 75 (8): 57–61.

Isadora, Rachel. 2000. *Listen to the City*. New York: Putnam.

Iyengar, Malathi Michelle. 2009. *Tan to Tamarind: Poems about the Color Brown*. Illus. Jamel Akib. San Francisco: Children's Book Press.

Jacobs, Paul DuBois, Jennifer Swender, and Selina Alko. 2004. *My Subway Ride*. Salt Lake City: Gibbs Smith.

Jenkins, Steve. 1997. *Biggest, Strongest, Fastest*. New York: Houghton Mifflin.

Jenkins, Steve, and Robin Page. 2003. *What Do You Do with a Tail Like This?* New York: Houghton Mifflin.

Jiménez, Francisco. 1997. *The Circuit: Stories from the Life of a Migrant Child*. New York: Houghton Mifflin.

Johnson, Angela. 1992. *The Leaving Morning*. Illus. David Soman. New York: Orchard Books.

———. 1995. *One of Three*. Illus. David Soman. New York: Orchard Books.

———. 2007. *A Sweet Smell of Roses*. Illus. Eric Velasquez. New York: Simon and Schuster Children's Publishing.

Johnson, Patricia. 1981. "Effects of Reading Comprehension of Language Complexity and Cultural Background of a Text." *TESOL Quarterly* 15 (2): 169–81.

Johnston, Tony. 2001. *Uncle Rain Cloud*. Illus. Fabricio Vanden Broeck. Watertown, MA: Charlesbridge.

———. 2003. *Any Small Goodness*. New York: Scholastic.

———. 2009. *My Abuelita*. Illus. Yuyi Morales. Orlando: Houghton Mifflin.

Joosse, Barbara. 2004. *Stars in the Darkness*. Illus. R. Gregory Christie. San Francisco: Chronicle Books.

———. 2004. *Hot City*. Illus. R. Gregory Christie. New York: Philomel.

Jules, Jacqueline. 2010. *Freddie Ramos Takes Off (Zapato Power)*. Illus. Miguel Benítez. New York: Albert Whitman and Company.

Kalman, Bobbie. 2007. *The ABCs of Habitats*. New York: Crabtree Publishing.

———. 2009. *What Is Religion?* New York: Crabtree Publishing.

Keats, Ezra Jack. 1960. *My Dog Is Lost!* New York: Viking.

———. 1964. *Whistle for Willie*. New York: Viking.

———. 1972. *Pet Show!* New York: Viking.

———. 1976. *The Snowy Day*. New York: Viking.

———. 1998. *A Letter to Amy*. New York: Puffin.

———. 1998. *Goggles*. New York: Puffin.

————. 1998. *Peter's Chair*. New York: Puffin.

————. 1999. *Apt. 3*. New York: Puffin.

————. 2001. *Louie's Search*. New York: Puffin.

Kena, Grace, Lauren Musu-Gillette, Jennifer Robinson, Xiaolei Wang, Amy Rathbun, Jijun Zhang, Sidney Wilkinson-Flicker, Amy Barmer, and Erin Dunlop Velez. 2015. *The Condition of Education 2015* (NCES 2015-144). U.S. Department of Education, National Center for Education Statistics. Washington, DC. http://nces.ed.gov/pubsearch.

Khan, Rukhsana. 2010. *Big Red Lollipop*. Illus. Sophie Blackall. New York: Viking Juvenile.

Kiefer, Barbara. 2007. *Charlotte Huck's Children's Literature*, ninth edition. Boston: McGraw Hill Publishing.

Kirkland, David E. 2011. "Books Like Clothes: Engaging Young Black Men with Reading." *Journal of Adolescent and Adult Literacy* 55 (3): 199–208. DOI:10.1002/JAAL.00025.

Kittinger, Jo S. 2010. *Rosa's Bus: The Ride to Civil Rights*. Illus. Steven Walker. Honesdale, PA: Boyds Mills Press.

Kletzien, Sharon B., and Robert J. Szabo. 1998. "Information Text or Narrative Text? Children's Preferences Revisited." Paper presented at the National Reading Conference, Austin, TX, December 1–4.

Klingner, Janette K., Alfredo Artiles, Elizabeth Kozleski, Beth Harry, Shelley Zion, William Tate, Grace Zamora Duran, and David Riley. 2005. "Addressing the Disproportionate Representation of Culturally and Linguistically Diverse Students in Special Education through Culturally Responsive Educational Systems." *Education Policy Analysis Archives* 13 (38): 1–40.

Krull, Kathleen. 2003. *Harvesting Hope: The Story of Cesar Chavez*. Illus. Yuyi Morales. Boston: Harcourt.

Ladson-Billings, Gloria. 1992. "Reading between the Lines and beyond the Pages: A Culturally Relevant Approach to Literacy Teaching." *Theory into Practice* 31 (4): 312–20.

————. 1995. "Toward a Theory of Culturally Relevant Pedagogy." *American Educational Research Journal* 32 (3): 465–91.

La Flesche, Francis. 1990. *The Middle Five: Indian Boys at School*. Boston: Small, Maynard & Co.

Ladson-Billings, Gloria. 2009. *The Dreamkeepers: Sucessful Teachers of African American Children*, second edition. San Francisco: Jossey-Bass.

Laínez, René Colato. 2010. *From North to South*. Illus. Joe Cepeda. San Francisco: Children's Book Press.

Larrotta, Clarena, and Jesse Gainer. 2008. "Text Matters: Mexican Immigrant Parents Reading Their World." *Multicultural Education* 16 (2): 45–48.

Laughlin, Lynda. 2014. "A Child's Day: Living Arrangements, Nativity, and Family Transitions: 2011." *Current Population Reports, P70-139*. Washington, DC: U.S. Census Bureau.

Lazar, Althier, Patricia Edwards, and Gwendolyn McMillon. 2012. *Bridging Literacy and Equity: The Essential Guide to Social Equity Teaching.* New York: Teachers College Press.

Lee, Carol D. 2000. "Signifying in the Zone of Proximal Development." In *Vygotskian Perspectives on Literacy Research: Constructing Meaning through Collaborative Inquiry,* edited by Carol D. Lee and Peter Smagorinsky, 191–225. Cambridge: Cambridge University Press.

Lee, Carol D., and Peter Smagorinsky. 2000. "Introduction: Constructing Meaning through Collaborative Inquiry." In *Vygotskian Perspectives on Literacy Research: Constructing Meaning through Collaborative Inquiry,* edited by Carol D. Lee and Peter Smagorinsky, 1–18. Cambridge: Cambridge University Press.

Lee, J., W. Grigg, and P. Donahue. 2007. *The Nation's Report Card: Reading 2007* (NCES 2007–496). National Center for Education Statistics, Institute of Education Sciences, U.S. Department of Education, Washington, DC.

Lee and Low. 2011. "Classroom Guide for *Estela's Swap*: About the Author and the Illustrator." *Teachers.* http://www.leeandlow.com/p/estela_tg.mhtml.

Lee and Low. 2013. "Literary Agents Discuss the Diversity Gap in Publishing." *The Open Book.* http://blog.leeandlow.com/2013/11/06/literary-agents-discuss-the-diversity-gap-in-publishing/.

Lepola, Janne, Marja Vauras, and Hanna Maki. 2000. "Gender Differences in the Development of Academic Self-concept of Attainment from the 2nd to the 6th Grade: Relations with Achievement and Perceived Motivational Orientation." *Journal of Hellenic Psychological Society* 7:3–21.

Levine, Ellen. 2007. *Henry's Freedom Box: A True Story from the Underground Railroad.* Illus. Kadir Nelson. New York: Scholastic.

Liao, Jimmy. 2006. *The Sound of Colors: A Journey of the Imagination.* New York: Little, Brown and Company.

Li, Chen-Hong, and Shu-Fen Lai. 2012. "The Functions of Cultural Schemata in the Chinese Reading Comprehension and Reading Time of College Students in Taiwan." *Journal of International Education Research* 8 (2): 105–12.

Lipson, Marjorie Youmans. 1983. "The Influence of Religious Affiliation on Children's Memory for Text Information." *Reading Research Quarterly* 18 (4): 448–57.

Lohfink, Gayla, and Juana Loya. 2010. "The Nature of Mexican American Third Graders' Engagement with Culturally Relevant Picture Books." *Bilingual Research Journal* 33 (3): 346–63.

Look, Lenore. 2001. *Henry's First Moon Birthday.* New York: Atheneum Books for Yound Readers.

Lopez, Loretta. 1997. *The Birthday Swap.* New York: Lee and Low Books.

López-Robertson, Julia. 2011. "'Yo el otro dia vi, um, un mojadito': Young Latino Children Connecting with Friends from the Other Side." *New England Reading Association Journal* 46 (2): 52–59.

Low, William. 1997. *Chinatown.* New York: Henry Holt.

———. 2012. *Machines Go to Work in the City.* New York: Henry Holt.

Lukens, Rebecca. 2002. *A Critical Handbook of Children's Literature*, seventh edition. Boston: Allyn and Bacon.

Lynch-Brown, Carol, Carl Tomlinson, and Kathy Short. 2010. *Essentials of Children's Literature*, 4th edition. Upper Saddle River, NJ: Pearson.

Madrigal, Patricia, Camille Cubillas, David B. Yaden, Jr., Anamarie Tam, and Danny Brassell 1999. Creating a Book Loan Program for Inner-city Latino Families. The Center for the Improvement of Early Reading Achievement (CIERA Report #2-003). Ann Arbor: University of Michigan.

Mak, Kam. 2001. *My Chinatown: A Year in Poems*. New York: HarperCollins.

Malik, Ali A. 1990. "A Psycholinguistic Analysis of the Reading Behavior of EFL-Proficient Readers Using Culturally Familiar and Culturally Nonfamiliar Expository Texts." *American Educational Research Journal* 27 (1): 205–23.

Manning, Maurie J. 2008. *Kitchen Dance*. New York: Clarion Books.

Marsh, Herbert W., and Martin, Andrew J. 2011. "Academic Self-Concept and Academic Achievement: Relations and Causal Ordering." *British Journal of Psychology* 81:59–77.

Martel, Cruz. 1993. *Yagua Days*. Illus. Jerry Pinkney. Scholastic.

Martin, Bill, and John Archambault. 1997. *Knots on a Counting Rope*. Illus. Ted Rand. New York: Henry Holt.

Martin, Jacqueline Briggs. 2013. *Farmer Will Allen and the Growing Table*. Illus. Eric Larkin. Bellevue, WA: Readers to Eaters.

Martin, Michelle H. 2004. *Brown Gold: Milestones of African American Children's Picture Books, 1845–2002*. New York: Routledge.

Martinez, Miriam, and Marcia Nash. 1998. "Children's Books: A Look at How We Evaluate and Select Them." *Journal of Children's Literature* 24:6–19.

Mathis, Sharon Bell. 1971. *Sidewalk Story*. New York: Penguin.

———. 2001. *Ray Charles*. New York: Lee and Low Books.

McCoy, Henrika, and Cassandra McKay. 2006. "Preparing Social Workers to Identify and Integrate Culturally Affirming Bibliotherapy into Treatment." *Social Work Education* 25:680–93.

McGinley, William, George Kamberelis, Timothy Mahoney, Daniel Madigan, Victoria Rybikci, and Jeff Oliver. 1997. "Re-visioning Reading and Teaching Literature through the Lens of Narrative Story." In *Reading Across Cultures: Teaching Literature in a Diverse Society*, edited by Theresa Rogers and Anna Soter, 42–68. New York: Teachers College Press.

McKenna, Michael C., Dennis Kear, and Randolph A. Ellsworth. 1995. "Children's Attitudes Toward Reading: A National Survey." *Reading Research Quarterly* 30 (4): 934–56.

McKissack, Patricia. 2006. *Abby Takes a Stand*. Illus. Gordon James. New York: Puffin.

———. 2008. *A Song for Harlem*. Illus. Gordon James. New York: Puffin.

McNair, Jonda C. 2008. "The Representation of Authors and Illustrators of Color in School-Based Book Clubs." *Language Arts* 65 (3): 193–201.

———. 2013. "'I Never Knew There Were So Many Books about Us:' Parents and Children Reading and Responding to African American Children's Literature Together." *Children's Literature in Education* 44:191–207.

McNamee, Gillian D. 2015. *The High-Performing Preschool: Story Acting in Head Start Classrooms*. Chicago: University of Chicago Press.

Mead, Alice. 1995. *Junebug*. New York: Farrar, Straus and Giroux.

———. 2002. *Junebug in Trouble*. New York: Farrar, Straus and Giroux.

Medina, Meg. 2011. *Tía Isa Wants a Car*. Illus. Claudio Muñoz. Somerville, MA: Candlewick Press.

———. 2013. *Yaqui Delgado Wants to Kick Your Ass*. Somerville, MA: Candlewick Press.

———. 2015. *Mango, Abuela, and Me*. Somerville, MA: Candlewick Press.

Medina, Tony. 2003. *Deshawn Days*. Illus. R. Gregory Christie. New York: Lee and Low Books.

Meier, Terry. 2008. *Black Communications and Learning to Read: Building on Children's Linguistic and Cultural Strengths*. New York: Lawrence Erlbaum Associates.

Mendoza, Jean, and Debbie Reese. 2001. "Examining Multicultural Picture Books for the Early Childhood Classroom: Possibilities and Pitfalls." *Early Childhood Research and Practice* 3 (2): 1–27. http://ecrp.uiuc.edu/v3n2/mendoza.html.

Michelson, Richard. 2006. *Across the Alley*. Illus. E. B. Lewis. New York: G. P. Putnam's Sons.

Milich, Zoran. 2003. *The City ABC Book*. Toronto: Kids Can Press.

———. 2005. *City 1 2 3*. Toronto: Kids Can Press.

———. 2006. *City Colors*. Toronto: Kids Can Press.

Miller, Carolyn R. 1984. "Genre as Social Action." *Quarterly Journal of Speech* 70 (2): 151–67.

Miller, Debbie. 2002. *Reading with Meaning*. Portland, ME: Stenhouse Publishers.

Mo, Weimin, and Wenju Shen. 2003. "Accuracy Is Not Enough: The Role of Cultural Values in the Authenticity of Picture Books." In *Stories Matter: The Complexity of Cultural Authenticity in Children's Literature*, edited by Dana L. Fox and Kathy G. Short, 198–212. Urbana, IL: National Council of Teachers of English.

Mohr, Kathleen. 2006. "Children's Choices for Recreational Reading: A Three-Part Investigation of Selection Preferences, Rationales, and Processes." *Journal of Literacy Research* 38 (1): 81–104.

Moll, Luis. 1992. "Bilingual Classroom Studies and Community Analysis: Some Recent Trends." *Educational Researcher* 21 (2): 20–24.

———. 2000. "Inspired by Vygotsky: Ethnographic Experiments in Education." In *Vygotskian Perspectives on Literacy Research: Constructing Meaning through Collaborative Inquiry*, edited by Carol D. Lee and Peter Smagorinsky, 256–68. Cambridge: Cambridge University Press.

———. 2014. *L. S. Vygotsky and Education*. New York: Routledge.

Moll, Luis, Cathy Amanti, Deborah Neff, and Norma Gonzalez. 1992. "Funds of Knowledge for Teaching: Using a Qualitative Approach to Connect Homes and Classrooms." *Theory into Practice* 31 (2): 132–41.

Moll, Luis, and Joel Dworin. 1996. "Biliteracy in Classrooms: Social Dynamics and Cultural Possibilities." In *Child Discourse and Social Learning*, edited by Deborah Hicks, 221–46. Cambridge: Cambridge University Press.

Moll, Luis, and James Greenberg. 1990. "Creating Zones of Possibilities: Combining Social Contexts for Instruction." In *Vygotsky and Education*, edited by Luis Moll, 319–48. Cambridge: Cambridge University Press.

Montes, Marisa. 2003. *Get Ready for Gabí: A Crazy Mixed-Up Spanglish Day*. Illus. Joe Cepeda. New York: Scholastic.

Mora, Pat. 2001. *The Bakery Lady/La Señora de la Panadería*. Illus. Pablo Torrecilla. Houston, TX: Piñata Books.

———. 2001. *Love to Mamá: A Tribute to Mothers*. Illus. Paula Barragán. New York: Lee and Low Books.

———. 2005. *Gracias Thanks*. New York: Lee and Low Books.

———. 2008. *Join Hands!* Illus. George Ancona. Watertown, MA: Charlesbridge.

Morales, Yuyi. 2013. *Niño Wrestles the World*. New York: Roaring Book Press.

Moreillon, Judi. 2003. "The Candle and the Mirror: One Author's Journey as an Outsider." In *Stories Matter: The Complexity of Cultural Authenticity in Children's Literature*, edited by D. L. Fox and K. G. Short, 61–77. Urbana, IL: National Council of Teachers of English.

Morgan, Paul, and Douglas Fuchs. 2007. "Is There a Bidirectional Relationship between Children's Reading Skills and Reading Motivation? *Exceptional Children* 73 (2): 165–83.

Morrell, Ernest, and Jodene Morrell. 2012. "Multicultural Readings of Multicultural Literature and the Promotion of Social Awareness in ELA Classrooms." *NERA Journal* 47 (2): 10–16.

Morris, Vanessa Irvin. 2012. *The Readers' Advisory Guide to Street Literature*. Chicago: American Library Association.

Moss, Barbara. 2003. *Exploring the Literature of Fact: Children's Nonfiction Trade Books in the Elementary Classroom*." New York: Guilford Press.

———. 2004. "Teaching Expository Text Structures through Information." *The Reading Teacher* 57:710–18.

Moss, Barbara, and Evangeline Newton. 2002. "An Examination of the Informational Text Genre in Basal Readers. *Reading Psychology* 23:1–13.

Myers, Christopher. 1999. *Black Cat*. New York: Scholastic.

———. 2000. *Wings*. New York: Scholastic.

———. 2001. *Fly*. New York: Jump at the Sun Publishers.

———. 2012. *H.O.R.S.E.: A Game of Basketball and Imagination*. New York: Egmont USA.

Myers, Walter Dean. 1969. *Where Does the Day Go?* New York: Parents' Magazine Press.

———. 1997. *Harlem*. Illus. Christopher Myers. New York: Scholastic.

———. 2003/1989. *Malcolm X: A Fire Burning Brightly*. Illus. Leonard Jenkins. New York: Amistad.

———. 2009. *Looking Like Me*. Illus. Christopher Myers. New York: Egmont USA.

———. 2010. *The Cruisers*. New York: Scholastic.

———. 2012. *Just Write: Here's How*. New York: HarperTeen.

———. 2014. "Where Are the People of Color in Children's Books?" *New York Times*, March 15, 2014. http://nyti.ms/1e4BYMc.

———. 1975. *Fast Sam, Cool Clyde, and Stuff*. New York: Viking.

———. 1988. *Fallen Angels*. New York: Scholastic.

———. 1988. *Scorpions*. New York: Harper & Row.

———. 1994. *Darnell Rock Reporting*. New York: Delacorte Press.

———. 1999. *At Her Majesty's Request: Am African Princess in Victorian England*. New York: Scholastic.

———. 1999. *Monster*. New York: HarperCollins.

———. 2000. *The Blues of Flats Brown*. New York: Holiday House.

———. 2000. *Malcolm X: A Fire Burning Brightly*. Illus. Leonard Jenkins. New York: HarperCollins.

———. 2001. *Bad Boy: A Memoir*. New York: HarperCollins.

———. 2004. *Antarctica: Journeys to the South Pole*. New York: Scholastic.

———. 2006. *Jazz*. New York: Holiday House.

———. 2006. *Toussaint L'overtoure: The Fight for Haiti's Freedom*. New York: Simon & Schuster Books for Young Readers

———. 2008. *Ida B. Wells: Let the Truth Be Told*. New York: HarperCollins.

———. 2008. *Sunrise Over Fallujah*. New York: Scholastic.

———. 2009. *Amiri and Odette*. New York: Scholastic.

———. 2010. *Lockdown*. New York: HarperCollins.

———. 2010. *Riot*. New York: Egmont USA.

———. 2011. *Carmen*. New York: Egmont USA.

———. 2013. *Darius and Twig*. New York: HarperCollins.

———. 2014. *On a Clear Day*. New York: Crown Books for Young Readers.

Naidoo, Jamie. 2008. "Opening Doors: Visual and Textual Analyses of Diverse Latino Subcultures in Américas Picture Books." *Children and Libraries* 6 (2): 27–35.

———. 2011. *Celebrating Cuentos: Promoting Latino Children's Literature and Literacy in Classrooms and Libraries*. Santa Barbara, CA: Libraries Unlimited.

Nassaji, Hossein. 2007. "Schema Theory and Knowledge-Based Processes in Second Language Reading Comprehension: A Need for Alternative Perspectives." *Language Learning* 57 (1): 79–113.

National Education Association. 2014. "Research Talking Points on English Language Learners." http://www.nea.org/home/13598.htm.

National Equity Project. 2012. "5 Ways to Create a Culturally Responsive Classroom." http://blog.nationalequityproject.org/2012/08/22/5-ways-to-create-a-culturally-responsive-classroom/.

National Governors Association Center for Best Practices, Council of Chief State School Officers. 2010. *Common Core State Standards*. Washington, DC.

———. 2011. *Common Core State Standards*. http://www.corestandards.org/.

National Institute of Child Health and Human Development. 2000. *Report of the National Reading Panel. Teaching Children to Read: An Evidence-Based Assessment of the Scientific Research Literature on Reading and Its Implications for Reading Instruction.* Washington, DC: U.S. Government Printing Office.

Nelson, Kadir. 2011. *Heart and Soul: The Story of America and African Americans.* New York: Balzer and Bray.

Neri, G. 2007. *Chess Rumble.* Illus. Jesse Joshua Watson. New York: Lee and Low Books.

———. 2013. *Ghetto Cowboy.* Illus. Jesse Joshua Watson. New York: Candlewick.

Neubecker, Robert. 2004. *Wow! City!* New York: Hyperion Books for Children.

New York City Department of Education. 2015. *Department of English Language Learners and Student Support, School Year 2013–2014 Demographic Report.* http:// schools.nyc.gov/Academics/ELL/default.htm.

Niemann, Christoph. 2010. *Subway.* New York: HarperCollins.

Nicholson, Janice I., and Quinn M. Pearson. 2003. "Helping Children Cope with Fears: Using Children's Literature in Classroom Guidance." *Professional School Counseling* 7:15–19.

Nieto, Sonia. 1993. "We Have Stories to Tell: A Case Study of Puerto Ricans in Children's Books." In *Teaching Multicultural Literature in Grades K–8*, edited by Violet Harris, 173–201. Norwood, MA: Christopher-Gordon.

———. 1994. "Affirmation, Solidarity, and Critique: Moving Beyond Tolerance in Multicultural Education." *Multicultural Education*, 1 (4): 9-12, 35-38.

———. 1997. "We Have Stories to Tell: Puerto Ricans in Children's Books." In *Using Multiethnic Literature in the K–8 Classroom*, edited by Violet Harris, 59–93. Norwood: Christopher-Gordon Publishers.

Nieto, Sonia, and Patty Bode. 2011. *Affirming Diversity: The Sociopolitical Context of Multicultural Education*, sixth edition. New York: Pearson.

Nikola-Lisa, W. 2003. "'Around My Table' Is Not Always Enough." In *Stories Matter: The Complexity of Cultural Authenticity in Children's Literature*, edited by Dana L. Fox and Kathy G. Short, 46–49. Urbana, IL: National Council of Teachers of English.

———. 2009. *How We Are Smart.* Illus. Sean Qualls. New York: Lee and Low Books.

Nolen, Jerdine. 2002. *Raising Dragons.* Illus. Elise Primavera. Orlando, FL: Harcourt Books.

Noll, Elizabeth. 2003. "Accuracy and Authenticity in American Indian Children's Literature: The Social Responsibility of Authors and Illustrators." In *Stories Matter: The Complexity of Cultural Authenticity in Children's Literature*, edited by Dana L. Fox and Kathy G. Short, 182–97. Urbana IL: National Council of Teachers of English.

Norman, Lissette. 2006. *My Feet Are Laughing.* Illus. Frank Morrison. New York: Farrar, Straus and Giroux.

Norton, Donna E. 2012. *Multicultural Children's Literature: Through the Eyes of Many Children*, fourth edition. Upper Saddle River, NJ: Pearson.

Nye, Naomi Shihab. 1997. *Sitti's Secrets*. Illus. Nancy Carpenter. New York: Simon and Schuster.

O'Dell, Scott. 1998. *Island of the Blue Dolphins*. New York: Houghton Mifflin Harcourt.

O'Neill, Alexis. 2007. *Estella's Swap*. Illus. Enrique O. Sanchez. New York: Lee and Low Books.

Opitz, Michael F. 1998. "Text Sets: One Way to Flex Your Grouping—In First Grade, Too!" *The Reading Teacher* 51 (7): 622–24.

Ortiz, Robert W., and Rosario Ordoñez-Jasis. 2005. "Leyendo Juntos (Reading Together): New Directions for Latino Parents' Early Literacy Involvement." *The Reading Teacher* 59 (2): 110–21.

Painter, Gary, and Zhou Yu. 2008. "Leaving Gateway Metropolitan Areas: Immigrants and the Housing Market." *Urban Studies* 45:1163–91.

Pahlke, Erin, Rebecca S. Bigler, and Marie-Anne Suizzo. 2012. "Relations between Colorblind Socialization and Children's Racial Bias: Evidence from European American Mothers and Their Preschool Children." *Child Development* 83 (4): 1164–79.

Paradise, Ruth, and Barbara Rogoff. 2009. "Side by Side: Learning by Observing and Pitching in." *Ethos* 37 (1): 102–38.

Park, Frances, and Ginger Park. 2008. *The Have a Good Day Café*. Illus. Katherine Potter. New York: Lee and Low Books.

Partners Against Hate. 2012. "The Importance of Multicultural Children's Books." http://www.partnersagainsthate.org/educators/books.html.

Paschen, Elise, and Dominique Raccah. 2010. *Poetry Speaks Who I Am*. Naperville, IL: Sourcebooks Jabberwocky.

Pashler, Harold, Patrice Bain, Brian Bottge, Arthur Graesser, Kenneth Koedinger, Mark McDaniel, and Janet Metcalfe. 2007. *Organizing Instruction and Study to Improve Student Learning*. Washington, DC: National Center for Education Research, Institute of Education Sciences, U.S. Department of Education. http://ncer.ed.gov.

Payán, Rose M., and Michael T. Nettles. 2008. *Current State of English-Language Learners in the U.S. K–12 Student Population*. Princeton, NJ: Educational Testing Service.

Payne, Charles. 2008. *So Much Reform, So Little Change: The Persistence of Failure in Urban Schools*. Cambridge: Harvard Education Press.

Pearson. 2012. "Opening the World of Learning." http://www.pearsonlearning.com/microsites/owl/main.cfm.

Pérez, Amada Irma. 2000. *My Very Own Room/Mi Propio Cuartito*. Illus. Maya Christina Gonzalez. New York: Children's Book Press.

———. 2007. *Nana's Big Surprise/Nana, ¡Qué Sorpresa!* Illus. Maya Christina Gonzalez. New York: Children's Book Press.

———. 2009. *My Diary from Here to There/Mi diario de aqui hasta allá*. Illus. Maya Christina Gonzalez. New York: Children's Book Press.

Pinkney, Andrea Davis. 2010. *Sit-In: How Four Friends Stood Up by Sitting Down*. Illus. Brian Pinkney. New York: Little, Brown Books for Young Readers.

Pockell, Leslie. 2009. *100 Essential American Poems*. New York: Thomas Dunne Books.

Polacco, Patricia. 1994. *Pink and Say*. New York: Philomel.

———. 2001. *The Keeping Quilt*. New York: Simon and Schuster.

Politi, Leo. 2009/1946. *Pedro, The Angel of Olvera Street*. Los Angeles: Getty Publications.

———. 2009/1947. *Juanita*. Los Angeles: Getty Publications.

Pransky, Ken. 2009. "There's More to See." *Educational Leadership* 66 (7): 74–78.

Prater, Mary Ann, Marissa L. Johnstun, Tina T. Dyches, and Marion R. Johnstun. 2006. "Using Books as Bibliotherapy for At-Risk Students: A Guide for Teachers." *Preventing School Failure* 50 (4): 5–13.

Price, Marie, and Lisa Benton-Short. 2008. *Migrants to the Metropolis: The Rise of Immigrant Gateway Cities*. Syracuse, NY: Syracuse University Press.

Pritchard, Robert. 1990. "The Effects of Cultural Schemata on Reading Processing Strategies." *Reading Research Quarterly* 25(4): 273–95.

Ramsey, Calvin Alexander, and Gwen Strauss. 2013. *Ruth and the Green Book*. Illus. Floyd Cooper. New York: Scholastic.

Ramsey, Patricia G. 1991. "The Salience of Race in Young Children Growing Up in an All-White Community." *Journal of Educational Psychology* 83 (1): 28–34. DOI: 10.1037/0022-0663.83.1.28.

Read, Nicholas. 2012. *City Critters: Wildlife in the Urban Jungle*. Custer, WA: Orca Book Publishing.

Reading Is Fundamental (RIF). 2012. "Reading Is Fundamental Offers Expansive Multicultural Book Collection Aiming to Help Close Achievement Gap." Washington, DC.

Reese, Debbie A., and Naomi Caldwell-Wood. 1997. "Native Americans in Children's Literature." In *Using Multiethnic Literature in the K–8 Classroom*, edited by V. J. Harris. Norwood, MA: Christopher Gordon.

Reynolds, Ralph. E., Marsha A. Taylor, Margaret S. Steffensen, Larry L. Shirey, and Richard Anderson. 1982. "Cultural Schemata and Reading Comprehension." *Reading Research Quarterly* 17 (3): 353–66.

Rich, Motoko. 2012. "For Young Latino Readers, an Image Is Missing." *New York Times*, December 5.

Ringgold, Faith. 1991. *Tar Beach*. New York: Dragonfly Books.

———. 2002. *Cassie's Word Quilt*. New York: Dragonfly Books.

Roberts, Brenda C. 2004. *Jazzy Miz Mozetta*. Illus. Frank Morrison. New York: Farrar, Straus and Giroux.

Robles, Anthony D. 2006. *Lakas and the Makibaka Hotel*. Illus. Carl Angel. San Francisco: Children's Book Press.

Rodman, Mary Ann. 2007. *My Best Friend*. Illus. E. B. Lewis. New York: Puffin.

Rodriguez, Alma D. 2009. "Culturally Relevant Books: Connecting Hispanic Students to the Curriculum." *GiST Colombian Journal of Bilingual Education* 3:11–29.

Rogoff, Barbara. 2003. *The Cultural Nature of Human Development*. New York: Oxford University Press.

Rosenblatt, Louise M. 1978. *The Reader, the Text, the Poem: The Transactional Theory of the Literary Work*. Carbondale, IL: Southern Illinois University.

Rueda, Robert. 2011. "Cultural Perspectives in Reading: Theory and Research." In *Handbook of Reading Research*, vol. 4, edited by Michael L. Kamil, P. David Pearson, Elizabeth Birr Moje, and Peter P. Afflerbach, 4–99. New York: Routledge.

Ryan, Camille. 2013. "Language Use in the United States: 2011." Washington, DC: U.S. Census Bureau. https://www.census.gov/prod/2013pubs/acs-22.pdf.

Saul, Wendy, and Donna Dieckman. 2005. "Choosing and Using Information Trade Books." *Reading Research Quarterly* 40 (4): 502–13.

Schofield-Morrison, Connie. 2014. *I Got the Rhythm*. Illus. Frank Morrison. New York: Bloomsbury, USA.

Schroeder, Alan. 2012. *Baby Flo: Florence Mills Lights Up the Stage*. Illus. Cornelius Van Wright and Ying-Hwa Hu. San Francisco: Lee and Low Books.

Schulman, Janet. 2008. *Pale Male: Citizen Hawk of New York City*. Illus. Meilo So. Knopf Books for Young Readers.

Seskin, Steve, and Allen Shamblin. 2006. *A Chance to Shine*. Illus. R. Christie. Berkeley, CA: Tricycle Press.

Shanahan, Timothy, Kim Callison, Christine Carriere, Nell K. Duke, P. David Pearson, Christopher Schatschneider, and Joseph Torgesen. 2010. *Improving Reading Comprehension in Kindergarten through 3rd Grade: A Practice Guide* (NCEE 2010-4038). Washington, DC: National Center for Education Evaluation and Regional Assistance, Institute of Education Sciences, U.S. Department of Education. whatworks.ed.gov/publications/practiceguides.

Shannon, George. 2015. *One Family*. Illus. Blanca Gomez. New York: Farrar, Straus and Giroux.

Shields, Carolyn M. 2004. "Diologic Leadership for Social Justice: Overcoming Pathologies of Silence." *Educational Administration Quarterly* 40:109–32.

Shin, Sun Yung. 2004. *Cooper's Lesson*. Illus. Kim Cogan. San Francisco: Children's Book Press.

Short, Kathy. 2006. "Ethics and Cultural Authenticity in International Children's Literature." Speech presented to the International Board on Books for Young People (IBBY), Basal, Switzerland, August 23–26. http://www.ibby.org/index.php?id=675.

———. 2013. "Common Core State Standards: Misconceptions about Text Exemplars." January 7. http://wowlit.org/blog/2013/01/07/common-core-state-standards-misconceptions-about-text-exemplars/.

Siegel, Siena Cherson. 2006. *To Dance: A Ballerina's Graphic Novel*. Illus. Mark Siegel. New York: Atheneum Books for Young Readers.

Silverstein, Shel. 2005. *Falling Up: Poems and Drawings*. New York: HarperCollins.

Sims, Rudine. 1983a. *Shadow and Substance: Afro-American Experience in Contemporary Children's Fiction*. Urbana, IL: National Council of Teachers of English.

———. 1983b. "What Has Happened to the 'All-White' World of Children's Books?" *Phi Delta Kappan* 64:650–53.

———. 1983c. "Strong Black Girls: A Ten-Year-Old Responds to Fiction about Afro-Americans." *Journal of Research and Development in Education* 16 (3): 21–28.

Singer, Marilyn. 2001. *Didi and Daddy on the Promenade*. Illus. Marie-Louise Gay. New York: Houghton Mifflin.

Sís, Peter. 2000. *Madlenka*. New York: Farrar, Straus and Giroux.

———. 2010. *Madlenka Soccer Star*. Madeira Park, BC: D and M Publishers.

———. 2010. *The Wall*. New York: Farrar, Straus and Giroux.

Smalls, Ciara, Rhonda White, Tabbye Chavous, and Robert Sellers. 2007. "Racial Ideological Beliefs and Racial Discrimination Experiences as Predictors of Academic Engagement among African American Adolescents." *Journal of Black Psychology* 33 (8): 299–330.

Smith, Cynthia Leitich. 2002. *Indian Shoes*. New York: HarperCollins.

Smith, Elizabeth B. 1995. "Anchored in our Literature: Students Responding to African American Literature." *Language Arts* 72:571–74.

Smith, Hope Anita. 2003. *The Way a Door Closes*. Illus. Shane W. Evans. New York: Henry Holt.

———. 2008. *Keeping the Night Watch*. Illus. E. B. Lewis. New York: Henry Holt.

Smitherman, Geneva. 1993. "'The Blacker the Berry, the Sweeter the Juice': African American Student Writers and the National Assessment of Educational Progress." Paper presented at the annual meeting of the National Council of Teachers of English, Pittsburgh, PA, November 17–22.

Smothers, Ethel F. 2003. *The Hard-Times Jar*. Illus. John Holyfield. New York: Farrar, Straus, and Giroux.

Soto, Gary. 1991. *Taking Sides*. Orlando, FL: Harcourt.

———. 1997. *Buried Onions*. Orlando, FL: Harcourt.

———. 2005. *Neighborhood Odes*. Illus. David Diaz. Orlando, FL: HMH Books for Young Readers.

Spencer, Margaret Beale. 1982. "Preschool children's social cognition and cultural cognition: A cognitive developmental interpretation of race dissonance findings." *Journal of Psychology: Interdisciplinary and Applied* 112:275–86.

———. 1984. "Black Children's Race Awareness, Racial Attitudes, and Self-Concept: A Reinterpretation." *Journal of Child Psychology and Psychiatry* 25 (3): 433–41.

Spinelli, Eileen. 2000. *Night Shift Daddy*. Illus. Melissa Iwai. New York: Hyperion Books.

Stanovich, Keith E. 1986. "Matthew Effects in Reading: Some Consequences of Individual Differences in the Acquisition of Literacy." *Reading Research Quarterly* 21:360–407.

Stead, Rebecca. 2009. *When You Reach Me*. New York: Yearling.

Steffenson, Margaret S. 1987. "The Effect of Context and Culture on Children's L2 Reading: A Review." In *Research in Reading in English as a Second Language*, edited by Joanne Devine, Patricia L. Carrell, and David E. Eskey, 41–54. Washington, DC: Teachers of English to Speakers of Other Languages.

Steffenson, Margaret S., Chitra Joag-Dev, and Richard Anderson. 1979. "A Cross-Cultural Perspective on Reading Comprehension." *Reading Research Quarterly* 15 (1): 10–29.

Stephens, Kathy. 2008. "A Quick Guide to Selecting Great Informational Books for Young Children." *The Reading Teacher* 61 (6): 488–90.

Steptoe, Javaka. 1997. *In Daddy's Arms I Am Tall*. New York: Lee and Low Books.

———. 2003. *The Jones Family Express*. New York: Lee and Low Books.

———. 2004. *Hot Day on Abbott Avenue*. New York: Clarion Books.

Steptoe, John. 1970. *Uptown*. New York: Harper and Row.

———. 1971. *Train Ride*. New York: HarperCollins.

———. 1986/1969. *Stevie*. New York: HarperCollins.

———. 2003. *Creativity*. Illus. E. B. Lewis. Boston: HMH Books for Young Readers.

Stewart, Michelle P. 2002. "Judging Authors by the Color of Their Skin? Quality Native American Children's Literature." *The Society for the Study of the Multi-Ethnic Literature of the United States (MELUS)* 27 (2): 179–96.

Style, Emily. 1996. "Curriculum as Window and Mirror." *Social Science Record* (Fall): 35–42. http://www.library.wisc.edu/edvrc/docs/public/pdfs/SEEDReadings/CurriculumWindows.pdf.

Suen, Anastasia. 2008. *Subway*. Illus. Karen Katz. New York: Viking.

Swanson, Dena P., Michael Cunningham, Joseph Youngblood II, and Margaret B. Spencer. 2009. "Racial Identity Development during Childhood." In *Handbook of African American Psychology*, edited by Helen Neville, Brendesha Tynes, and Shawn Utsey. Thousand Oaks, CA: Sage.

Sweller, John. 1988. "Cognitive Load during Problem Solving: Effects on Learning." *Cognitive Science* 12 (2): 257–85.

Taback, Simms. 2009. *City Animals*. Maplewood, NJ: Blue Apple Books.

Tarpley, Natasha. 2002. *Bippity Bop Barbershop*. Illus. E. B. Lewis. New York: Little, Brown and Company.

———. 2004. *Destiny's Gift*. Illus. Adjoa J. Burrowes. New York: Lee and Low Books.

Tarry, Ellen. 1942. *Hezekiah Horton*. Eau Claire, WI: E. M. Hale.

Tarry, Ellen, and Marie Hall Ets. 1946. *My Dog Rinty*. New York: Viking Juvenile.

Tatum, Alfred W. 2006. "Engaging African American Males in Reading." *Educational Leadership* 63 (5): 44–49.

———. 2008. "Adolescents and Texts." *English Journal* 98 (2): 82–85.

Taylor, Debbie. 2004. *Sweet Music in Harlem*. Illus. Frank Morrison. New York: Lee and Low Books.

Taylor, Gail S. 1997. "Multicultural Literature Preferences of Low Ability African American and Hispanic American Fifth Graders." *Reading Improvement* 34:37–48.

Teachers and Writers Collaborative. 2012. *A Poem as Big as New York City: Little Kids Write about the Big Apple*. Illus. Masha D'yans. New York: Universe Publishing.

Teale, William H., and Elizabeth Sulzby. 1987. "Literacy Acquisition in Early Childhood: The Roles of Access and Mediation in Storybook Reading." In *The Future of Literacy in a Changing World*, edited by Daniel Wagner, 111–30. New York: Pergamon Press.

Teitelbaum, Michael. 2010. *Jackie Robinson: Champion for Equality*. New York: Sterling.

Temple, Charles, Miriam Martinez, and Junko Yakota. 2011. *Children's Books in Children's Hands: An Introduction to Their Literature*, fourth edition. Boston: Allyn and Bacon.

TESOL International Association. 2015. "Levels of Language Proficiency." http://www.tesol.org/advance-the-field/standards/prek-12-english-language-proficiency-standards.

Thome, Catherine. 2013. "Bringing the Common Core Standards to Life in the Classroom." http://www.readinga-z.com/research/bringing-the-common-core-standards-to-life-in-the-classroom.pdf.

Thong, Roseanne. 2000. *Round Is a Mooncake: A Book of Shapes*. Illus. Grace Lin. San Francisco: Chronicle Books.

———. 2007. *Gai See: What You Can See in Chinatown*. Illus. Choi Yangsook. New York: Abrams.

———. 2013. *Round Is a Tortilla: A Book of Shapes*. Illus. John Parra. San Francisco: Chronicle Books.

Tomlinson, C. A., and M. B. Imbeau. 2013. *Leading and Managing a Differentiated Classroom*. Independence, KY: Cengage Learning.

Tonatiuh, Duncan. 2010. *Dear Primo: A Letter to My Cousin*. New York: Abrams.

Torres, Leyla. 1997. *The Subway Sparrow*. New York: Square Fish Publishing.

Uchida, Yoshiko. 1995. *The Invisible Thread*. New York: Beech Tree Books.

———. 2005. *Journey to Topaz*. Berkeley, CA: Heyday Books.

Uegaki, Chieri. 2005. *Suki's Kimono*. Illus. Stephanie Jorisch. Toronto: Kids Can Press.

U.S. Census Bureau. 1990. "Urban and Rural Definitions." Washington, DC: Bureau of the Census.

———. 2012. September 27. "2010 Census Shows Multiple-Race Population Grew Faster Than Single-Race Population." U.S. Department of Commerce. http://www.census.gov/newsroom/releases/archives/race/cb12-182.html.

———. 2015. State and County QuickFacts. Washington, DC: U.S. Department of Commerce. http://quickfacts.census.gov/qfd/states/00000.html.

U.S. Department of Education. National Center for Education Statistics. 2013. *Common Core of Data (CCD), Public Elementary/Secondary School Universe Survey, 2010–2011 (version 2a)*. http://nces.ed.gov/programs/coe/indicator_tla.asp.

Unrau, Norman, and Jonah Schlackman. 2006. "Motivation and Its Relationship with Reading Achievement in an Urban Middle School." *Journal of Educational Research* 101 (2): 81–101.

Uro, Gabriella, and Alejandra Barrio. 2013. "English Language Learners in America's Great City Schools: Demographics, Achievement and Staffing." Washington, DC: Council of Great City Schools.

Valdes, Alisa. 2012. "Finding Minority Voices in Children's Fiction." *Huff Post Live.* http://live.huffingtonpost.com/r/segment/finding-minority/50bf67612b8c2a5d82 00099f.

Van Leeuwen, Jean. 1967. *Timothy's Flower.* Illus. Moneta Barnett. New York: Random House.

Velasquez, Eric. 2001. *Grandma's Records.* New York: Walker and Company.

———. 2010. *Grandma's Gift.* New York: Walker and Company.

Vicente, Antonio. 2010. *Marina and the Little Green Boy: In the City/Marina y el niño verde: en la ciudad.* Illus. Miguel Ordonez. London: Bilingual Readers.

Vygotsky, Lev. 1978. *Mind in Society.* Translated by Michael Cole. Cambridge, MA: Harvard University Press.

Wahl, Jan. 2004. *Candy Shop.* Illus. Nicole Wong. Watertown, MA: Charlesbridge.

Wakim Dennis, Yvonne, and Arlene B. Hirschfelder. 2003. *Children of Native America Today.* Watertown, MA: Charlesbridge.

Wang, Judy H., and John T. Guthrie. 2004. "Modeling the Effects of Intrinsic Motivation, Extrinsic Motivation, Amount of Reading, and Past Reading Achievement on Text Comprehension between U.S. and Chinese Students. *Reading Research Quarterly* 39: 162–86. DOI: 10.1598/RRQ.39.2.2.

Weatherford, Carole Boston. 2006. *Sidewalk Chalk.* Illus. Dimitrea Tokunbo. Boston: Wordsong.

———. 2014. *Sugar Hill: Harlem's Historic Neighborhood.* Illus. R. Gregory Christie. Park Ridge, IL: Albert Whitman Company.

Weill, Cynthia. 2009. *Opuestos: Mexican Folk Art Opposites in English and Spanish.* Illus. Martin Santiago and Quirino Santiago. El Paso, TX: Cinco Puntos Press.

Weinstein, Carol, Saundra Tomlinson-Clarke, and Mary Curran. 2004. "Toward a Conception of Culturally Responsive Classroom Management." *Journal of Teacher Education* 55 (1): 25–38.

Wigfield, Allan. 2004. "Motivation for Reading during the Early Adolescent and Adolescent Years." In *Bridging the Literacy Achievement Gap, Grades 4–12,* edited by Dorothy S. Strickland and Donna E. Alvermann. New York: Teacher College Press.

Wigfield, Allan, and Jacquelynne S. Eccles. 2000. "Expectancy-Value Theory of Achievement Motivation." *Contemporary Educational Psychology* 25:68–81. DOI:10.1006/ceps.1999.1015.

Wigfield, Allan, and John T. Guthrie. 1997. "Relations of Children's Motivation for Reading to the Amount and Breadth of Their Reading." *Journal of Educational Psychology* 89:420–32.

Wilkins, Julia, and Robert Gamble. 1998. "Evaluating Multicultural Literature for Use in the Classroom." *Educational Considerations* 26 (2): 28–31.

Williams-Garcia, Rita. 2010. *One Crazy Summer.* New York: HarperCollins.

———. 2013. *P.S. Be Eleven*. New York: HarperCollins.

Williamson, Mel, and George Ford. 1972. *Walk On!* Illus. George Cephas Ford. Chicago: Odarkai Books/Third Press.

Willems, Mo. 2003. *Don't Let the Pigeon Drive the Bus!* New York: Hyperion Books for Children.

———. 2004. *Knuffle Bunny: A Cautionary Tale*. New York: Hyperion Books.

Winter, Jonah. 2009. *Sonia Sotomayor: A Judge Grows in the Bronx/La juez que crecio en el Bronx*. Illus. Edel Rodriguez. New York: Atheneum Books for Young Readers.

Witte, Anna. 2011. *Lola's Fandango*. Illus. Micha Archer. Cambridge, MA: Barefoot Books.

Wolf, Bernard. 2003. *Coming to America: A Muslim Family's Story*. New York: Lee and Low Books.

Wong, Carol A., Jacquelynne S. Eccles, and Arnold Sameroff. 2003. "The Influence of Ethnic Discrimination and Ethnic Identification on African American Adolescents' School and Socioemotional Adjustment." *Journal of Personality* 71 (6): 1197–232.

Wong, Janet S. 2006. *Apple Pie 4th of July*. Illus. Margaret Chodos-Irvine. Boston: HMH Books for Young Readers.

———. 2006. *Minn and Jake's Almost Terrible Summer*. Illus. Genevieve Cote. New York: Farrar, Straus and Giroux.

Woodson, Jacqueline. 1997. *We Had a Picnic This Sunday Past*. Illus. Diane Greenseid. New York: Hyperion Books for Children.

———. 1998. "Who Can Tell My Story?" *Horn Book Magazine* 74 (1): 34–38.

———. 2001. *The Other Side*. Illus. E. B. Lewis. New York: Putnam.

———. 2002. *Last Summer with Maizon*. New York: Puffin.

———. 2002. *Visiting Day*. New York: Scholastic.

———. 2003. *If You Come Softly*. New York: Penguin.

———. 2003. "Who Can Tell My Story?" In *Stories Matter: The Complexity of Cultural Authenticity in Children's Literature*, edited by Dana L. Fox and Kathy G. Short, 41–45. Urbana, IL: National Council of Teachers of English.

———. 2013. *This Is the Rope*. New York: Nancy Paulsen Books.

Wyeth, Sharon D. 2002. *Something Beautiful*. Illus. Chris K. Soentpiet. New York: Dragonfly Books.

Yep, Laurence. 2000. *The Magic Paintbrush*. Illus. Suling Wang. New York: HarperCollins.

Yezerski, Thomas F. 2011. *Meadowlands: A Wetlands Survival Story*. New York: Farrar, Straus and Giroux.

Yokota, Junko. 1993. "Issues in Selecting Multicultural Children's Literature." *Language Arts* 70:156–67.

Yolen, Jane. 1987. *Owl Moon*. Illus. John Schoenherr. New York: Philomel.

Yoo, Paula. 2010. *Sixteen Years in Sixteen Seconds: The Sammy Lee Story*. Illus. Dom Lee. New York: Lee and Low Books.

Yopp, Ruth H., and Hallie K. Yopp. 2012. "Young Children's Limited and Narrow Exposure to Informational Texts." *The Reading Teacher* 65 (7): 480–90.

Young, Ed. 1989. *Lon Po Po: A Red-Riding Hood Story from China*. New York: Philomel.

~

Index

~

About the Authors

Jane Fleming, PhD
Jane Fleming is a reading specialist with more than twenty years of experience working in urban public schools in Chicago, St. Louis, and Washington, D.C. She is cofounder of Kids Like Us, a nonprofit organization dedicated to research, professional development, and advocacy around teaching with culturally relevant texts. She is a frequent consultant for schools, professional organizations, and teacher education programs on the use of urban children's literature to support reading and writing achievement.

Susan Catapano, EdD
Susan Catapano is Professor and International Coordinator in the Watson College of Education at the University of North Carolina Wilmington. Susan has a doctorate in higher education with concentrations in adult learning and early childhood education. She teaches both undergraduate and graduate courses in curriculum, instruction, and supervision. Her research focus is supporting the development of cultural competence in beginning teachers working with diverse learners.

Candace M. Thompson, PhD
Candace Thompson is an associate professor at the University of North Carolina Wilmington. She received her PhD in social foundations of education from the University of South Carolina in 2008. Her research interests include culturally responsive applied learning in teacher preparation, and

youth empowerment. She lives this work by immersing her beginning education students (and herself) in local urban elementary and middle schools and the communities they serve.

Sandy Ruvalcaba Carrillo, MS

Sandy Ruvalcaba Carrillo earned her undergraduate degree in bilingual/bicultural education from Western Illinois and completed a graduate degree in early childhood education at Erikson Institute. In her seventeen years in the education field, she has worked with children from preschool to sixth grade. She currently works as a resource teacher of English learners in a school on the Southwest side of Chicago. Her interests are in language acquisition, culturally relevant pedagogy, and culturally relevant literature.

Made in the USA
Monee, IL
04 August 2020

37589861R00152